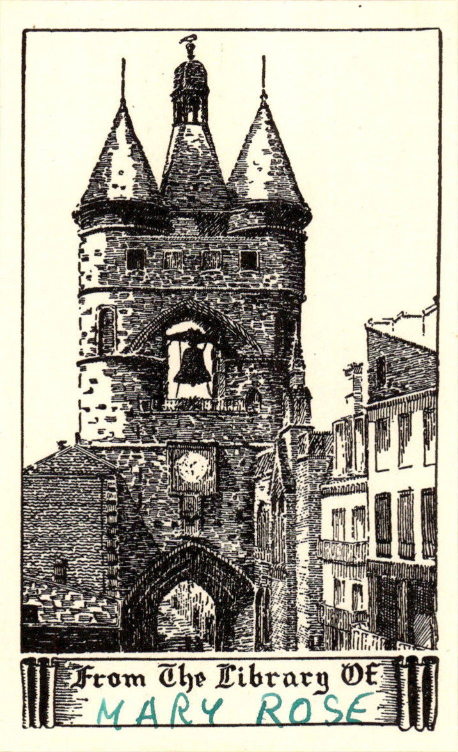

MARCH '46

THE WAY OF WESTERN ART

1776–1914

LONDON : HUMPHREY MILFORD
OXFORD UNIVERSITY PRESS

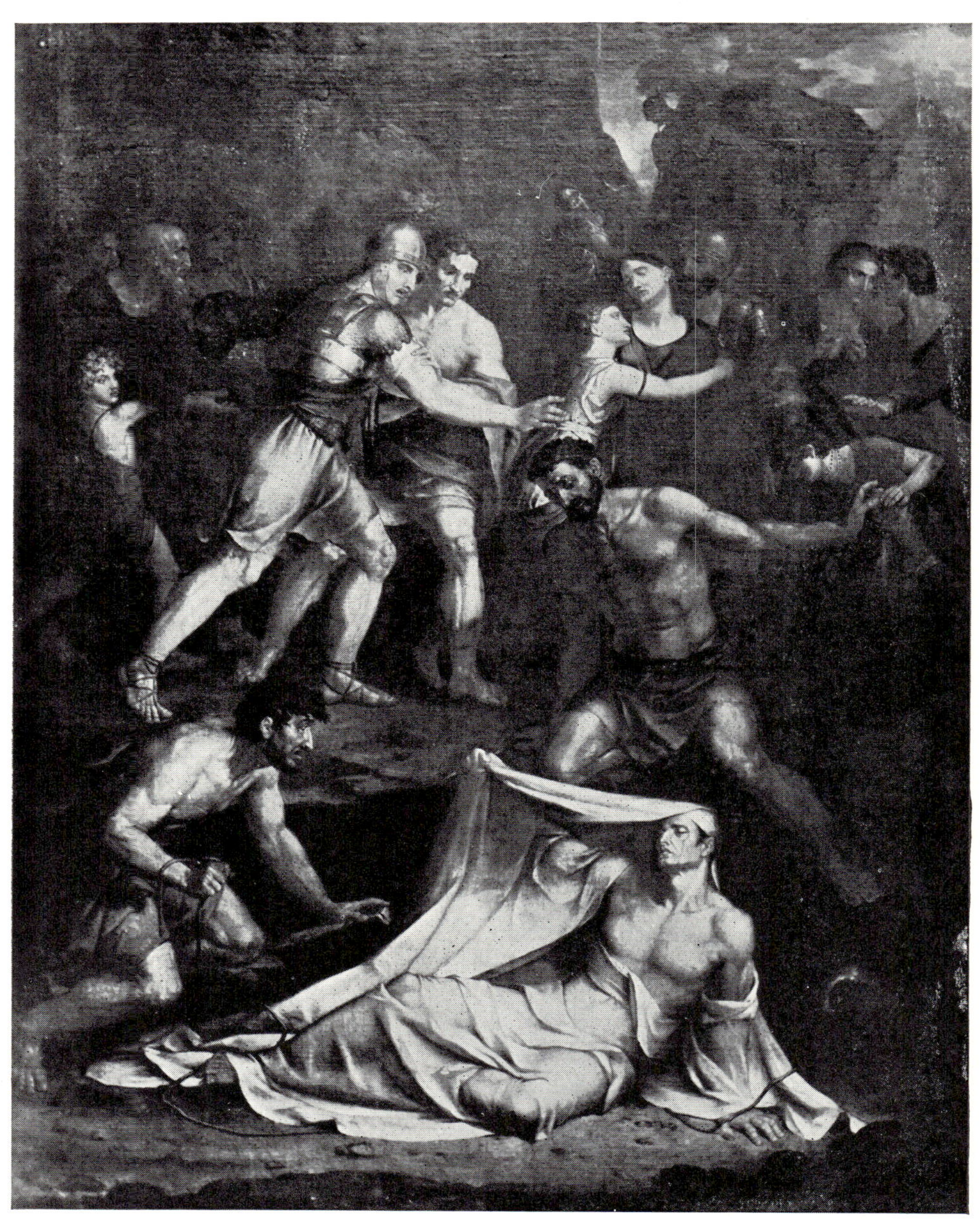

Allston: The Dead Man Restored to Life by the Bones of Elijah. 1813

THE WAY OF WESTERN ART

1776–1914

BY

EDGAR PRESTON RICHARDSON

The Detroit Institute of Arts

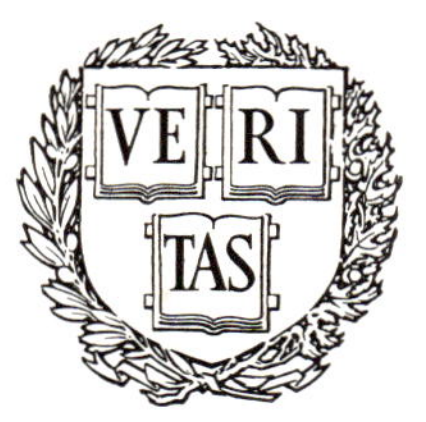

CAMBRIDGE, MASSACHUSETTS

HARVARD UNIVERSITY PRESS

1939

PREFACE

THIS ESSAY is a study of modern western art as a unity which embraces the nations of western Europe and America. There are, it is true, certain modern philosophies which would like to deny that there is such a unity and prefer to divide men according to race or economic status rather than culture. But most men who have thought about the matter will agree that there is such a thing as western civilization, an entity in the world's life to which both America and Europe belong. Other generations have had a clearer comprehension than we of the wholeness of our civilization. In the eighteenth century a sturdy local patriotism does not seem to have interfered, at least in educated men, with the consciousness of a wider tradition of life in which we all shared. This happy combination of an international mind and patriot emotions faded with the coming of the romantic movement in the nineteenth century. The poets and antiquaries who delved so lovingly into the legends of the past cultivated an exclusive racial consciousness in the light of which most of our histories have since been written. Yet it is clear to all students that a large degree of interconnection exists between the modern national traditions of America and Europe; and in the arts perhaps quite as large a degree of interconnection, I am inclined to venture, as in the medieval centuries which are held up to us as examples of the unity of Christendom, but which reveal upon closer study that they also had their share of national hostilities and jealousies. There still exists, in short, a general consciousness, or western mind, within which nations and men carry on their individual development.

Generalization as a method is not now in very good repute. Nonetheless, beside analysis there is always need for synthesis, and the problem in which I am interested calls for the latter treatment. And since those who are better equipped than I (as I am well aware) for such a task are busy with other problems, I have not hesitated to attempt it. But it is not an easy task, in this day of research, to include within one's view the art of the west and the life which is its source and background;

and to those who will understand the difficulties of the problem, I offer my apologies for any inadequacies they may find in the following pages.

My essay begins with the period of the American and French revolutions, not only because the political separation of America from Europe began then but because the cataclysm of these revolutions, which were intellectually and morally interwoven, marks the beginning of the modern world. I have ended with the Great War, not because it put a period to any development, for the currents of the years before 1914 run through and beyond the war with surprising continuity, but simply because the post-war years are too close for our perspective. Our view will be arbitrarily limited, except in rare instances, to America, England, France, Germany, and Austria. It is true that the creative activity of the western mind was by no means limited to these countries, but within these limits one can see the main currents of art and the most conspicuous personalities.

This essay is the result of an attempt to understand the place of American art within that larger development. There is a common, though I believe entirely fallacious notion that a connection between our culture and that of other countries is a sign of weakness or provincialism. On the contrary, we would in my opinion most certainly be provincial if we had no connection with the rest of the western world, as an individual is provincial if, being deprived of education, he is cut off from the intellectual heritage of his race and the development of his time. It is impossible for me to conceive of civilization except as a cumulative thing, to which each generation adds a little, while receiving infinitely more from the past; nor can I conceive that any man or people is benefited by being cut off from the accumulated best that the human race has produced, which is the spiritual inheritance of us all. The notion that a nation or an individual is harmed by that inheritance and must refashion the whole of civilization for itself is romantic nonsense. Thoreau, who is somewhat of a patron saint among these partisans of spiritual isolation, was not such a rattlebrain as they would have him. Did he not have Homer and the Upanishads open on his table in the Walden Woods? The fact that we have shared with our contemporaries abroad both the great past of our world and the mental climate of our age, and that our contributions to the common sum are not always the least interesting, will perhaps be the conclusion also of the reader of this book.

The attempt to study western art as a unit is not, of course, new. It has been undertaken from various points of view by Continental scholars, in such notable compilations as Michel's *Histoire de l'art* and the Propylaean *Kunstgeschichte*, as well as in the work of individual critics. But English-speaking scholars have struck hardly more than a glancing blow at the problem, and, in particular, no one has touched upon the relation of American art to the general development of art in the western world. The relation of America to Europe is one of the most interesting questions in the history of our art; yet it has remained almost undealt with. Once the problem is stated, it seems obvious that there is need for a study of the part which American art takes in the larger development. The wonder is that we in this country have left it so long unattempted. The omission is perhaps the result of too severe a conscience on the part of the scholars who have developed the study of American art (and of whose researches I have made grateful use), for generalization as a method is now apt to be considered too easy. I confess I have not found it so.

Since one of my main objects is to relate American art to the tradition to which it belongs, I make no apology for sometimes emphasizing American art at the expense of European parallels. The American examples are the unknown which it is my chief purpose to study. It is, I believe, safe to leave to the taste and intelligence of the reader his own estimate of the relative values within the larger relationships which are to be established.

A study of relationships may easily become a mere table of "influences" or a kind of genealogical table of artists' names. I do not believe, however, that ideas are objects passed along from mind to mind unchanged, as something goes from hand to hand in a parlor game. They live in personalities and as part of them, and cannot be followed in a mere genealogical tree from name to name. Furthermore, art is by definition a form of creation. Only second-rate figures are imitators. To an artist strong enough to be a force in his generation the example of another man's work may open a door, but it cannot determine what he will do after he goes through. An artist does, however, take his start from the advancing experience of the race and the spirit of his age. I have attempted to give this element its value and to show the varying stamp given by national and individual temperament to what is drawn from this underlying reservoir of experience.

Modern taste in America has tended to ignore many artists discussed in this essay who happen to represent an age of taste different from our own. No one will deny that many — and, in common sense, most of the artists of the nineteenth and twentieth centuries are minor men if compared with Jan van Eyck or Michelangelo. But no one who is aware how hard it is to do anything at all in creative work can feel that it is a little thing to have filled the minds of one generation with images, even if those images have since lost some of their original power. And it seems to me that we miss the social value of the artist if we pay attention only to the rare artists who form the peaks of history and dismiss the others from our reckoning, for these, too, helped to form the mental climate of their age. Our taste is much given to annihilating enthusiasms. Now Bruegel or El Greco or Bach (as once it was Raphael or Sargent or Wagner) is pronounced the great one, while all others are rolled impatiently into oblivion. I have derived a great deal of pleasure, I confess, from artists whom one would never think of elevating to such a company, and it grieves me to see their contribution to our inheritance treated so brutally. It is like seeing one's friends — talented, useful people, givers of pleasant dinners and good conversation — sent to the scaffold because they are not Napoleons or Julius Caesars.

Finally, this essay is the product of much reading and thought over a period of years, much of it done without the intention of writing the book. It would be impossible for me, therefore, to quote all the sources I have used, nor does it seem essential to this kind of study, since the material is well known and accessible to all. This essay makes no pretense of taking the place of the many detailed studies of artists and movements, but is intended rather to suggest certain links which may help in the matter of perspective. The reader will discover for himself my indebtedness to Croce's *History of Europe in the Nineteenth Century.*

I should like also to mention my indebtedness to Mr. Christopher B. Coleman and Miss Dorothy Tyler, and to my colleagues, Mr. Robert H. Tannahill and Dr. William R. Valentiner. I am deeply grateful for their kindness in reading the manuscript, in whole or in part, and for their advice and suggestions.

E. P. R.

Detroit, *September,* 1939

CONTENTS

ILLUSTRATIONS

THE WAY OF WESTERN ART
1776–1914

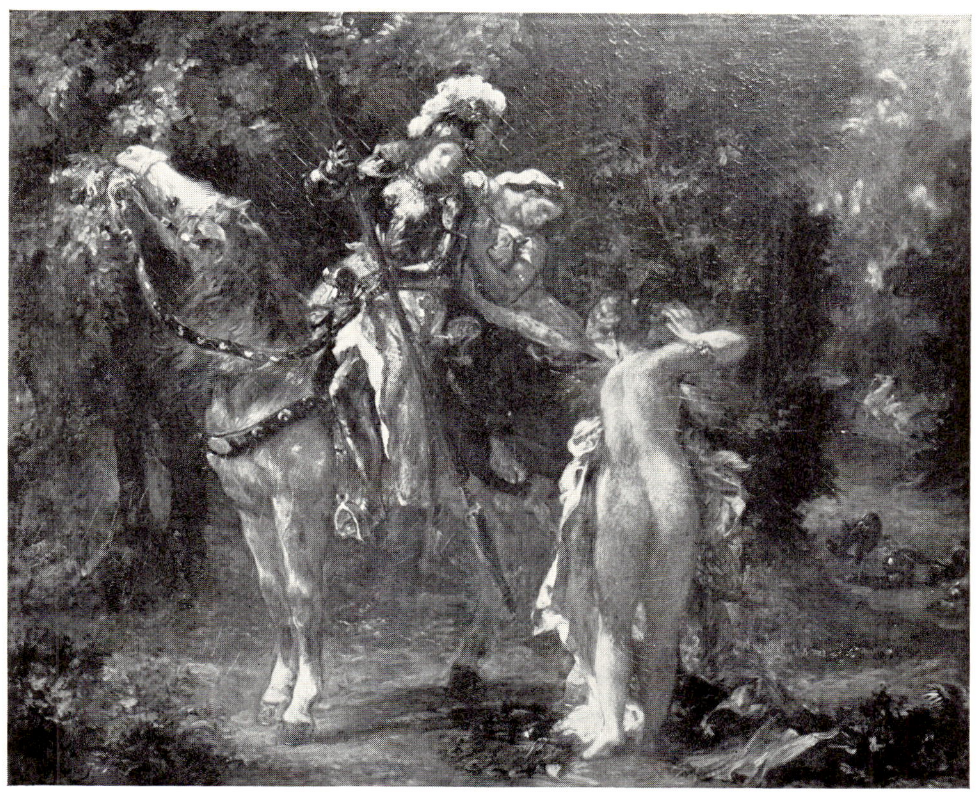

1. Delacroix: Marphise

CHAPTER I

BACKGROUND

THE PERIOD in western art from 1776 to 1914 was one filled with swift changes and conflicts of thought. Ideas of great power, rising both within and without our culture, exerted enormous strains upon the tradition of western art, and again and again (so it seemed to contemporaries) altered it almost beyond recognition. To a large degree these forces can be recognized as the great fructifying but conflicting tendencies out of which our civilization is built. Western civilization was formed by the union of four great historical traditions, which by no means live easily together; and while one can believe proudly that it has brought out the best that the human being is capable of, because it unites the varied extremes of achievement to which the human mind can rise, nonetheless the balance of its vivid and disparate elements has been kept only by constant effort. One of these historical roots is the mysticism of the Orient, whose greatest representative in our thought is Christianity. Although the western or Latin form of Christianity absorbed both Greek philosophy and Roman discipline, it retained the unworldly Oriental inwardness of mind, to which the only true values are spiritual and beyond the reach both of man's reason and of his self-help. A second root is the free, secular spirit of Hellenic learning, skeptical and rationalistic in character, whose exploration of the possibilities of human reason conflicted with and counterbalanced the mystical absorption in God. A third source is the political tradition of Rome, which contributed the ideas of citizenship, social discipline, and the rule of laws rather than of personalities. The fourth, the contribution of the barbarian invaders, is the Germanic ideal of freedom and the northern warriors' code of comradeship, courage, and devotion to a personal leader, which later became the basis of feudalism and the chivalric ideal.

From these four ancient sources developed the richest and most fruitful of human traditions. But it has paid for its riches by the instability of its balance. It is a thing of irreconcilables. Reason and intuition, logic and mysticism, social discipline and personal liberty have fought a long battle through its history. The Middle Ages, one may say, were predominantly formed by Christian mysticism and social order. The Renaissance replaced these by individualism and a rationalistic view of the world which prevailed down to about the year 1800. Since that time the struggle between reason and intuition seems, perhaps because of our nearness to the event, to have grown more intense and its revolutions more rapid. In the field of taste the rationalistic classicism [1] of Winckelmann and David, still rooted in antiquity, first gave place to an emotional romanticism which discovered its foundation in a kinship with the Middle Ages and with the Orient, and substituted for the international mind of the eighteenth century the instincts of race and

---

[1] The English vocabulary of criticism is so vague that one can never feel sure that well-known words, such as "classic," "romantic," "realistic," will mean to the reader exactly what one intends to convey. "Classic" is popularly applied to any work of art of standard

locality. The struggle entered a second phase in the 1840's, when a scientific materialism, descended from the rationalistic mind of the Renaissance, rose to dominate the remainder of the century. Since the opening of the twentieth century a revival of the emotional and intuitive comprehension of the world, which looked for support to romanticism and to the Middle Ages, and borrowed deeply from the mystical arts of the Orient and of primitive man, has again completely transformed the face of the arts.

The arts have also varied with the natural alternations of interest which take place with each generation. The satisfactions of the mind are clarity, order, definiteness, a general validity of statement. The satisfactions of the heart are warmth and spontaneity of feeling, excitement, strangeness and variety. The alternations between these satisfactions are the source of many of the changes in nineteenth- and twentieth-century art. Because these alternations have come in modern times with great rapidity, and because there is a strong human tendency to resist a change of habits, the modern period, far more than any other of which we have knowledge, is a period of esthetic controversy.

Another and still more fertile source of trouble and heartburning is the influx of ideas from outside the western tradition.

The nineteenth was a century of expansion such as had never before been experienced. At its beginning, with the exception of a few merchants and sailors, the peoples of Europe were confined to their own small peninsula jutting off from the land mass of Eurasia, while America consisted of five million souls (three and a half million white) of whom all but a few hundred thousand were within a hundred miles of tide-

---

value; more properly, to any Greek or Roman object from certain centuries. I have used it to describe the antique, likewise the early nineteenth-century attempt to revive the forms of antique art, of which Jacques Louis David's historical paintings and the Roman and Greek revivals in architecture are examples. But I have also used it to describe the direction of thought of which these two classes of objects are conspicuous illustrations. This is the tendency to follow the clarifying and unifying lead of the intellect toward the norm of an experience, to seek the generalization that lies at the center of our range of sensibility. The opposing tendency to push outward to the frontiers of experience, toward the strange, the unique, the overwhelming, the marvelous, is to follow the lead of the emotions, which crave excitement as the reason craves surety. For this latter tendency I have used the term "romantic."

water. When the century ended, the white race controlled most of the globe. The culture of western Europe had been carried over the earth; more than that, it had acted as an irresistible solvent upon all other cultures. The collapse of all non-European arts at the touch of western life is certainly one of the most important events of the nineteenth century; but it lies outside our study. The return tide of influence is a different matter. Beginning with the interest in Egypt awakened by Napoleon's expedition in 1798, the newborn science of archaeology advanced to the discovery of Egypt, Assyria and Babylon, Persia and prehistoric Greece, Stone Age man, Crete, Sumeria, the Hittites, and Europe's own Celtic and Teutonic past. Meanwhile works of art in vast quantities were brought back by travelers from China, Japan, India, the South Seas, Africa, and the territories of the American Indian. All these objects were gathered in museums (institutions which are essentially a development of the nineteenth century), where they were studied by scholars and artists. One by one their qualities were recognized. The attitude of unquestioned superiority to all other cultures, which permeated every paragraph of the articles on non-European arts in the *Encyclopaedia Britannica* of the eighties, gave way within another generation to one of respect and admiration. That change carried away not only the moral basis of nineteenth-century imperialism but the ancient boundary marks of western art. The non-European arts sprang from different philosophical bases than ours, and differed radically in both style and content from what Europe had been developing since the Renaissance. The most obvious difference is that, judged by the standard of nineteenth-century naturalism,[2] all are stylistic rather than natural in their representation of the world. From 1850 onward western artists experimented with and adopted a steady succession of forms from these non-European arts. The effect upon our tradition has been enormous.

The revolutions which inaugurated our era brought to power an educated professional class whose strong ethical, social, and literary

[2] I have tried to distinguish *realism* from *naturalism* throughout this essay, reserving the former word to describe the use of exact natural detail as a means of expression, the

interests found their expression in a historical and literary art. The lawyers, merchants, and country gentlemen who composed the Constitutional Convention of 1787 and the *états généraux* of 1789 gave extraordinary prestige to writers. If one remembers the strongly literary make-up of the government of France from 1789 to 1850, one will not be surprised that art, too, showed traces of the dominating influence of literature. Eighteenth-century rationalistic philosophy and literature had created an image of the ideal man in an ideal society which the revolutionary generation attempted to translate into reality. In the struggle they called for morally stirring historical compositions to represent their ideal. This was the foundation for the classic style to which, in France, the painter Jacques Louis David gave a definitive form.

It was the destiny of the revolutionary generation to unleash emotional forces of which no one at that time had any comprehension. Before the giant passions of nationality, race, locality, of liberty and equality and democracy, the ideals of an older world faded like candles in the glare of a forest fire. In a long generation of war the international thought of the eighteenth century gave place to a fierce love of one's own race and soil. The generalized decorations of rococo painting, which had flourished in a world educated in good manners and in the classic poets, grew pallid. The ancient imagery of Christianity faded before the new religion of liberty and the dream of freedom of peoples. It continued to be the fashion of the coming generation of romantic artists to create images of an ideal world rather than the one in which they lived. But the thunder of the Napoleonic Wars had called home men's attention from Plutarch's antique heroes to their own. The romantic painters turned to the pageant of the national past, where through the mists of time and sentiment gleamed the proud triumphs of national heroes — Bruce and the Black Douglas, Charlemagne and Richard Cœur de Lion, Roland and Siegfried. The picturesque splendor of the Near East, which romanticism also discovered, was less valued for itself than as an exotic backdrop, against which Byron and Scott could place

---

latter for an unimaginative imitation of nature as an end in itself. Both tendencies were powerfully stimulated by the scientific materialism which dominated later nineteenth-century thought.

the noble and unhappy heroes who were the type figures of the romantic cry for freedom and hatred of restraint.

In France the romantic painters and sculptors, and writers like Victor Hugo, created this new ideal world. In Germany the Nazarenes, the Düsseldorf and Munich painters, reflected, with less technical ability, the old German folklore which the romantic poets were rediscovering. In England the historical painters turned to illustrations of Queen Elizabeth or the Hundred Years' War, or to the Italy of the city republics. In the United States Washington Irving and Cooper, Allston, and a score of forgotten historical painters turned to the legends of America as well as to the pageantry of English and German romantic literature.

The tendency toward localism implicit in this trend of thought became stronger in the 1830's. As the older generation died out, there died with it the afterglow of eighteenth-century culture, which lingered in those born before the great revolutions. As the last embers of the aristocratic world went out, society shifted still farther toward democracy. Andrew Jackson's election to the presidency in 1828 transferred power in the United States from the tidewater gentry to the frontier democracy. The English Reform Bill of 1832 ended the long rule of the great landowners and brought the trading and manufacturing classes of the towns into power. The year 1830 saw the bourgeois monarchy of Louis Philippe installed on the throne of the Bourbons, and a sporadic stirring and change over all Europe.

Another aspect of the democracy of these times was the rise of the cities. The great cities of the modern world — Vienna, Berlin, Munich, Paris, and London, as well as Boston and New York — are in their present form products of the nineteenth century. As a new urban life appeared, a new world of self-conscious and politically powerful crowds produced the periodical press, and with it the nineteenth-century illustrator of books and magazines. The techniques of lithography and of wood and steel engraving were born or refashioned in the first half of the nineteenth century. But painting, as well as black-and-white illustration, showed an interest in the common life of town and country. There was a great increase in realistic landscape and genre, in which the small citizen could find a portrait of himself and his world. The charming Biedermeier [3] art of Austria and Germany, Barbizon realism in France, the landscape and genre of Victorian England and of the Hudson River school in America were the expression of another side of romanticism. The literary prototype of this movement was Wordsworth, the poet of nature and of simple, humble life, as the prototype of the other side of romanticism was Byron, the poet of escape from simple realities and of hatred of home. Romantic realism, as I prefer to call this return to nature, in contrast to the romantic idealism of the other wing, had its roots in a new middle-class society, somewhat local and limited in horizon, and, whether one finds it in the suburbs of Vienna or an American frontier town, equally unaccustomed to the interests of the *haut monde*, but nonetheless thoughtful and ready for an art to express its life.

In the 1840's romantic realism began to give way before the new force of scientific materialism. Darwin had then returned from his cruise on the *Beagle* to settle into his life of research, Lyell and Agassiz were studying the traces of the Deluge and discovering the glacial period and historical geology, and Science, which had been growing in power ever since Bacon and Pascal, assumed control of the mind of the age. The appetite for observation of physical fact, which was coupled in the second half of the century with a scorn for all forms of ideal thought, such as religions and philosophies, did more than upset the faith of a few sensitive minds like Matthew Arnold. The whole temper of western life was changed. The moralistic view of society that had ruled through the period of idealism gave way to the materialistic and economic. Freedom, which had been the religion of the first half of the century, gave way to the religion of railroads and factories, needle-guns and African colonies, as the dream of the liberty of peoples faded before the *Realpolitik* of Bismarck. Objective realism became the next phase of art. In the

[3] Originally the name of a Philistine but lovable comic character, Gottlieb Biedermeier, in the poems of Ludwig Eichrodt, the term Biedermeier has been applied to the tranquil domestic life of a whole period in German culture between the fall of Napoleon and the Revolution of 1848. Its artistic expression in interior decoration was a style springing out of the late eighteenth-century English styles and the Empire style, characterized by sober charm and usefulness but ornamented and made cheerful by the use of beautiful wood inlays. In painting it is used to designate the movement of naïve and intimate realism which stood in marked contrast to the idealistic school, in Germany as elsewhere.

middle of the century the period of the factual dispassionate eye began in the arts. The objective realist looked upon the romantic with virulent contempt. Mark Twain's scorn for Sir Walter Scott is a good example of the feeling of this generation for its predecessors.

It is difficult to overstate the importance of the break in the tradition of art which objective realism implied. From the time of Giotto the Latin tradition of art had been that of form: art was an orderly, noble, and serene harmony imposed by the mind upon the chaos of nature. Side by side with the tradition of form went the northern tradition of sensibility, illustrated by Rembrandt, that had made art the expression of distilled and concentrated emotion (the "emotion recollected in tranquillity" of Wordsworth's definition of poetry). In either case art was an activity of the spirit, springing from within the mind and shaping the images of the world which the artist used into a more intense and transcendent spiritual reality. In place of this, objective realism substituted the direct transcript of nature, stated without comment or overtone of feeling. Theoretically, the sights before an objective realist's eyes ought to be transferred by his brain through his hands to his canvas without anything's happening to them during their journey through his personality. It is true, of course, that the profound emotions of discoverers of a new vision of reality live within the works of the great realists of this time, and that great gifts of style transferred their work to another plane than that of nature. But the conception of art as an objective process applied to nature, which made Courbet paint nymphs as peasant women, led Wagner to impose naturalistic stage settings upon the opera, and left Monet helpless to paint except before his "subject," had grave weaknesses which in the next generation produced a violent reaction.

But idealism never came wholly to an end. Although the early nineteenth-century idealism died away in the commonplaces of sentimental painters like Couture, Ary Scheffer, and Delaroche in France, and Cornelius in Germany, the impulse still existed in artists to lift the phenomena of life by the exercise of imagination to a more significant level than mere observation of fact. A new form of idealistic painting began in the middle of the century, of which the first signs appear in

France with the mural paintings of Chassériau. The leaders of this movement, Puvis de Chavannes in France, Marées in Germany, and John La Farge in America, used the luminous atmospheric color and the realistic detail of their period to attempt again the creation of a monumental form of art. They were less successful, however, in forming new ideas to animate their style, a field in which their age could offer little assistance. The leadership, therefore, gradually passed to the men we term the Post-Impressionists, who accepted their age more completely and, without trying to use abstract ideas, achieved monumentality within the small scale and realistic subject matter of Impressionism. Degas, Cézanne, Seurat, Gauguin accepted all that Impressionism had to give, then went on to reassert the concept of art as an order and a harmony, springing from within the mind rather than from nature. Van Gogh, and in a lesser degree Inness, were likewise witnesses of the value of emotional expression, until the twentieth century appeared to champion it once more.

Across the great alternation of reason and instinct, logic and emotion, played other forces. In choosing what we admire from the art of the past, taste seems to lead us to admire our own opposite and to prefer the arts that supply what is lacking in the mental climate of our own world. The provincial United States of the early nineteenth century admired the painters of the Italian High Renaissance and the Baroque, finding in these sophisticated products of an overcivilized world a balance for its own provincialism. Similarly, it was the England of Prince Albert's prime which discovered, through Ruskin and Eastlake, the austere nobility of early Italian art, just as it was in the gilt pseudo-rococo salons of the French Second Empire (whose favorite painter was Meissonier) that admiration was born for the cool restraint and arbitrary stylization of Japanese prints. At the end of the century, in the period of Whistler and Oscar Wilde, the robust vitality of Frans Hals and the objective force of Velásquez were recovered after centuries of neglect. And as the liberal dream faded at the close of the century, in the world of Bismarck and the partition of Africa, as men multiplied comforts and read Schopenhauer, poets and artists arose to express the world's nostalgia for a life close to earth and for the simple faith of the peasant. The poets of the Irish Renaissance fled to the last outer islands, where Europe goes down into the sea, to find a primitive peasant culture; and Gauguin fled from the studio atmosphere of Paris to live among primitive men on the coral beaches of the South Seas. It is hardly a coincidence that, again, in our own restless and introspective century, whose lack of grand ideas is revealed by the lack of subject matter in our art, we should have admired the arts of the Far East, in whose heart lies the silence and peace of Buddhist mysticism, or the strong, objective fire of primitive art.

It would be ridiculous to ignore the fact that national temperaments also played a part in the development of the nineteenth century, however much one must protest against the mistaken notion that they existed in isolation one from another. The more one studies the arguments for and against the concept of race, the more one is inclined to belief that there is no such thing, but that there very definitely is what one may call the French, or American, or English, or German mind. Whatever may be the mechanism that accomplishes the result, millions of mixed blood think alike in a manner recognizable (to taste and common sense, if not to laboratory tests) as French, while other equally mixed millions think in an American, or English, or German manner. To ignore the influence of these groupings of mental traits upon nineteenth- and twentieth-century art would be as illogical as to assert that they explain the whole process. The logic and sense of form of the French; the combined idealism, reverence for fact, and sentimentalism of the German; the characteristics of a deep-rooted countryman in the Englishman, with his dislike of strangers and strange ideas, his clannishness and silent sentiment; the sentiment, idealism, and dislike of metaphysics of the American — all these national temperaments have played their part in forming our art.

The logical sequence of French art since the Revolution (so pleasing to the historian) and the world-wide influence upon taste which France has exerted in the past three generations have led many acute critics, notably Walter Pach and Roger Fry, to identify the whole modern development with the French tradition. It is true that no other country produced so unbroken a series of great painters throughout the entire one hundred and fifty years. Nowhere else was the technical tradition preserved on so high a level. In Germany, England, and the United States the break with the eighteenth century involved the loss of the craft tradition of art, with a consequent decline in technique that placed a heavy handicap upon the individual artist.

It is not to deny the preëminence of French artists in the nineteenth century, however, to say that the French contribution was predominantly formal and intellectual. French rationalism, with its clear logic and its deference to rules and authority, was at once the strength and the weakness of the nineteenth century. It created the classic tradition of David, which reëchoed Poussin and Raphael, and restated in modern terms the concept of art as a formal harmony and a projection of the cultured mind upon the chaos of life. This faith in formal pictorial order was the central thread of French art, which it defended with all the ardor and intelligence of the French temperament against the onslaught of romantic sentimentalism, scientific materialism, and Freudian introspection.

At first glance it may seem impossible to sustain this generalization through the long line of French development, from the classicism of David or Ingres through the romanticism of Delacroix and the objective realism of Courbet and Manet, through Impressionism and the Post-Impressionism of Renoir and Cézanne, and through the mingled currents of the last fifty years: Seurat's pointillism, the exoticism of Gauguin, the color patterns of the Fauves, and the rigors of Cubist theory. If one compares the French with other artists, however, one will see how slight are the invasions of sentiment or naturalism in French romanticism or objective realism. Delacroix, for example, so far as he was a romantic, was inspired by the English and German authors who had created and nourished romanticism, but his true painter-ancestors were, first, Rubens, who tamed the realism of a Flemish mind to the discipline of a Latin sense of form, and, second, Poussin, the archetype of formal painting, whose baroque bacchanals are essentially as passionless and formal as Delacroix's Moroccan hunts or medieval battles. To Delacroix romantic subjects were an opportunity to create a harmony of forms in movement instead of the static groups of the classicists. And, so far as he was influential in the logic of the French development, it was not as a master of sentiment but as a stylist and a formal colorist whose interweaving of pure tints (which he called *flochetage*) led the way to the color of the second half of the century.

And if one compares Courbet, the realist, not with other French artists but with Menzel in Berlin or Eakins in Philadelphia, how slight are the innovations of subject matter which he allows himself! The human figure, draped or undraped, was his great theme; and the female nude, posed in the studio, plays nearly as important a part in his work as in that of Ingres. What makes his work seem novel and un-French is not so much realism of thought as the lack of the formal, picture-making faculty, which gives so many of his works the character of magnificent studies rather than compositions.

When Monet allowed his interest in light to lead him into painting directly from nature and ignoring construction, Degas protested caustically against the heresy. "Je n'éprouve pas le besoin de perdre la connaissance devant la nature," he said of him to Rothenstein.[4] Degas himself was by every instinct a classic draughtsman, proud of having seen and spoken to Ingres.

Vollard[5] tells a story of a lady who came to talk to Degas about her son.

"My son paints," she said winningly, "and he is so sincere about his work from Nature."

"And how old is he, madam?"

"He will soon be fifteen. . . ."

"So young and already so sincere about working from Nature? Well, madam, all I can say is that your son is lost!"

The lady departed, quite overcome, as might well be imagined.

Vollard: "But how else is a painter to learn his métier, Monsieur Degas?"

<hr>

[4] William Rothenstein, *Men and Memories*, I (New York, 1935), 104.
[5] Ambroise Vollard, *Degas, An Intimate Portrait* (New York, 1927), p. 95.

"He should copy the masters and re-copy them, and after he has given every evidence of being a good copyist, he might then reasonably be allowed to do a radish, perhaps, from Nature."

To Degas, in other words, art was a formal language, to be learned like any other language by study of its great examples.

"Good painting," said Michelangelo, "is a music and a melody, which intellect only can appreciate, and that with great difficulty." The Latin genius for form has probably never been more clearly put into words. Cézanne, after he had assimilated from Pissarro the objective eye and the broken color of Impressionism, devoted his life to restoring formal order to French painting, which had been rendered at once so delicious and so fragile by the transparence of the Impressionist palette. "L'art," he said, in words that recall Michelangelo, "est une harmonie parallèle à la nature." Seurat's artistic credo began with almost the same words: "Art is a harmony." Like Cézanne, he tried to save the coloristic charm of Monet while restoring the elaborate harmonies of form and tone and color that reflect the order of the intellect rather than the face of nature. Even Gauguin told his pupils at Pont Aven, "Let everything you do breathe peace and calm of soul," a sentiment which a Greek sculptor could not have bettered. And, as is well known, the tendency to geometrize the detail of nature (if one may be permitted the expression) so that the eye should see form exalted above reality was evident in French painting as early as the eighties, but it was carried to its logical extreme by the Cubists, who wished to make painting consist of form and nothing else.

The constancy with which the French carried on their tradition of formal pictorial order is the positive side of the medal; the reverse is the tendency toward academicism implicit in a formal tradition. There must always be a counterpoise to discipline and learning in freshness and individuality of spirit. The great figures of the French nineteenth century had both; not so the lesser. One might oversimplify the century into a generalization: in France, many geniuses, but few minor talents free of academic dullness; outside France, few great artists, but much spirited and interesting minor painting. In England, the United States, and Germany the force of sentiment, the love of life, the worship of individuality were stronger than the sense of style; from these sources came the contribution which they also had to make to modern art.

2. *Flaxman: Penelope's Dream.* 1805

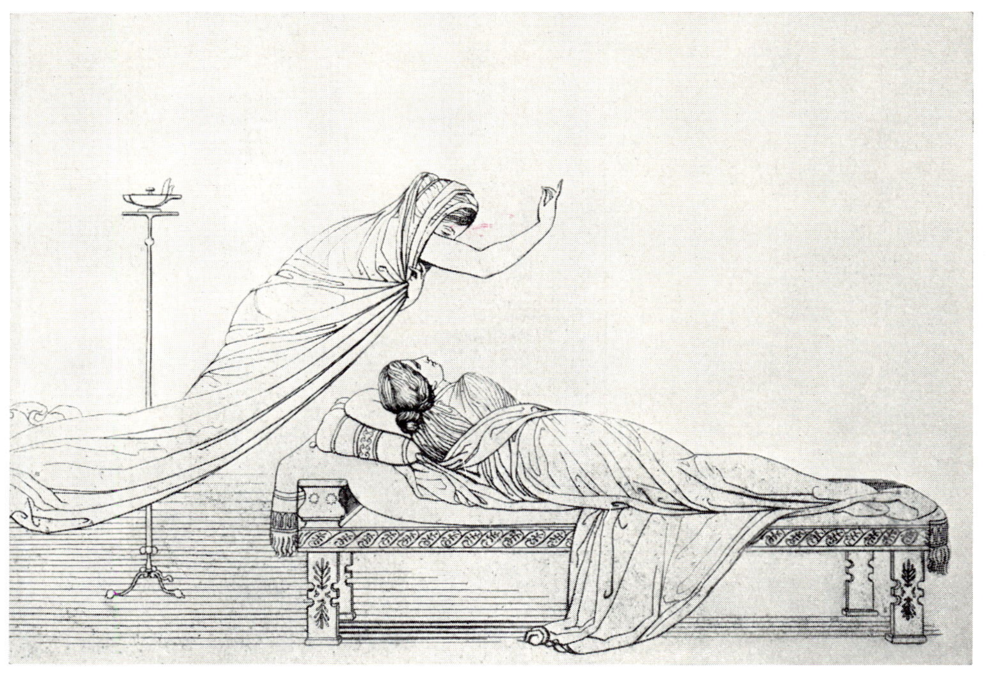

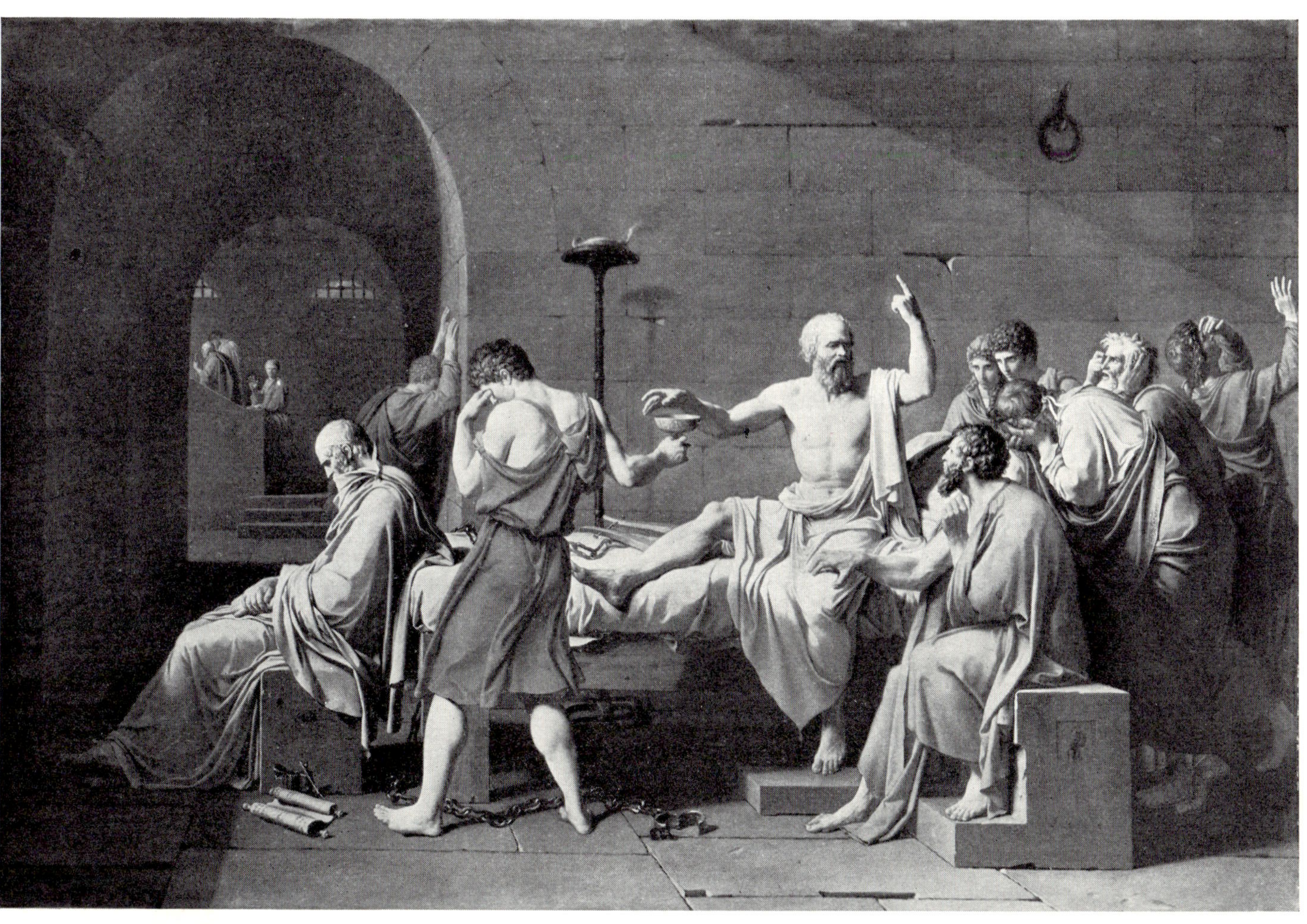

3. David: *The Death of Socrates.* 1787

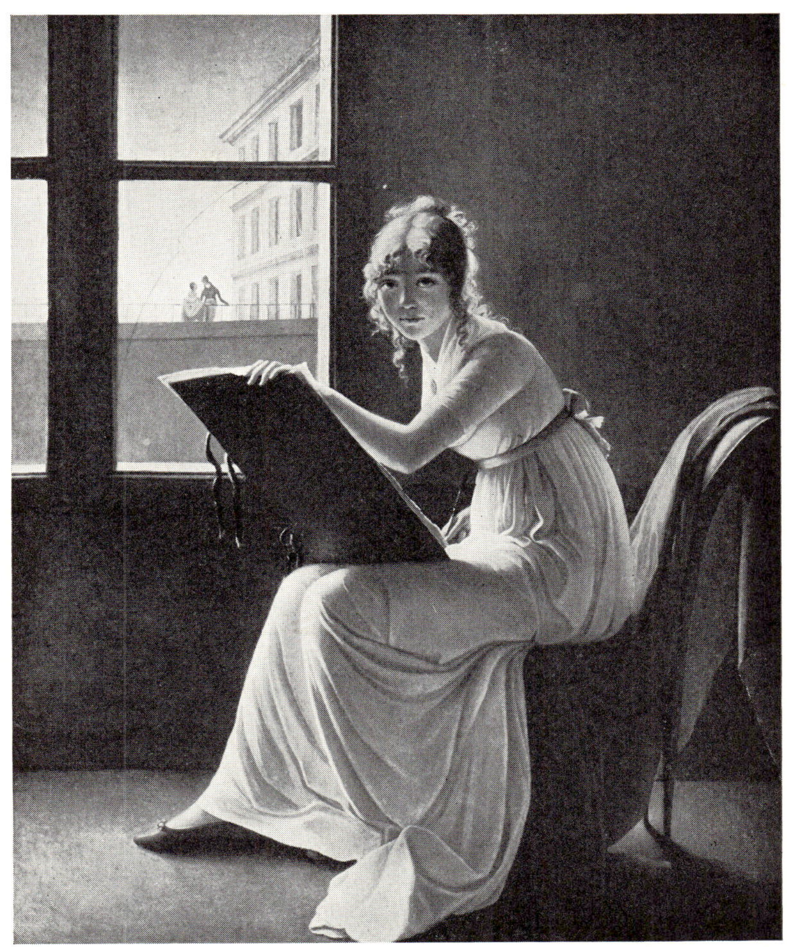

4. David: Mlle Charlotte du Val d'Ognes

CHAPTER II

CLASSIC AND ROMANTIC IDEALISM

WHEN THE American and French revolutions put a period to the Renaissance epoch, the newborn art of history was an intellectual fashion as all-pervading as psychology was in the 1920's. The excavations at Pompeii and Herculaneum, begun in the second quarter of the eighteenth century, had fascinated a world educated on the Latin poets. Never before had it been possible to recapture the past in such accurate detail. The eighteenth century not only created the science of archaeology but gave the art of history an entirely new character. The work of men like Gibbon and Voltaire, who used a comparative and critical study of sources to build up not a mere chronicle but the living portrait of civilization, had created written history in the modern sense. But the eighteenth century not only discovered in historical knowledge a new intellectual force of extraordinary interest; it also set for itself the task of remodeling the world upon historical models. Probably never before or since has literature been so influential as it was then, when the reconstruction of the world was undertaken under the guidance of historians, philosophers, and novelists. The writer was more powerful than kings; and all the other arts, today so jealous of their independence, willingly accepted the lead of literature.

The center of this intellectual revolution was France. In the long calm pause of French life in the decades before the Revolution, the peculiar tranquility of life prepared men to believe it would be an easy thing to change the customs of mankind. French philosophers had developed in the eighteenth century a new and deceptively attractive theory of human nature. For two thousand years Christianity had taught that the ills of society rose from the imperfection of the human soul. Now Rousseau and his fellows asserted that men were naturally good and plastic, that only their institutions were corrupt: change the institutions, they said, and all will be well.

It is impossible to understand the art of the period unless one can imagine the attraction exercised upon generous minds by this confident appeal. The moralists had found what they believed to be the pattern of a perfect society in the ancient republics of Greece and Rome, and of individual life in the examples of heroic civic virtue described in Plutarch's *Lives*, while the historians and archaeologists had created a dazzlingly complete vision of that vanished but perfect world. Godwin in England, Jefferson and Tom Paine and Joel Barlow in America, communicated the same enthusiasm for a new social order, made the same confident appeal to reason and justice as Rousseau in France, while in Germany the direction of philosophical idealism was all toward the power of the ideal over life. The men who made the liberal revolutions in America and Europe were well-educated men. As a result of their

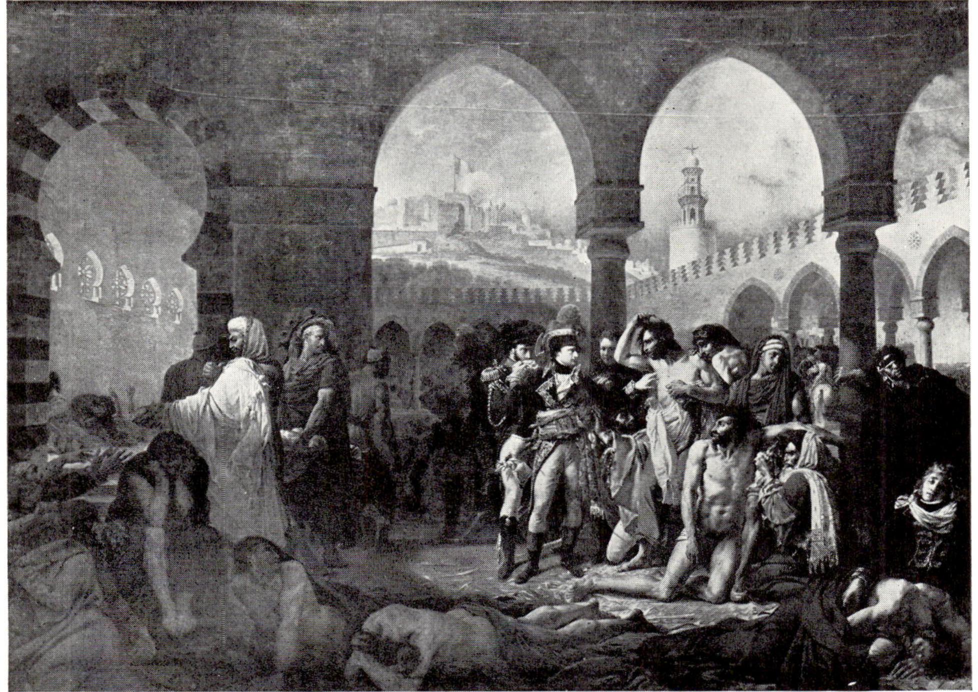

5. *Gros: Napoleon among the Plague-Stricken at Jaffa.* 1804

thorough acquaintance with the classics and with the literature of their day, their rise meant not mere reform but a complete break with what had gone before and an attempt to create an altogether new political, social, philosophical, and artistic machinery of life. Their rational, skeptical thought had no conception of the deep emotional needs and loyalties that bind men to their past and hold society together. Dissatisfied with their own world, they thought it an easy thing to seize the ready-made forms of a perfect past which history presented so vividly. Only if we remember the generous enthusiasms of this generation of philosophic aristocrats and gallant intellectuals can we realize how ardent and stirring to them were the pompous historical subjects that seem now to us so dead.

A historical eclecticism, an urge to break violently with the present and to set up in its place a historically accurate reconstruction of some past era, was the basis of both classic and romantic idealism. The romantics only changed their mind about the era which it was desirable

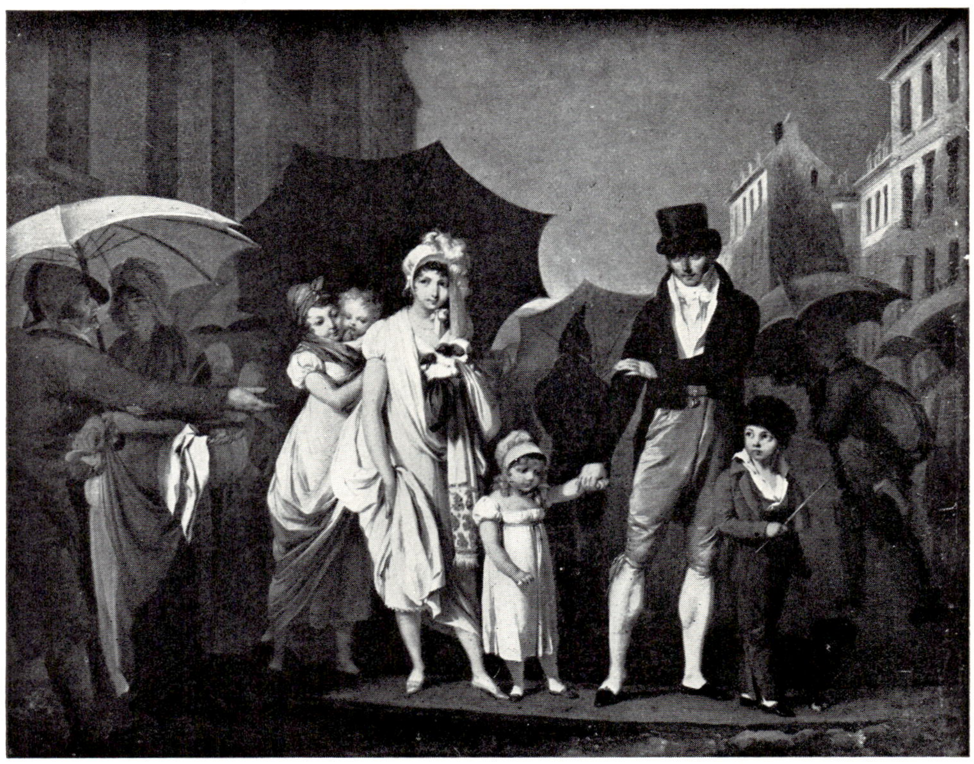

6. Boilly: The Shower. 1803

to reconstruct. The change in style that separates the two movements
in France has confused this fundamental likeness and made the difference between them seem greater than it is. In England, Germany, and
the United States the two movements are inextricably mixed.

The eighteenth-century interest in antique ruins, expressed with great
charm by Pannini, Piranesi, and Hubert Robert, was replaced in the
last quarter of that century by the strict esthetic of Winckelmann. His
dogma, which has a very strange sound in modern ears, may be sum-
marized as the doctrine of Ideal Beauty. Beauty, impersonal and universal, is not to be found in the diverse and changing face of Nature.
Art must therefore turn its back upon Nature. Nature is the object
of Sensation; Beauty is the conception of Reason. The stable and intellectual elements in art are drawing and design, which are the combination of geometric lines; color, variable and making its appeal to

the emotions, is a secondary matter. And, Winckelmann asserted, since antique sculpture had attained the perfection of serenity and nobility — that is to say, of Ideal Beauty — modern art should imitate antique sculpture.

Winckelmann's books provided a critical statement of the trend of the arts; but the eclectic movement was broader than Winckelmann. Its basis was the general belief of the age that art could simply abandon its entire practice and technical tradition to build a new one out of the contemplation of the distant past. Winckelmann's theories, current in Rome, were accepted by the German painter, Mengs, in 1761 and by J. L. David in the 1780's. But another expression of historical eclecticism, initiated in 1765 in London by the American painter, Benjamin West, was already in its second generation when David brought his classicism to Paris.

The greatest of the classic painters, Jacques Louis David (1748–1825), was already a mature artist, equipped with all the inherited skill of the baroque discipline, when he went to Rome and absorbed the theory of classicism. With his "Oath of the Horatii," exhibited in 1785 after

7. *Ingres: La Grande Baigneuse.* 1808   8. *Ingres: Comtesse d'Haussonville.* 1845

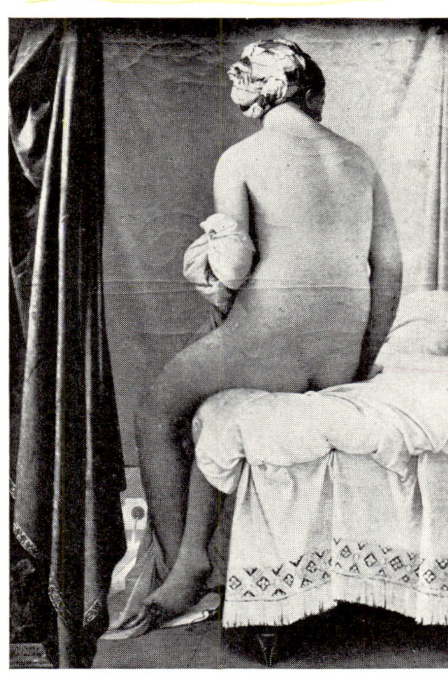

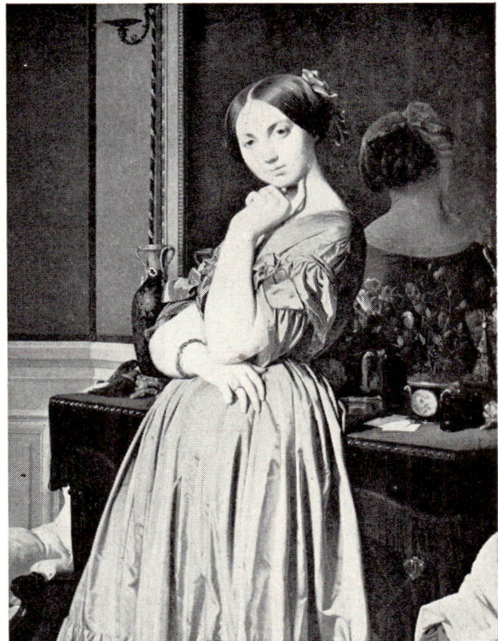

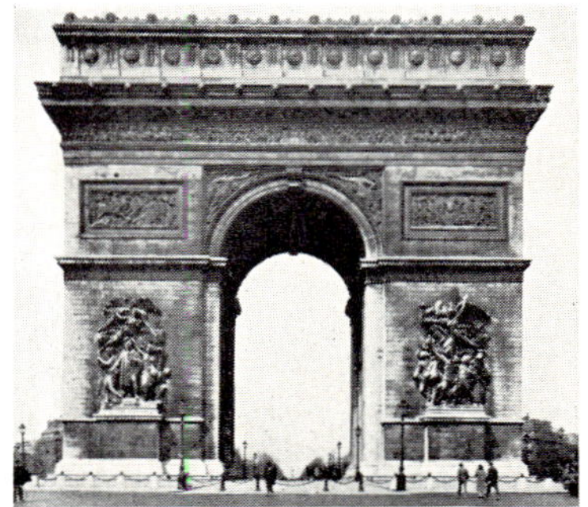

9. *Chalgrin: L'Arc de Tri- omphe de l'Étoile, Paris.* 1806–37

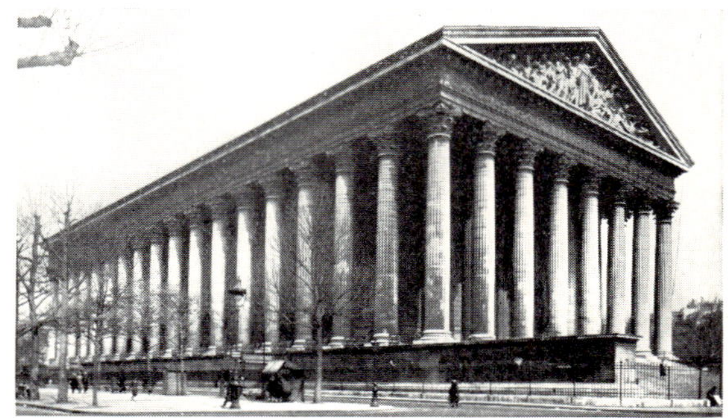

10. *Vignon: L'Église de la Madeleine, Paris.* 1806–42

his return to Paris, French art plunged into the great effort of historical idealism which was to absorb its energies for the next two generations. His "Death of Socrates" (1787; Fig. 3), now in New York, contains all the elements of great painting according to the theory of classical idealism: a heroic subject, embodying nobility of soul, civic virtue, and pathos; brilliance and energy of line; and composition in the manner of a bas-relief. David's subjects no longer have the life which only one moment of history could give them, but one must still consider him a great artist. His drawing has superb decision and energy. His color, although subordinate to line, is solid and agreeable. His austere idealism did not destroy his hold upon nature. He excluded rigidly from his historical paintings many qualities which we admire, but the exclusion was deliberate, and he still composed with the skill inherited from the great baroque tradition. There is no better test of his qualities, per- haps, than his portraiture. His "Mlle Charlotte du Val d'Ognes" (Fig. 4) portrays the simplicity and grace of a French girl with the effortless assurance of a master. The preceding centuries had been rich in such skill; after David it grew more and more rare.

There was, in fact, a strong undercurrent of realism in French classical idealism. It appears not only in David's portraits but in the elegant portraits of Gérard (1770–1837) and in Gros's (1771–1835) dramatic paintings of Napoleon's campaigns (Fig. 5). The sentiment and grace of the eighteenth century lingered also in the painterlike[1]

---

[1] *Painterlike* I have used as the opposite of *linear*, to designate the two types of vision

touch of Prud'hon (1758–1823) and the amiable genre of Boilly (1761–1845; Fig. 6). Even the national tradition was represented in the classic movement. Ingres, who was at first called a romantic, exhibited at the Salon of 1822 an "Entry of Charles V into Paris" that was inspired by medieval miniatures. French classicism was thus a matter of concentration, an emphasis placed upon line and form in a clear, cold manner, but it did not become academic in our sense of losing touch with life until it had passed into the second generation.

While David was the creator of the classic style, it was Ingres (1780–1867) who dominated the nineteenth century. For the nobility and pathos of David's historical subjects Ingres substituted the less difficult

------

which are so well described by Woelfflin. The painterlike vision sees color and tonal values, and subordinates the sharp delineation of shapes and details to masses of light and shade or of color. Rembrandt and Daumier are great examples. The linear vision subordinates richness of color and tone to the clear and exact delineation of form. Botticelli and J. L. David are examples in painting. Both of these categories apply to all the visual arts.

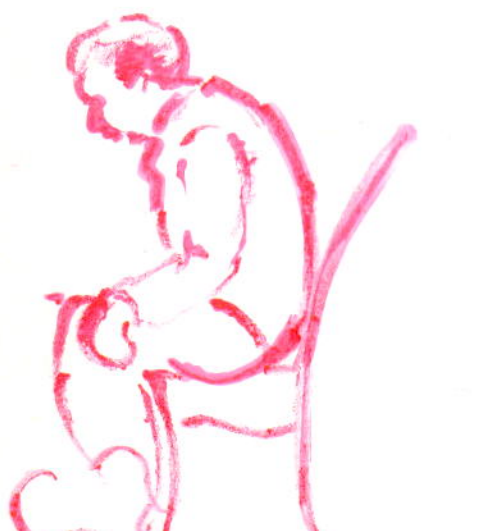

11. *Cortot: Coronation of Napoleon.*
1833

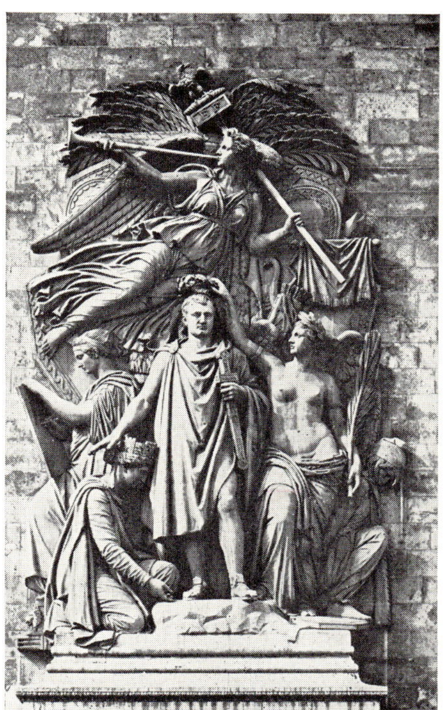

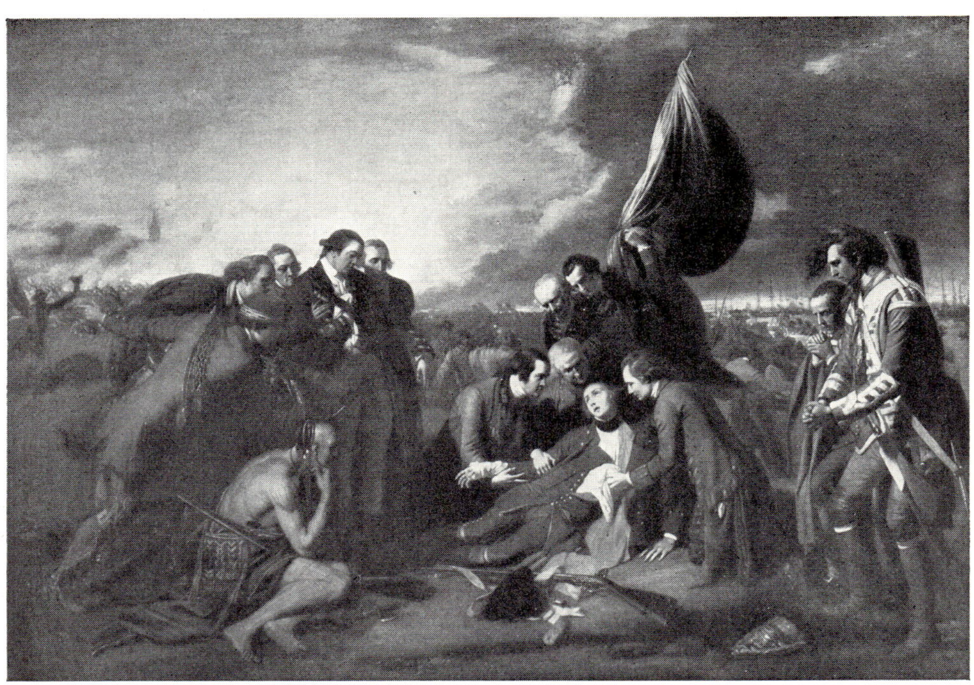

12. *West: The Death of Wolfe*

ideal of physical beauty. The classic purity of line assumed in his feminine nudes, such as "La Grande Baigneuse" (Fig. 7) or "La Source," a soft, sinuous grace that is to David's energetic draughtsmanship as Mino's sculpture is to that of Donatello. Or perhaps one should say as the work of Raphael is to that of Masaccio, for Ingres made of Raphael a cult as great as that of the antique. Ingres was the beginning of the modern academic tradition; his imagination had no driving force, and his big compositions were airless and lifeless collections of single figures, without pictorial or psychic unity. But in his portraits, which show clearly the formal nature of his art, his style reveals its power. Although Ingres was both frigid and external in perception of character, he was so able an observer of detail and so distinguished in style that his figures achieve a perfection of their own in what the French call the *portrait d'apparat*, the portrait of a person in his social setting (Fig. 8).

Ingres's diluted form of classicism was what later generations of academic painters chose to copy. But the real flowering of the classic movement took place at the beginning of the century, when an abstract style of line and plane permeated all the arts. In the decorative arts the austere lines of Directoire and Empire furniture and costume succeeded the coloristic profusion of rococo art. In architecture Chalgrin's Arc de Triomphe (1806; Fig. 9), with its severely geometrical outline and broad wall planes, and Vignon's Madeleine (begun in 1806 as a Temple de la Gloire for Napoleon; Fig. 10) are outstanding examples of this abstract feeling. In sculpture the monumental, if empty, dignity of Cortot's "Crowning of Napoleon" (1833; Fig. 11) on the Arc de Triomphe is the measure of the French achievement. And whatever may be one's personal sympathy or lack of sympathy for the statuesque form and the historical subject-matter of David and his immediate followers, no one can deny that at least the first generation of classic painters possessed the great and disciplined knowledge which has always been the strength of French painting. It is difficult for us today to realize how glowing their pompous subjects once seemed. It now requires, sad to say, a definite effort of historical knowledge on our part to understand that generation which once shook Europe, a generation whose dream was the moral dignity of man rather than the advancement

13. Fuseli: Titania and Bottom

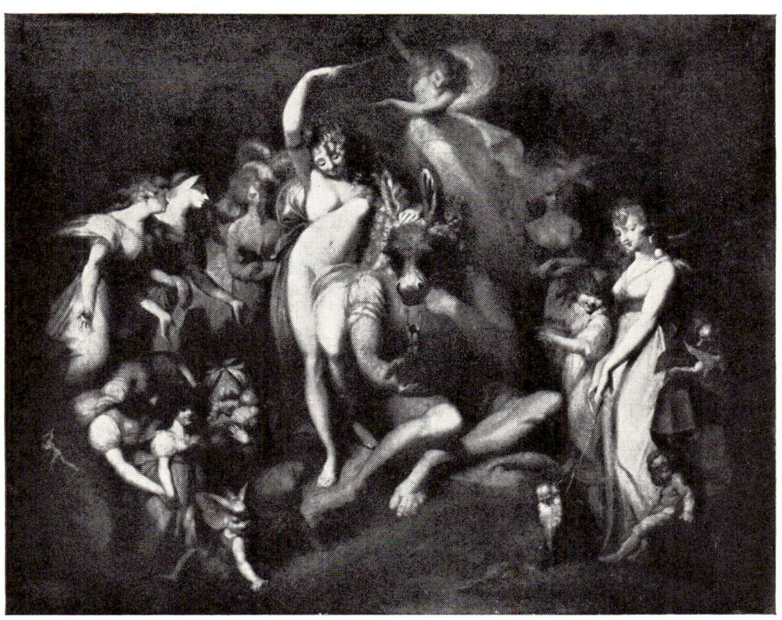

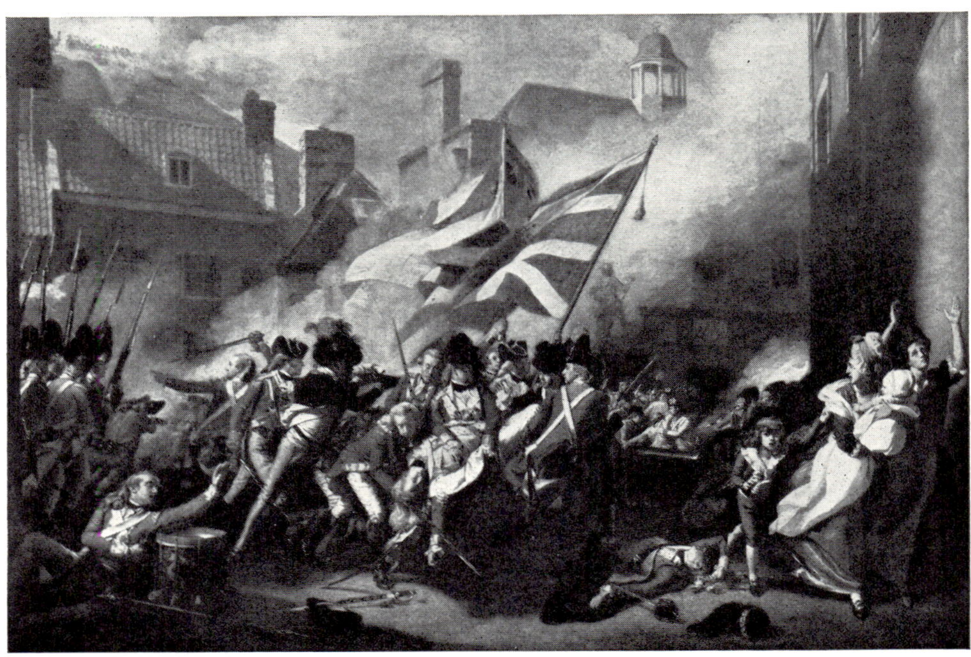

14. Copley: Death of Major Pierson. 1783

of a class, and who guided their lives not by statistics and tables of pur-chasing power but by the magnanimity of the antique hero.

In England no revolution separated the old world from the new, and the aristocratic grace of the eighteenth century cast a long afterglow over the opening decades of the nineteenth. English sentiment, which shows its predominance as a motive force even in architecture, came to an extraordinary flowering in the literature of this period: Burns, Chatterton, Byron, Scott, Coleridge, Wordsworth, Lamb, Hazlitt, Shelley, Keats, Jane Austen make this one of the great creative ages of the English mind. The paradox of the English plastic arts is that at the beginning of the nineteenth century they were at once more conservative and more advanced than the French: they looked backward in style to the painterlike eighteenth century while they explored the themes of a future romanticism. In painting, neither the dogmatic rule of the antique nor the precise linear technique of David's classicism ever took root. The historical school of painting arose even earlier in England than in France, but its leader, West, was trained in the painterlike style

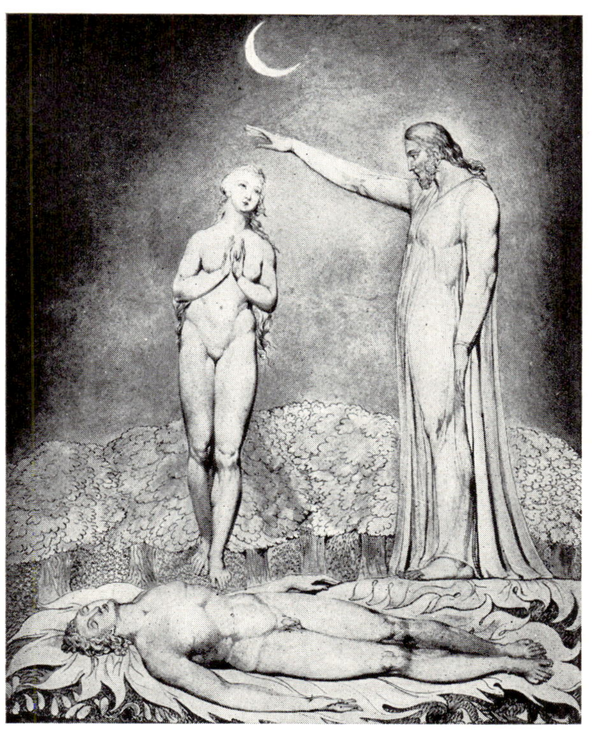

15. *Blake: The Creation of Eve*

16. *Soane: Bank of England, Interior of the Three Per Cent Consols Office*

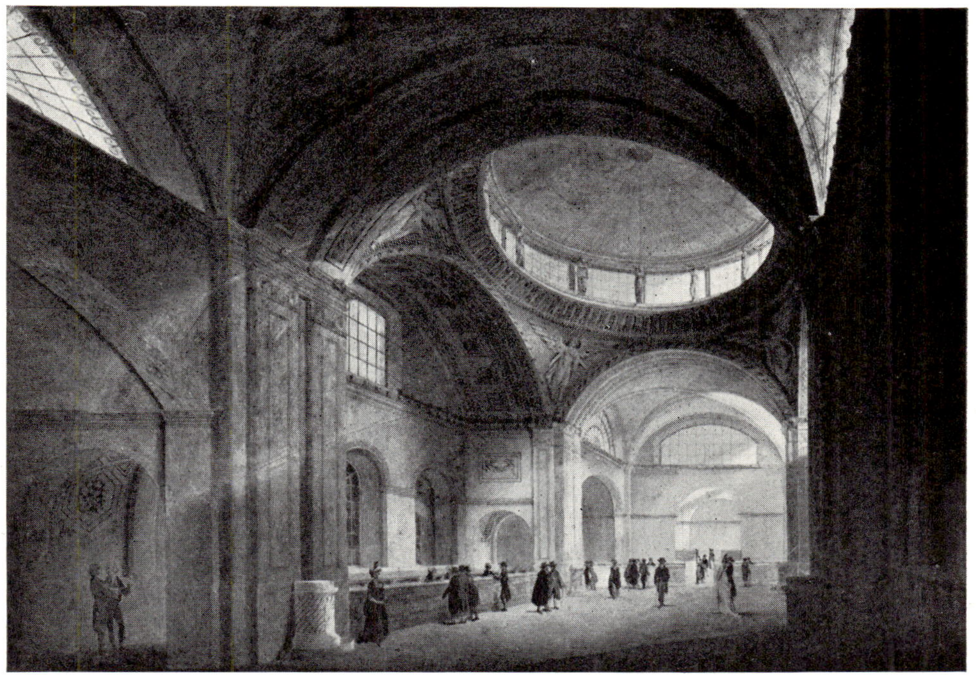

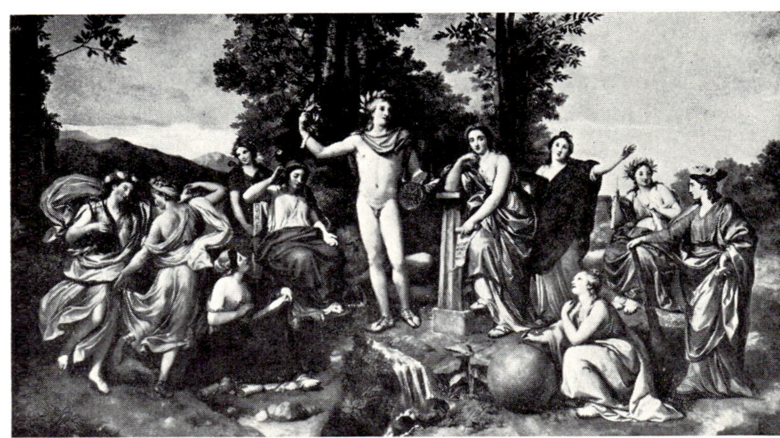

17. Mengs: Parnassus. 1761

of Reynolds. Landscape painting, which was one of the interests of romantic sentiment, developed without interruption from the eighteenth-century atmospheric technique of Gainsborough and Wilson, so that Constable and Crome (who will have their place in another chapter) began their development in the decade 1800–1810, while the French had to wait until 1830 for the revival of landscape. When Delacroix visited England in 1825 he was impressed not only by the character of the English painters but also by the technique of Constable, Bonington, and Lawrence. Through their influence upon Delacroix and the effect of Lawrence's stay in Vienna during the Congress of Vienna in 1814, the English painters led the way to a revival in the thirties and forties of a painterlike technique which had spread over the whole Continent by the middle of the century.

The historical school which corresponds in England with French classicism was led by the Pennsylvania-born Benjamin West (1738–1820; Fig. 12), to whom the patronage of the King gave an opportunity for vast canvases such as circumstances denied to Barry (1741–1806), Fuseli (1741–1825; Fig. 13), and Haydon (1786–1846). West had no rigid, clean-cut theory of the sort that French logic had developed for classicism; there was room in his ideal art for religious subjects, for scenes from national history, and even for contemporary events such as "The Death of Wolfe at Quebec." His work seems to us, therefore, less arid and remote in subject matter than the works of the French classicists. But the theatrical pathos which was part of the taste of the age was not sustained in his canvases (or in those of his school) by a style capable of true monumental effects. English painting was an art of sentiment, not of form, and sentiment is not the foundation of monumentality. With the exception of a few pictures such as Copley's "Death of Major Pierson" (Fig. 14), there is little left of the English historical school that one can look at with pleasure.

The great figure of the age of idealism in England was William Blake (1757–1827), though his style derived more from the Gothic sculpture in Westminster Abbey and from the *terribilità* of Michelangelo than from the Apollo Belvedere. Blake's style was as linear as that of the French classicists; his approach to the ideal world, however, was not through intellectual theory but through sentiment and mystical intuition. In the fabulous and haunting character of his work is visible the distinction between French and English idealistic art, as well as the inextricable mingling of classic and romantic in the English tradition (Fig. 15).

England's greatest achievements, however, were in architecture. Her

18. *Carstens: Night with Her Children.* 1795

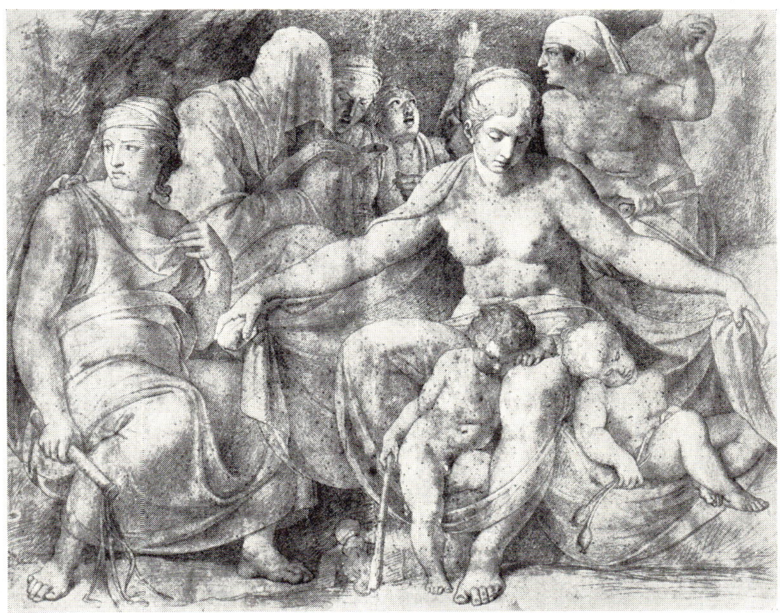

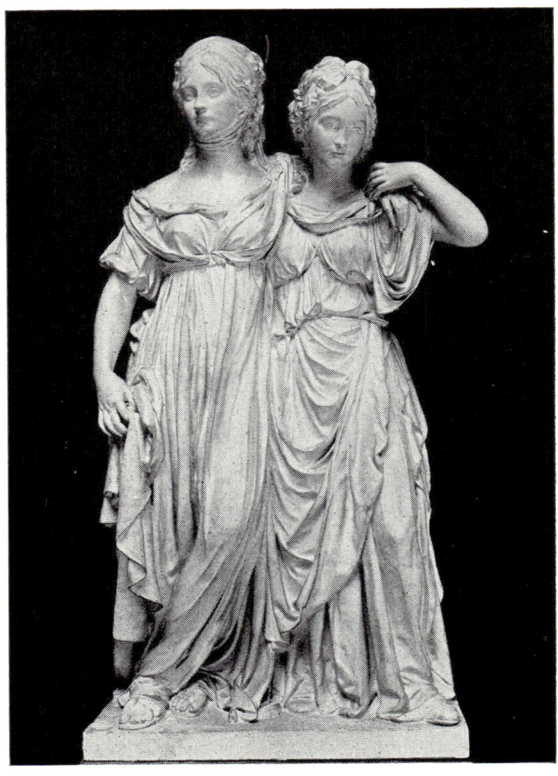

19. *Schadow: Two Royal Sisters.* 1797

long isolation from the Continent during the Napoleonic Wars caused
no separation there from the classic movement. The Adam brothers
had made a notable contribution to the eighteenth century's body of
accurate archaeological knowledge by their study of Diocletian's palace
at Spalato, and their delicate Pompeian motives in interior design became a national style. Their tradition was continued by Sir John Soane,
whose Bank of England (1788–1827) showed him as one of the few
nineteenth-century architects to grasp the fact that the secret of the
Roman style was a mastery of interior space. The sober solemnity of
his domed and vaulted halls in the Bank makes him the truest Roman
of them all (Fig. 16). In the later phase of classicism the attention of
architects turned to Hellenic forms, and William Hamilton's High
School, Edinburgh (1824–1829), excellent in line and in mass, is one
of the important achievements of the whole movement.

In sculpture the aim of the international style which stemmed from the Italian, Canova (1752–1822), was the cold, smooth surface quality and elegant line of the Apollo Belvedere. John Flaxman (1755–1826), in formal works such as the Nelson Monument in St. Paul's, showed himself master of its rather chilly grace. He also illustrated Homer and Aeschylus in engravings whose smooth-flowing, unmodulated line founded a new style of black and white and helped greatly to spread the taste of classicism. But his most important contribution was through his designs for the Wedgwood pottery. In his ceramic reliefs on a miniature scale he infused with poetry the cold purity of his line and created not only one of the happiest phases of classic decoration but a unique English tradition which has held its popularity until today (Fig. 2).

The Germanic world faced the nineteenth century with a divided mind. In contrast to the rationalism of France at the time of the Revolution, Germany was then entering its great period of philosophical idealism, which was to continue to the middle of the nineteenth century. This was also the great period of German literature. But in the arts the struggle between the idealistic and the factual mind, which disturbed all the nineteenth century, was complicated still further by that hunger

20. *Peter von Nobile: Temple of Theseus, Volksgarten, Vienna.* 1823

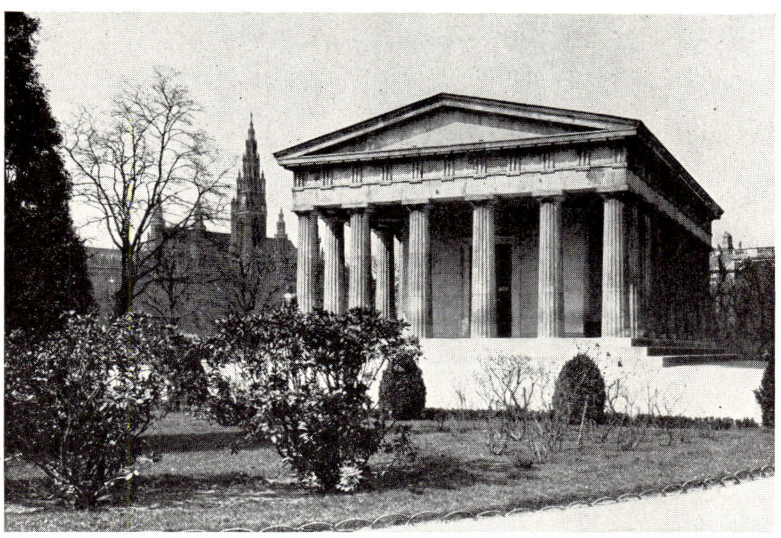

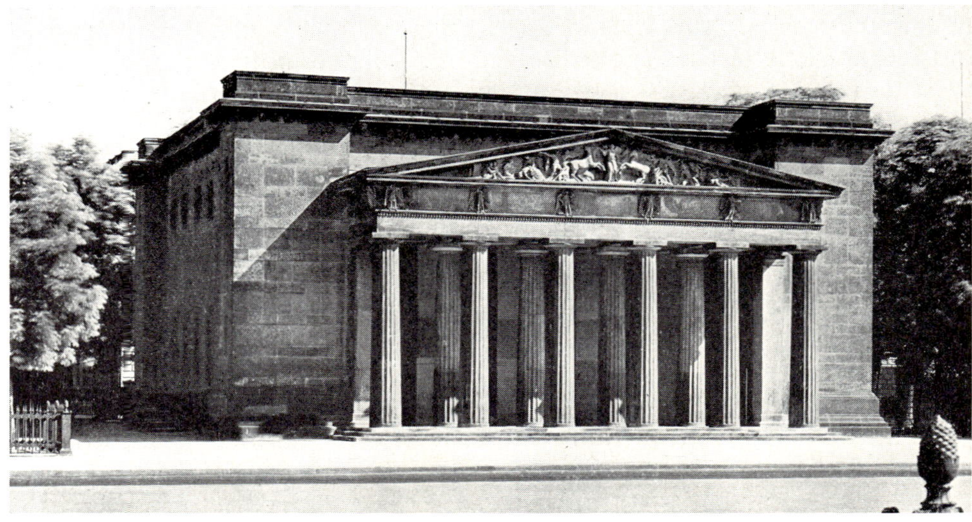

21. Schinkel: Neue Wache, Berlin. 1816–18

for the South which has made itself felt in Germans since Otto the Great crossed the Alps to refound the Holy Roman Empire, or, indeed, since the first barbarian invasions.

Winckelmann had in 1760 advanced his theory that art should break with the existing practice and remake itself in the image of antique sculpture. Goethe, in his youth a champion of Gothic art, eventually threw his influence upon the side of the antique. Winckelmann's first convert was the painter Mengs (1728–1779), who came in touch with his theory while director of the Academy in Rome. In the Villa Albani, built by the famous eighteenth-century collector, Cardinal Alessandro Albani, to house his collection of antique sculpture, Mengs painted a large fresco decoration, called "Parnassus" (Fig. 17), which began the period of eclecticism in German painting. In the one hundred years that followed, the architecture of Schinkel and Klenze, the painting of Carstens and Marées, the sculpture of Schadow, Rauch, and Hildebrand, show how great was the effort put forth by German art to capture the secret of Greece. But the immediate result of the eclectic theory that art could simply abandon its whole existing practice and build a new technical tradition out of contemplation of the distant past was to destroy in Germany an already weak technical tradition. The painter's craft was so impoverished by the break that when in the second decade

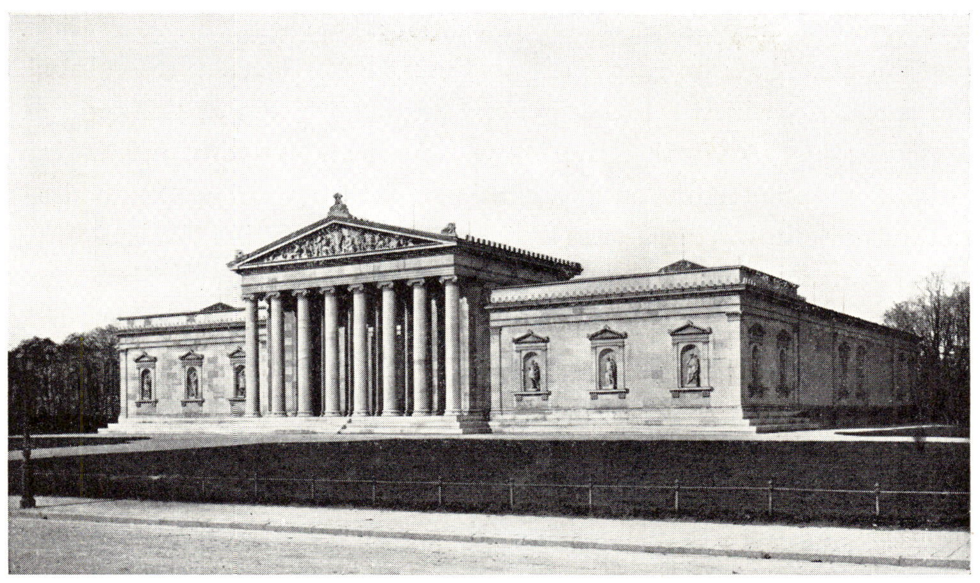

22. Klenze: Glyptothek, Munich. 1816–30

of the nineteenth century classicism slid over into the romanticism of
the Nazarenes the ability to paint large figure compositions had been
lost. The transition figures like Mengs and J. H. W. Tischbein, the
friend of Goethe, had a sound eighteenth-century training; after them
the eclectic theory was taken up by a group of ardent idealists who were
without the same technical preparation. Asmus Jacob Carstens (1754–
1798) was the first pure classicist (Fig. 18). He believed it possible to
throw away not only the painterlike rococo craft of painting but nature,
too, and to shut himself into an ideal world in which only antique
sculpture and Michelangelo were to be his guides. German classicism,
founded by Carstens upon abstract draughtsmanship alone, resulted in
a blight upon the development of the school. The group of German
painters who gathered in Rome in the early nineteenth century were
so woefully weak in technique that, although no idealistic artists were
more serious and sincere in intention, their work was stillborn. Josef
Anton Koch (1768–1839), who painted formal landscapes in the tradition of Claude, and Bonaventura Genelli (1798–1868), a refined
draughtsman, were perhaps the most living of the school.

In the opinion of that age sculpture was one of its most conspicuous achievements, an opinion which we cannot accept without reservation. Schwanthaler, in Munich, represents the taste for the cold, the colossal, and the static, which was that generation's conception of the antique. It is only just to say that the icy whiteness and smooth, mechanical surfaces of nineteenth-century classic sculpture were understood as methods of eliminating a too real effect and of elevating the sculptor's conceptions to the level of the ideal. In two Berlin sculptors, however, a sturdy realism was combined with the formal ideal. Schadow (1764–1850) was able to unite the clear, flowing line of classic sculpture with a charming naturalness and softness of touch which he inherited from the rococo; his "Two Royal Sisters" (1797) is deservedly famous (Fig. 19). Rauch (1777–1857), who recorded the heroes of the Napoleonic Wars as Schadow had those of the Seven Years' War, was a more commonplace mind, but he, too, shows the vitality of the combination of realism and classicism.

23. *Klenze and Gärtner: Hall of Liberation, near Kelheim. 1842–63*

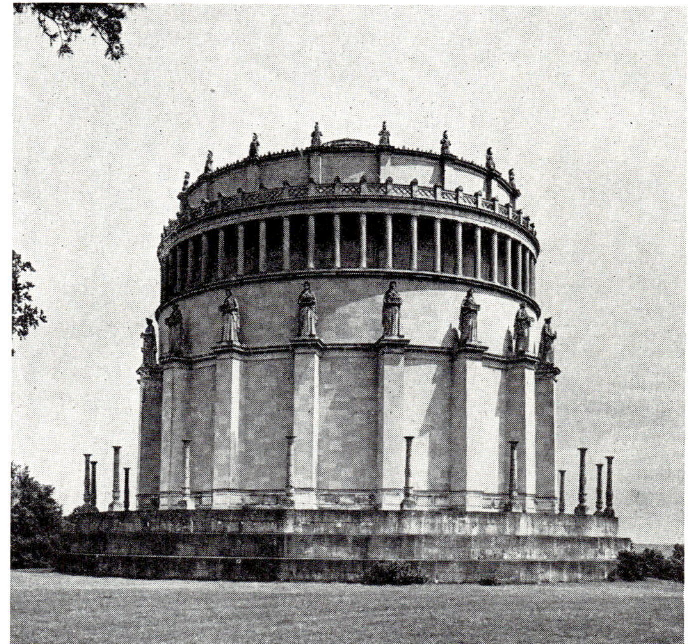

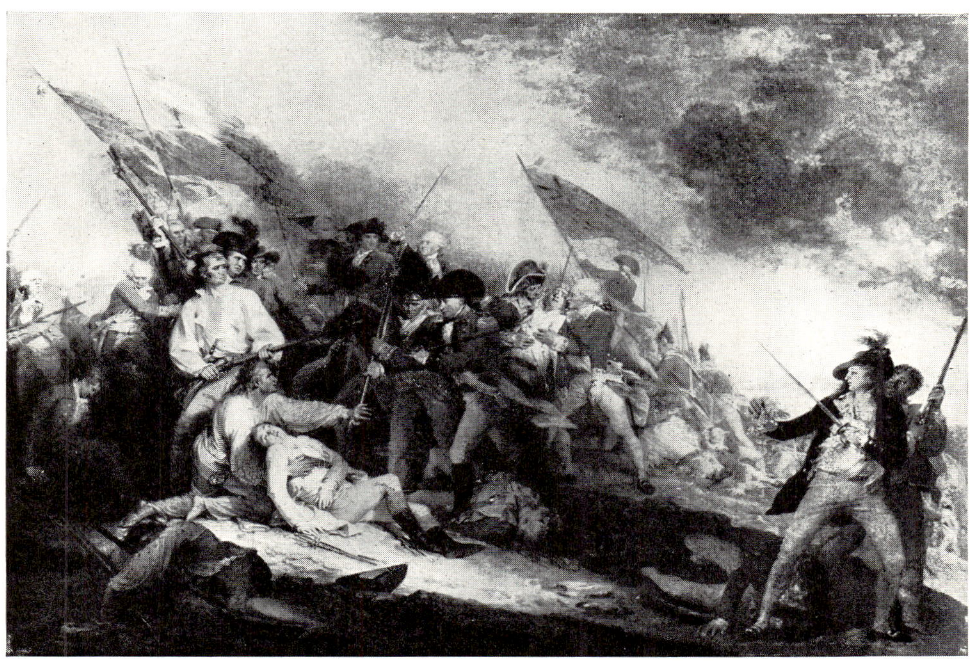

24. Trumbull: Battle of Bunker Hill. 1786

Like England, Germany did her most important work in architecture. After the Napoleonic Wars Berlin and Munich were the two great centers of building; Vienna, except for the charming Temple of Theseus in the Volksgarten, erected to house Canova's "Theseus" (Fig. 20), was to make its contribution later. In Berlin, Schinkel built the series of severely regular, strong, cold buildings that still create the character of the old center of the city (Fig. 21). In Bavaria Klenze and Gärtner built for Ludwig I an equally remarkable series of classic monuments. Leo von Klenze's Hall of Fame in Munich and his stately Walhalla on a hill overlooking the Danube near Regensburg are a direct imitation of the Parthenon in monumental buildings divorced from any practical necessity. But his other buildings, which were built for use, show how mistaken it is to think of this movement as mere archaeology. His Glyptothek (1816–1830), the first modern building designed to serve as a museum (Fig. 22), and his Propylaea (1846–1863), looking across at Ziebland's Corinthian Exhibition Hall (completed 1845), form one of the first and best of modern monumental civic groups. But Klenze's

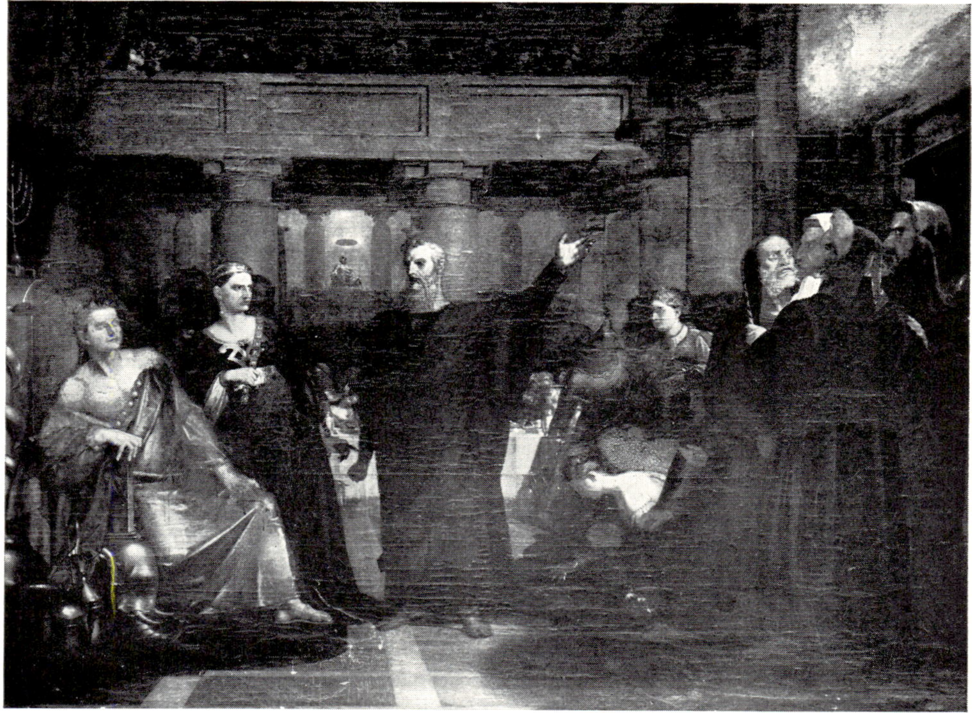

25. *Allston: Belshazzar's Feast*

design in these buildings and in his Hall of Liberation (Fig. 23), which was executed near the Walhalla in collaboration with Gärtner, is far less remarkable for archaeological correctness than for an architecture of pure form, in which strongly emphasized wall planes, stark geometric masses, and a noble harmony of mass and void are the impressive features. This architecture of Schinkel and Klenze was, in fact, a true architectural language, for one finds the same formal qualities in Klenze's Alte Pinakothek (1826–1836), executed with Renaissance ornament, and in Gärtner's monumental avenue, the Ludwigstrasse, in Munich, upon which he used Renaissance and even Romanesque detail in buildings which all harmonize in a single massive and severely monumental effect. There is no better illustration than the Ludwigstrasse of the fact that the imitations of the past were for the early nineteenth-century artist merely surface changes upon the stream of one great idealistic movement. We shall find Schinkel and Gärtner also among the architects of the medieval revival.

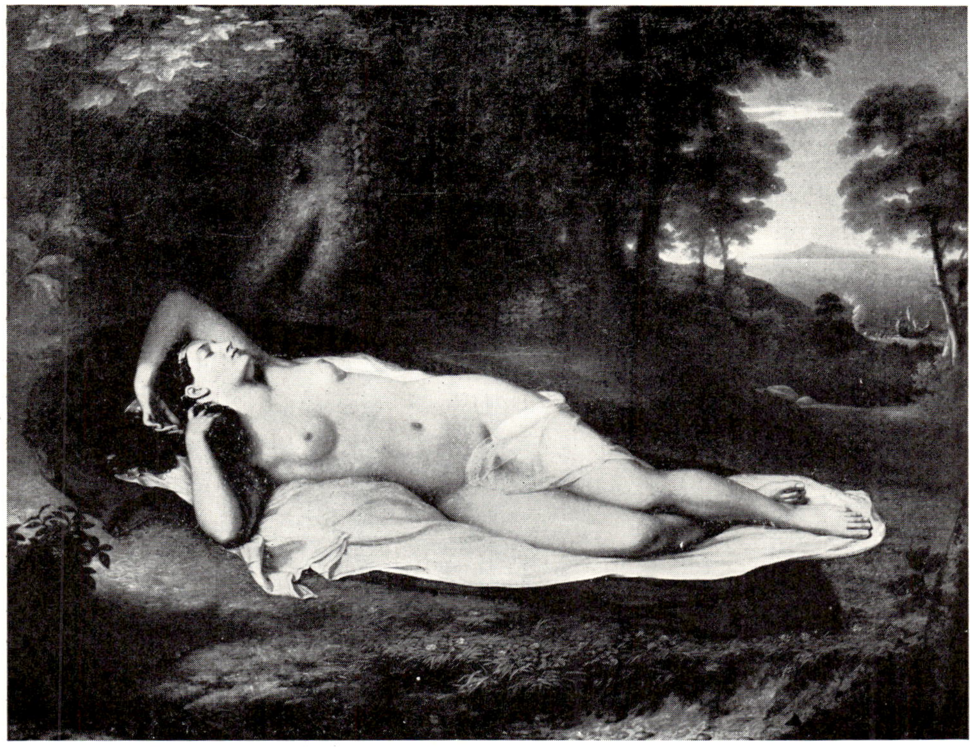

26. *Vanderlyn: Ariadne.* 1812

In American art, it is worth repeating, the historical and monumental aims of classical idealism were already in the second generation when David exhibited the "Oath of the Horatii" in Paris. In 1785 and 1786 John Trumbull, working in West's studio but already a better painter than his teacher, executed "The Battle of Bunker Hill" (Fig. 24) and "The Death of Montgomery in the Attack upon Quebec," the first two of his cycle of illustrations of the American Revolution. These paintings and David's were thus simultaneous efforts of two different cultures to raise life to the epic plane. But while David's effort led toward the abstract and the statuesque, Trumbull was still inspired by the ardor and realism of the baroque.

Nowhere was the historical mind stronger than in this country, among a people who had just erected the first modern republic upon the models of antiquity. John Trumbull (1756–1843) was a son of one of the New England leaders of the Revolution and had served in the army as an officer upon Washington's staff. He knew personally and on terms of equality the men in America, France, and England who were important in the history of the American Revolution. He was admirably equipped when in 1785 the idea came to him to paint the story of the Revolution while its principal actors were still alive to serve as models. Jefferson and Adams helped him choose twelve episodes from the military struggle and the founding of the new nation. Some of these subjects, like the surrender of Cornwallis, were unfortunately such as to defy all the artist's efforts to make them anything more than a collection of portraits. Yet his small studies for his compositions, together with the many small portrait heads of officers and statesmen made in preparation for the task, constitute not only a unique historical document but an artistic achievement as well. It was unfortunate for American art that the execution of the sketches in full scale was postponed twenty-seven years, until 1816, by the confusion of the French Revolution and the Napoleonic Wars. The four feeble paintings executed for the Rotunda of the Capitol in Washington between 1816 and 1824, when Trumbull was too old and embittered to do himself justice, have unjustly obscured the achievements of his early years. Trumbull

27. *Rush: Self-Portrait, c.* 1822   28. *Powers: Greek Slave.* 1843

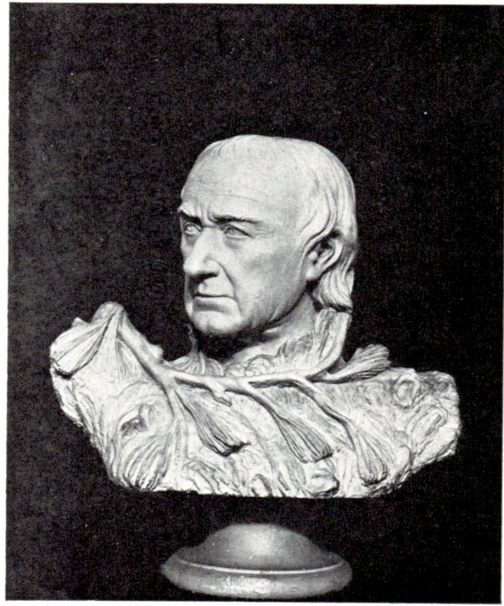

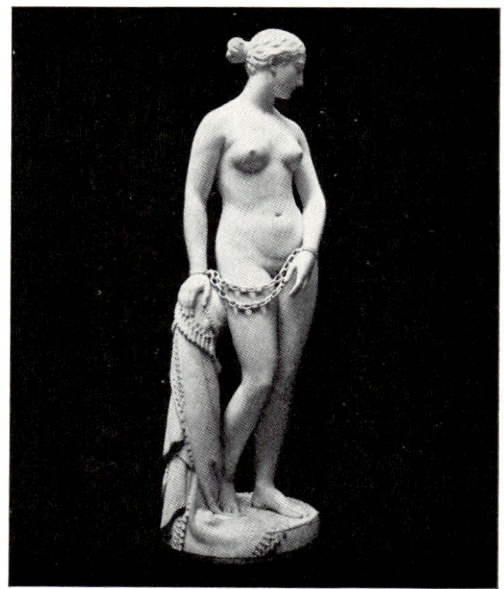

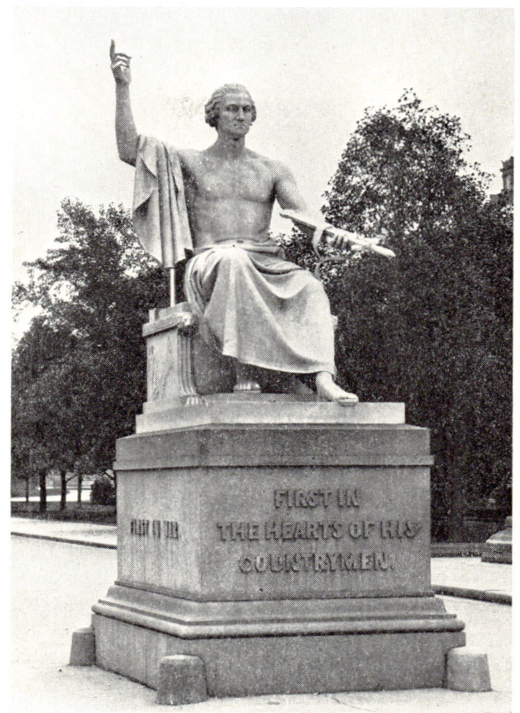

29. *Greenough: George Washington,*
Capitol, Washington

in 1785 was a man capable of forming a great idea, a master of the human figure, and a colorist equal to the best of his age. He, if anyone, might have created a monumental historical art in the United States.

In all, four generations of American artists devoted their lives to the effort to create an epic, ideal art, an effort which ended at last in almost total failure. The monumental and grandiose mural pretensions of the movement were its ruin. The natural gifts of Washington Allston (1779–1843), the greatest painter of the third generation, were romantic: he modeled his art upon Michelangelo's tragic grandeur and upon the color of the Venetians. Allston lived in Rome and in England from 1801 to 1818, and, helped by his personal charm and by his friendships with a circle of distinguished minds, attained an international reputation (Frontispiece). In 1812 his "Angel Releasing St. Peter" was commissioned by Sir George Beaumont, who had probably a better eye for talent than any English connoisseur at that time. But when Allston

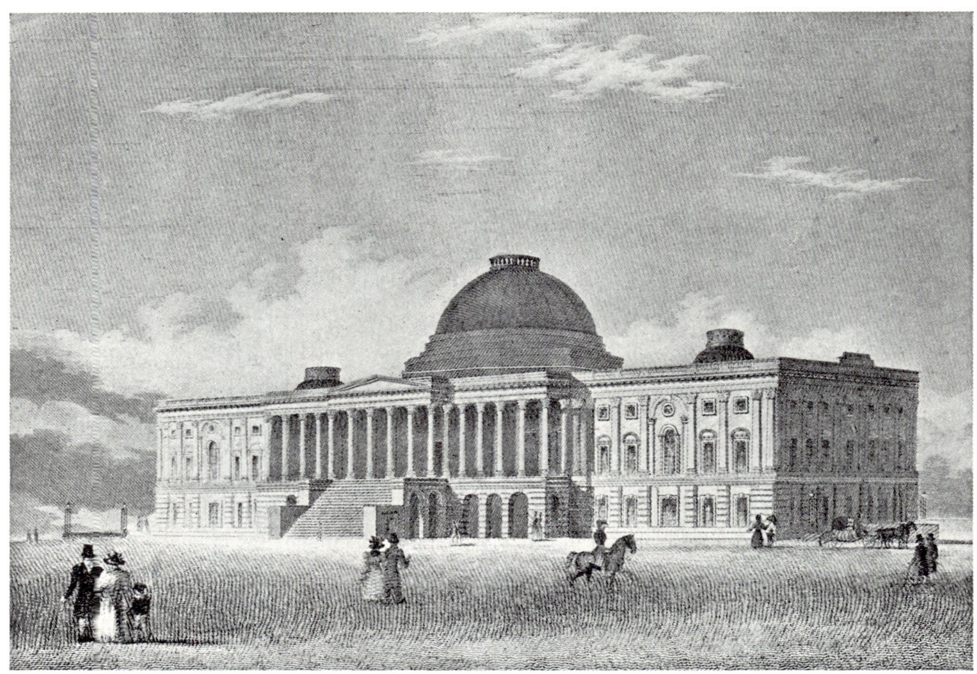

30. *Thornton, Latrobe, and Bulfinch: The Capitol of the United States in 1831*

returned to Boston in 1818 his delicate and subtle personality was over-whelmed by the problem of producing a monumental, ideal art in the unsympathetic atmosphere of a canny New England realism. He never completed the huge canvas of "Belshazzar's Feast" (Fig. 25) which he brought with him unfinished from England. His love of color, however, and his naturally romantic temperament (Washington Irving spoke of him as an inimitable teller of ghost stories) found an outlet in small pictures and drawings which were the most important stylistic influence upon the new generation.

Trumbull modeled his style upon Rubens, Allston upon the Venetians. John Vanderlyn (1775–1852), sprung from a family of Dutch portrait painters on the Hudson River, was the only American classicist to study in Paris. As a pupil of David he absorbed the French plastic tradition, and his "Ariadne" (1812) is the best formal nude painted in America before the 1870's (Fig. 26). His well-disciplined art might have formed a necessary base to American figure painting, but the same impossible gap between his ideals and the thin artistic soil of early nineteenth-century America that had defeated Trumbull and Allston defeated Vanderlyn. Unable to earn a livelihood by his art, he introduced the panorama into the United States. The rotunda which he built behind the City Hall, New York, for exhibiting his panoramas was the first American exhibition gallery. There he showed panoramas of Paris, Athens, Mexico, and Versailles. But when Congress finally gave him a commission to paint "The Landing of Columbus" (1846) for the Rotunda of the Capitol, he was too old to execute it. The canvas was done by assistants in Paris and proved a failure. All that is left of Vanderlyn's talent is the "Ariadne" and a few solid, disciplined portraits in the tradition of David.

While in painting American idealism was thus, to its profit, predominantly based upon the baroque, sculpture was allied with the formal tradition which had its center in Rome. For two generations the Venetian, Canova, and the Dane, Thorwaldsen (1770–1824), made

31. Strickland: Second United States Bank, Philadelphia. 1819–24

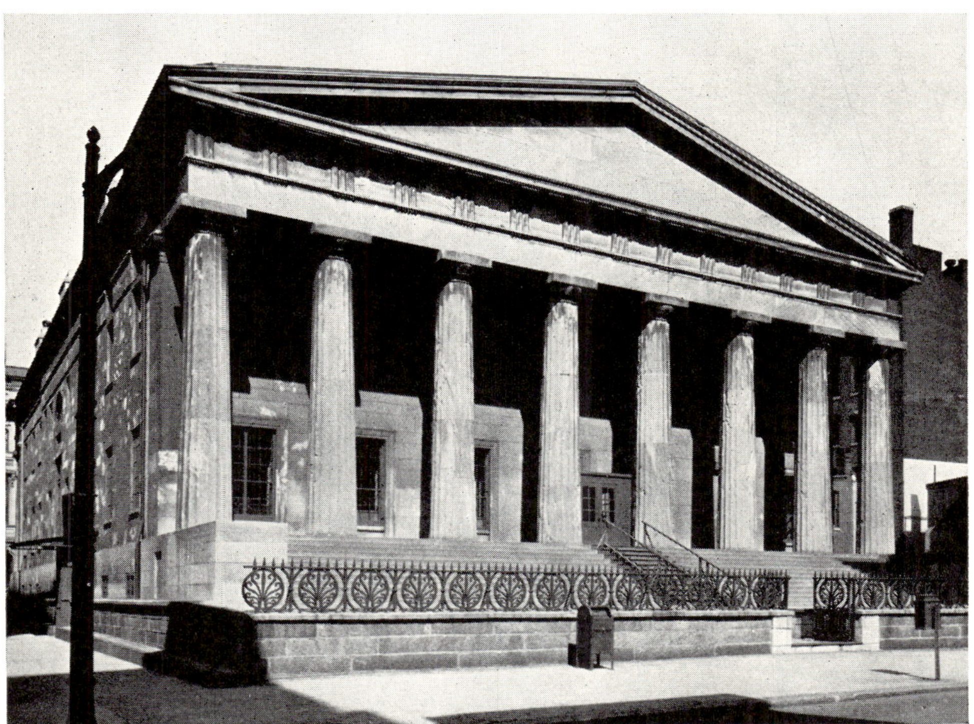

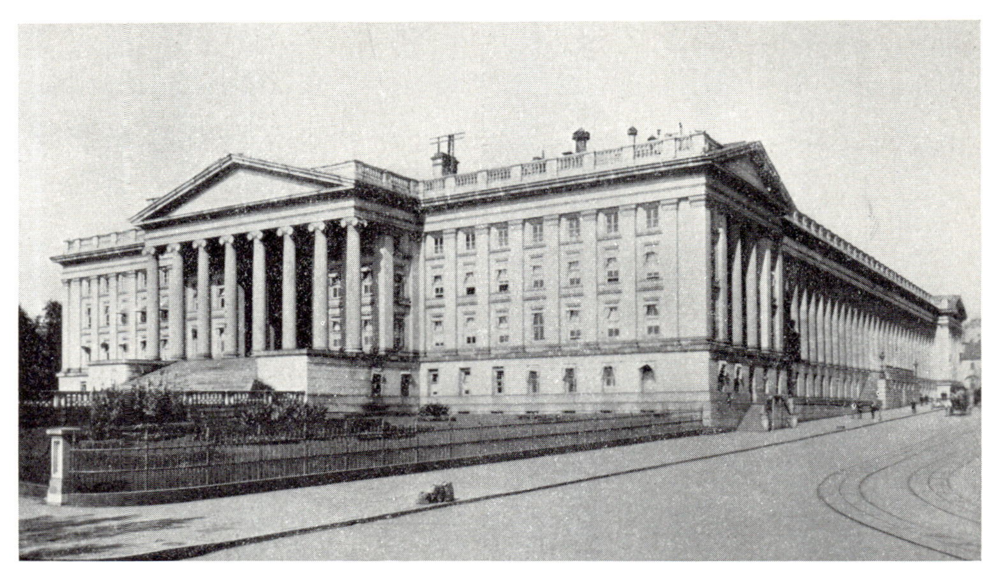

32. Mills: Treasury Building, Washington. 1836–42

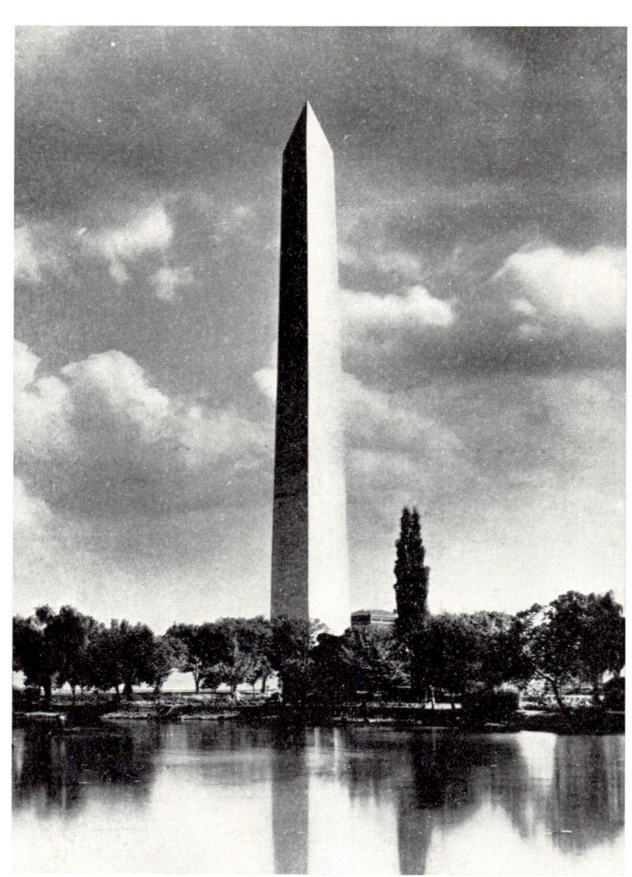

33. Mills and Casey: Washington Monument,
Washington. 1848–84

Rome play the part in the formation of classic sculpture which Paris later was to play in the development of Impressionist painting.

America had, it is true, one home-grown sculptor in William Rush (1756–1823), a wood carver who lived by making figure heads for the ships of Philadelphia's great merchant fleet. His ideal figures, like the "Girl with the Heron" at the old Waterworks (now the Aquarium), Philadelphia, are quite naïve, but his portrait heads show a power of characterization in their rugged realism that was not equaled by the next generation (Fig. 27).

The second generation of American classic sculptors lived in Italy, where Carrara marble and Italian stonecutters were available. The cold linear grace and sweetness of the nudes of Hiram Powers (1805–1873; Fig. 28) gave him great popularity in England and America. Horatio Greenough (1805–1852) had a bolder invention which led him toward the naturalism of a later generation (Fig. 29), while Crawford (1813–1857) might have done much had his life been longer. But in general the artificiality and technical weakness of American idealistic sculpture has made it as extinct as the passenger pigeon.

The failure to establish the historical style in America embittered the lives of Allston, Trumbull, and Vanderlyn, in whom we must recognize as high a degree of ability and promise as we have had. Yet the attempt to create a school of monumental painting was foredoomed in a country whose monumental architecture had yet to be born. The small wall areas, the narrow intercolumniations, the still more limited interior spaces of Thornton's Capitol in Washington (Fig. 30) — a vast building for those days and one whose dimensions rather awed Bulfinch when he took charge of its construction in 1818 — show how far the United States was even in its greatest building from a need for mural painting of heroic dimension. When Benjamin West sent his "Christ Healing the Sick" to the Pennsylvania Hospital in 1817, a special building had to be erected to house it, for the hospital had no room large enough. But the failure of the architects to create a setting for historical painting does not alter the fact that in architecture the classic style became a national idiom to a greater extent here than in any other country.

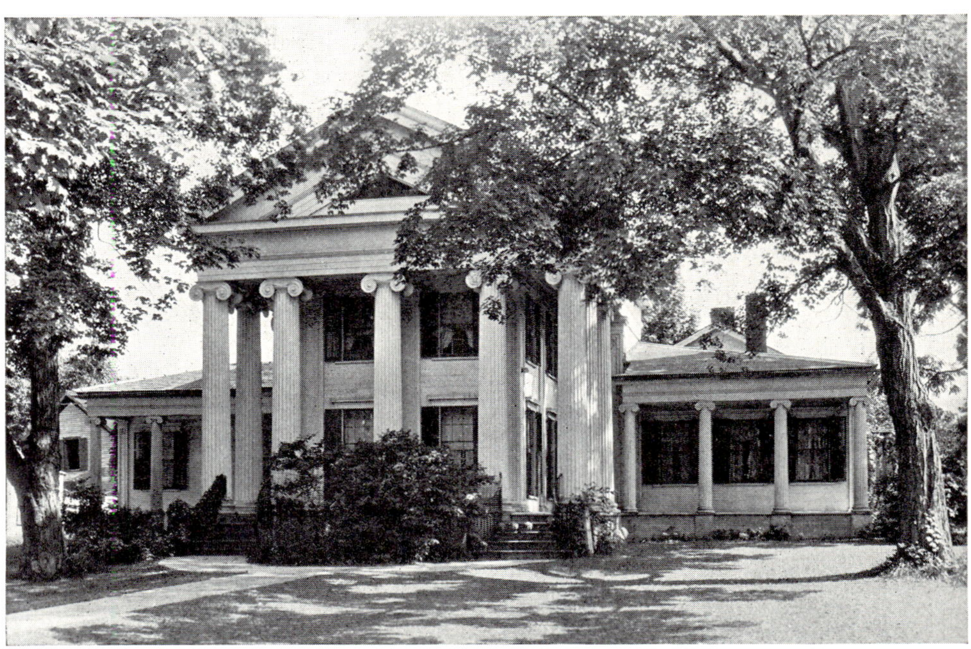

34. *The Manse, Castleton, Vermont*

Architecture, in fact, discovered a wealth of opportunity in the settlement of the country at the same time that it discovered a new classic
idiom of form. Architects were faced by no accumulation of ancient
buildings such as existed in Europe, but by a new continent to be
ornamented and a new nation to be housed. Added to this were other
favorable circumstances: a taste disciplined by a century of Palladian
design, scarcely touched by the rococo; the habit of wood construction,
which simplified or eliminated many structural problems; and the dry,
intense American sun, which, like the sun of Italy, emphasizes and
aids an art of form. Two generations of classic architects, Jefferson,
Latrobe, Bulfinch (a classicist in his later phase of the Federal and
Maine state capitols), Strickland, and Mills, furnished the great models
and imposed upon the native functionalism of the wooden house a
style of simple geometric masses, strongly emphasized wall planes, and
geometric detail, which became the vernacular from Maine and South
Carolina to the Mississippi. Nowhere but in the United States can one
see of what the classic style was capable when carried out by the united

taste of a people into every phase of building, from Mills's masterpieces of monumental design in Washington to a one-room house on the frontier.

The classic revival was begun in America by Thomas Jefferson, who, aided by professional architects, introduced in the Virginia state capitol (1789) the Roman temple form as the norm of design. He is also to be credited with the first truly monumental architectural group erected in this country, the University of Virginia (1818–1819). But the placing of the Rotunda as the focus of the latter group, which is the source of its dignity, was the suggestion of Benjamin Latrobe (1764–1820), the first of our professional architects and the man whose influence really established the classic style in the United States.

Latrobe's Baltimore Cathedral (completed 1821) was modeled upon the Roman Pantheon and remains even today an imposing use of in-

35. *Porch of a House in Portsmouth,*
New Hampshire

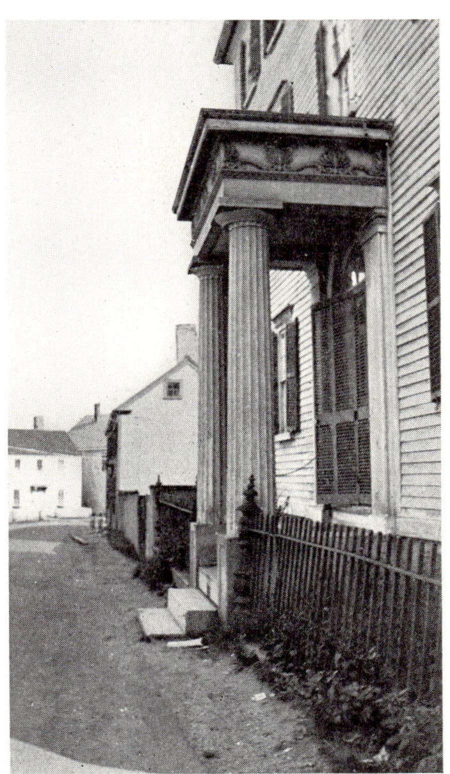

terior space. But with Latrobe's pupils the search for form turned from Roman to Greek models. The Second United States Bank, in Philadelphia, more than any other single building ushered in the new period of taste. Nicholas Biddle, the head of the bank and an enthusiastic amateur who had visited Greece, called for a building in the Greek style. Latrobe, in his design, based the front and rear elevations upon the Parthenon. After his death the commission fell to his pupil Strickland, who executed a design closely following Latrobe's plans, but characterized by his own admirable purity and vigor of form (Fig. 31). This Philadelphia bank, erected 1819–1824, anticipates by more than a decade similar use of the Parthenon model abroad; and the attempt to use a temple form for a building devoted to a practical activity like banking was an experiment of great boldness. Under the influence of Latrobe and his pupils, Strickland and Mills, American architecture became one of pure form. The use of ornamental detail such as porticoes and domes, derived from Greek and Roman building, gives the style its obvious eclectic and popular qualities. But it was a far more substantial style than this alone would indicate, as it spread throughout the continental range of the United States. The style-feeling was similar to what one finds in England or Germany — a design in geometric block-forms, with strongly emphasized wall planes and delicate linear detail, the whole being conceived rather as an exterior to please the eye by its formal order and balance than as a functional plan or a grouping of internal spaces. But it was flexible enough to allow a thousand variations and adaptations to personal fancy or to climate, giving to all its distinctive virtues of clarity, order, and harmony of form.

The culmination of this monumental, idealistic phase of American architecture came with Thomas U. Walter's Girard College, Philadelphia (1833–1847), a Corinthian temple with complete exterior colonnade, and Mills's two great designs in Washington, the colonnaded façade of the Treasury Building (1836–1842; Fig. 32) and the Washington Monument (1848–1884; Fig. 33). The final simplification and justness of proportion of the Washington Monument, which make it the greatest achievement of the classic revival, were however, the work of Colonel Thomas Lincoln Casey of the United States Army Engineers,

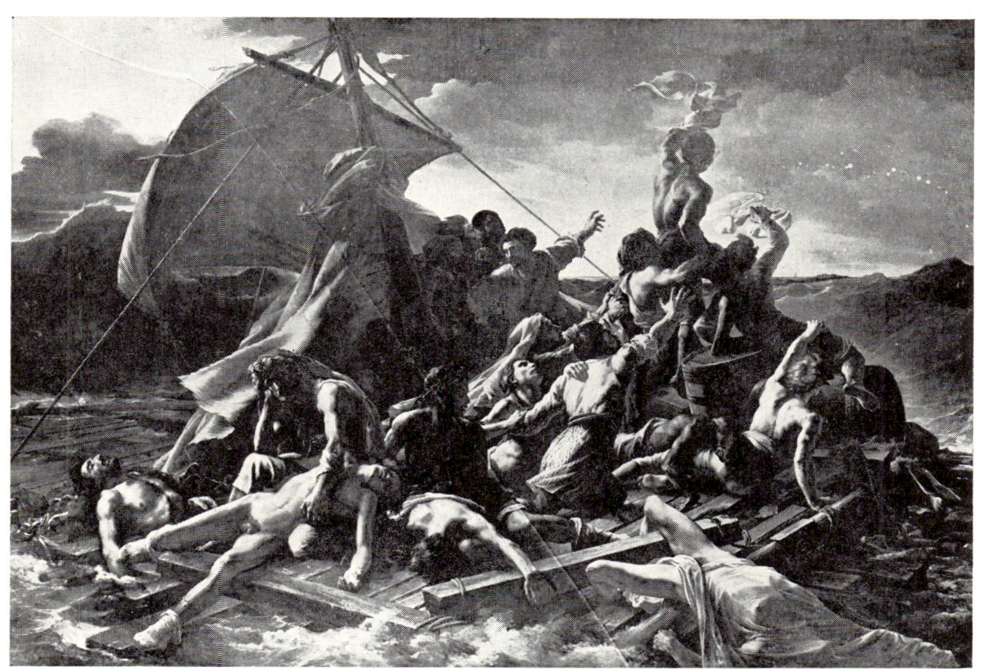

36. Géricault: The Raft of the Medusa. 1818

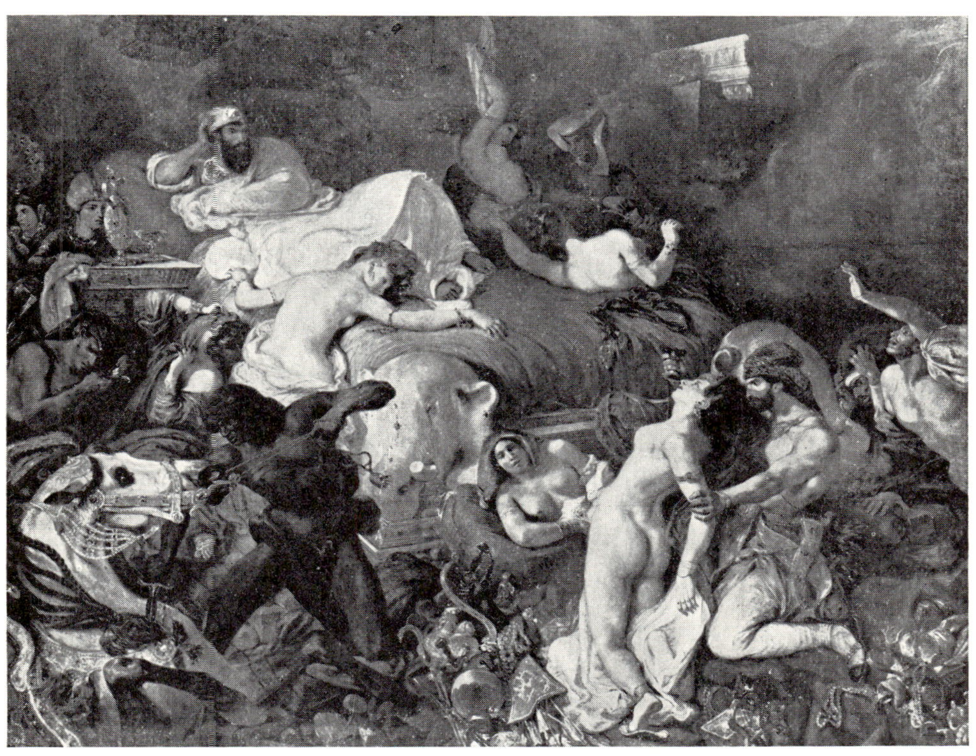

37. Delacroix: Death of Sardanapalus. 1827

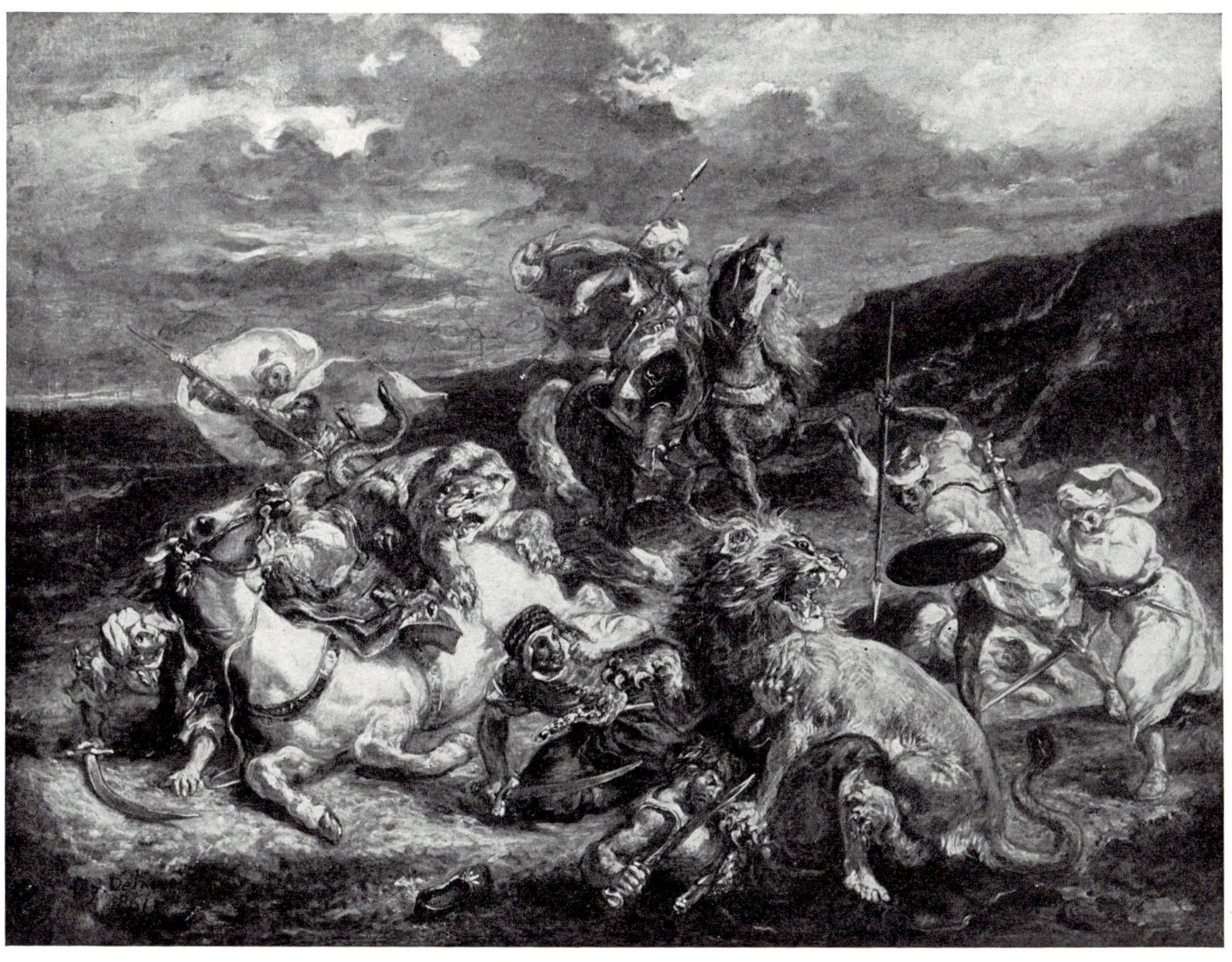

38. *Delacroix: The Lion Hunt.* 1861

carried out in the seventies in the face of a popular outcry against its noble and majestic simplicity.

What was unique in America, however, was the domestic architecture of classicism. Nicholas Biddle, one of the first Americans to visit Greece and the man who gave Latrobe the commission for the United States Bank, built the most elaborately archaeological of classic country houses, Andalusia (1834), on the Delaware River above Philadelphia, in the external form of a Greek temple with a surrounding Doric colonnade. Few houses, however, were carried so far toward archaeological accuracy as this. The temple portico and ornamental detail, both Greek and Roman, were freely adapted, in wood construction and generally on a small scale, wherever buildings were being erected. Along the Cherry Valley road and the Erie Canal through New York State, in the towns of New England and the Middle States, in the "big house" of innumerable plantations in the new South, and in innumerable farmhouses of smaller size in the old Northwest, the sense of form propagated by a few professional architects became the vernacular of the country. The local variations are too numerous to be mentioned, but a common emphasis upon simple geometric masses and flat wall planes (windows were generally flush with the exterior wall surface), a slender grace of proportion in the wooden columns, the happy dependence upon clapboarding and upon sunlight to ornament the white exteriors by shadows penciled in fine detail, give the style great distinction. A few towns, like Nantucket or Madison (Indiana) on the Ohio River, and certain undisturbed portions of the older eastern cities, show that American architecture in general spoke with a clearer and surer accent at that time than it ever has since. Duncan Phyfe was the most famous of the cabinetmakers who supplied the furniture to fit these simple and formal houses (Figs. 34 and 35).

By 1830 the temper of the times had changed. Classicism had been a tradition of logic and clear thinking, of order and authority. Romanticism, cutting across this intellectual tradition, was, as Paul Jamot expressed it, "an immense lyric and dramatic poem, sung by a thousand voices," in praise of passion and spontaneity, of instinct and introspec-

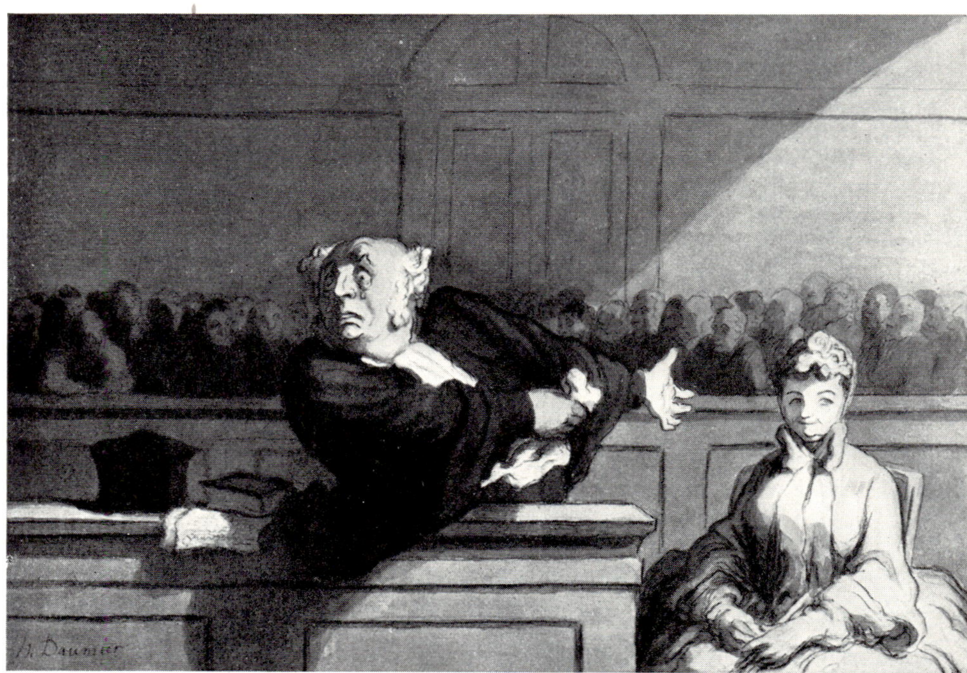

39. *Daumier: The Advocate*

tion. Men were still intent upon creating an ideal world different from the actual one in which they lived. But a generation of revolutions and wars for national survival had unloosed great emotional forces of race and locality, freedom and self-government, emotions which were mingled with the weariness and disappointment of a great post-war readjustment to form a new attitude of mind. The doctrine of the perfectibility of man, here and now, had taken too deep root for the world to return either to the eighteenth-century ideal of the golden mean or to the Christian belief in the essential imperfection of our human life on earth. Men were still Utopia-builders, still sought the ideal society. But the young generation had been nursed in disillusion and disappointment. Byron's poems, filled with melancholy, hatred of the normal, discontent with the social order, and longing for the unattainable, struck the keynote of the age and aroused the enthusiasm of the world.

One great source of romanticism was the mystical and philosophical movement of German thought. Another was the great group of English novelists and poets, who were read all over the world. In America the

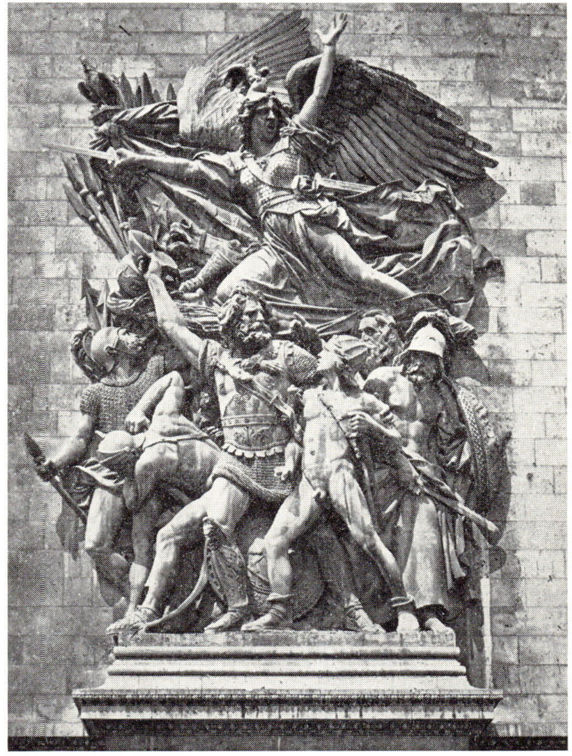

40. *Rude: The Marseillaise, Arc de Triomphe,
Paris.* 1833–36

Transcendentalists were the most gifted group in a mystical generation that filled the whole country with strange movements and sects, of which each held the secret of perfection and each demanded that one renounce the world as it existed. Emerson, the greatest of them, looked out upon an age of visionary ferment and with prophetic common sense noted in his diary (March 1845) that "after this generation one would say mysticism should go out of fashion for a long time."

In France alone the romantic revolution was more formal and stylistic than metaphysical. There had been even under David's rule artists who differed from his statuesque ideal: Gros, who painted the adventurous activity and the passion of the living heroes of the Napoleonic Wars, and Prud'hon, whose classicism had more to do with the gentle melancholy of Virgil than with Plutarch or the Apollo Belvedere. The romantic revolt from David's painting was toward movement, away

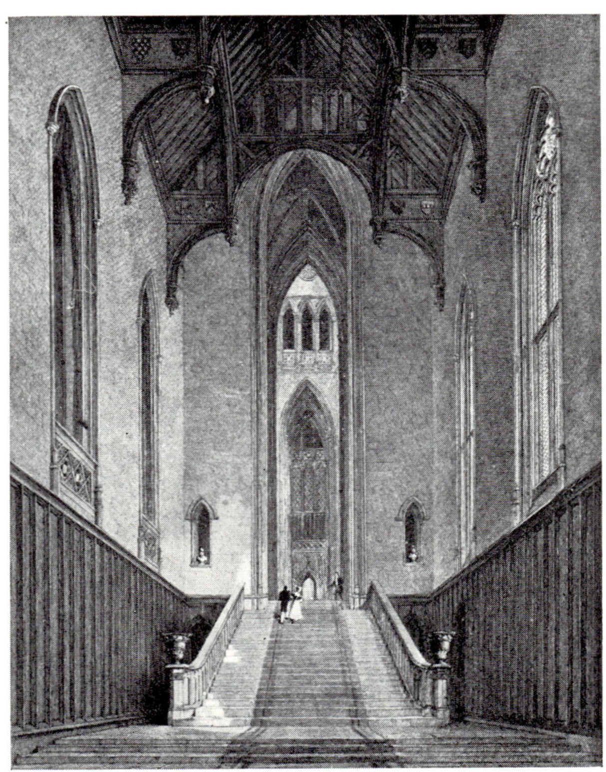

*41. Wyatt: Fonthill Abbey, The Great Western
Hall*

from statuesque repose, as one finds it in the famous "Raft of the Medusa (1818; Fig. 36) by Géricault (1791–1824). Yet even in this illustration of a contemporary shipwreck the figures appear as antique
nudes; and the emotions involved are the orthodox pity and terror of
the classic drama. In a few pictures done after a visit to England in
1820–1821, Géricault began to draw nearer to the simple, immediate
world about him, foreshadowing a later development.

French romanticism owes its character to Eugène Delacroix (1798–
1863). No nineteenth-century painter was more a man of culture and
intellect and less a creature of emotion than the reserved and aristocratic mind that is revealed in Delacroix's journals. His romanticism
was the product of thought and the influence of other artists rather
than of spontaneous impulse. It is doubtful whether he would have
been a romantic artist had he not been under the influence of English

literature. The change which he worked in French painting was one of style, therefore, rather than of content. His "Death of Sardanapalus" (Fig. 37), which he exhibited in the Salon of 1828, may be taken to mark the definite emergence of the romantic school: it was never again possible for the orthodox classicists to ignore or deny the existence of the new movement. In this painting, an illustration of a tragedy by Byron, the painter dealt with the extreme subject matter of romanticism: tragic grandeur, terror, madness, death. What impresses one in his treatment, however, is not the exaggerated romantic tragedy (which seems to us to verge rather on the ridiculous) but the essentially formal nature of his picture. The figures swirl in Rubens-like arabesques around the one fixed point in the composition — Sardanapalus' bearded, glowering head. French taste made even this subject, in other words, a problem of plastic, not psychological, expression. As Delacroix elaborated his technique, the color harmony became richer, more and more

42. *Barry: Houses of Parliament, London.* 1840–57

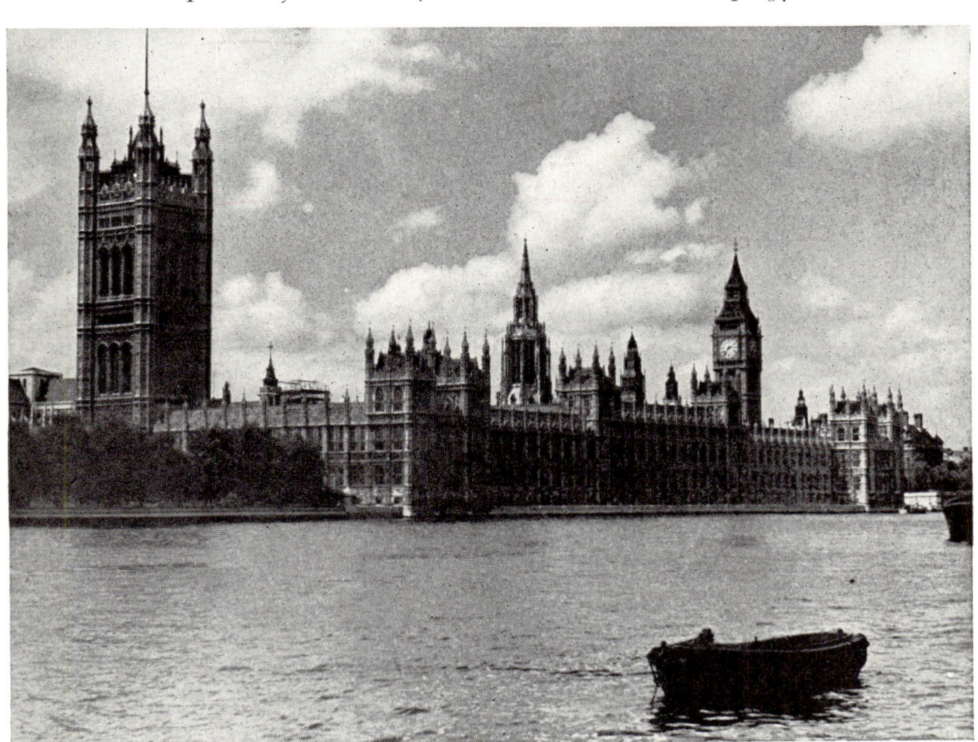

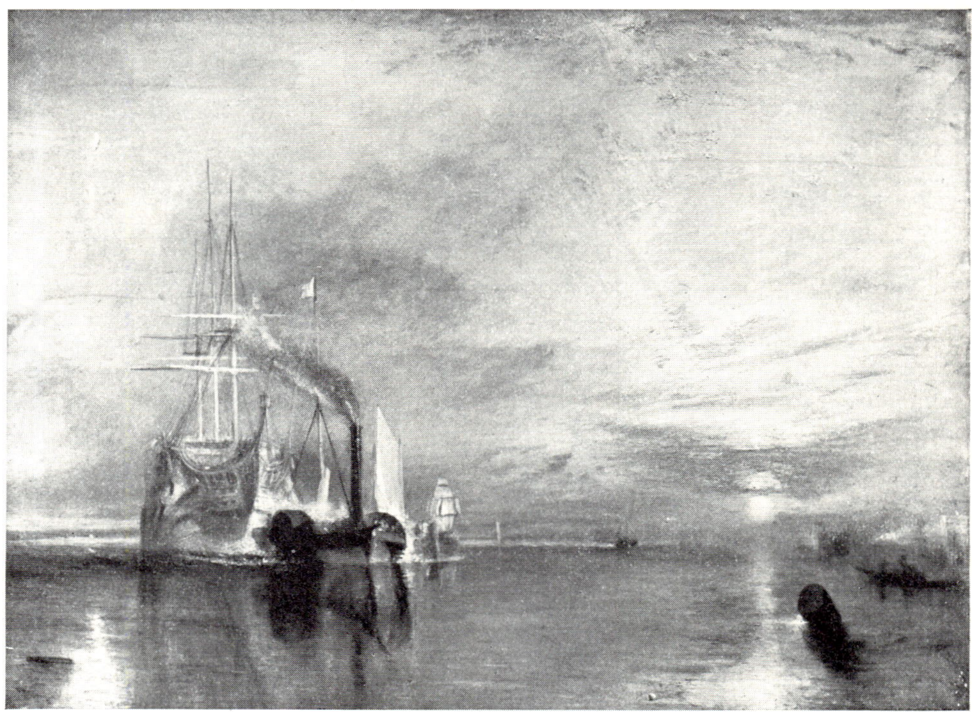

43. *Turner: The Fighting Téméraire Towed to Her Last Berth.* 1838

a ripple of floating tints (*flochetage*), until he had prepared the way for the atmospheric painting of the colorists to come.

Delacroix took his subject matter from romantic poetry and novels, from Shakespeare, and from the literature of the Middle Ages, but he was also the greatest, if not the first, of the Orientalists. Morocco, which he visited in the 1830's, offered him exotic charm, movement, and color, in contrast to the cold statuesque subjects of the classicists. It was he who introduced the Orient as a theme in French nineteenth-century painting (Fig. 38). It was taken up by lesser figures of his school, Diaz and Isabey, Fromentin and Decamps, until it became a standard source of imagery for all French colorists.

Delacroix's romanticism springs from the brain and the sense of style. To non-French taste his large dramatic compositions, therefore, seem artificial machines. His gifts were plastic: it is not by accident that he was admired by Cézanne. For romanticism in its aspect of a passionate outpouring of the heart one looks to Daumier (1810–1879). He was a

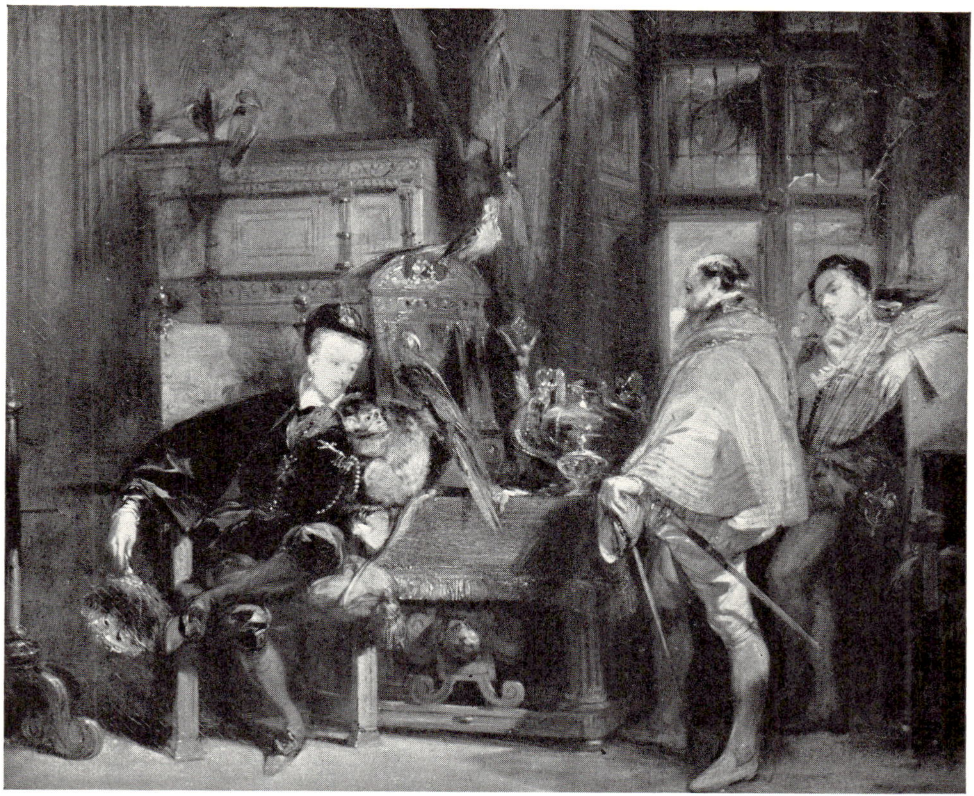

44. Bonington: Henri III and the English Ambassador

product of the newly risen periodical press, a bitter and daring cartoonist famous for his lampoons of the Bourbon and Orleanist governments.
Hardly considered an artist by his own time, and, indeed, active as a
painter only after 1848, he enriched French painting by unique gifts
of satire, humor, and feeling for character. In his paintings, which are
in style typical of the warm, coloristic atmosphere sought by the romantic artist, one can find preserved better than anywhere else the religion
of liberty which burned so fiercely in that liberal age — the love of
humanity, the hatred of all injustice and entrenched privilege, the
passionate faith in the common man and scorn for all other faiths,
combined with an individual greatness of mind that makes his work
art rather than propaganda. Yet the grandeur of his design, which
admits only the essential and the type, shows how Latin was his genius
also (Fig. 39).

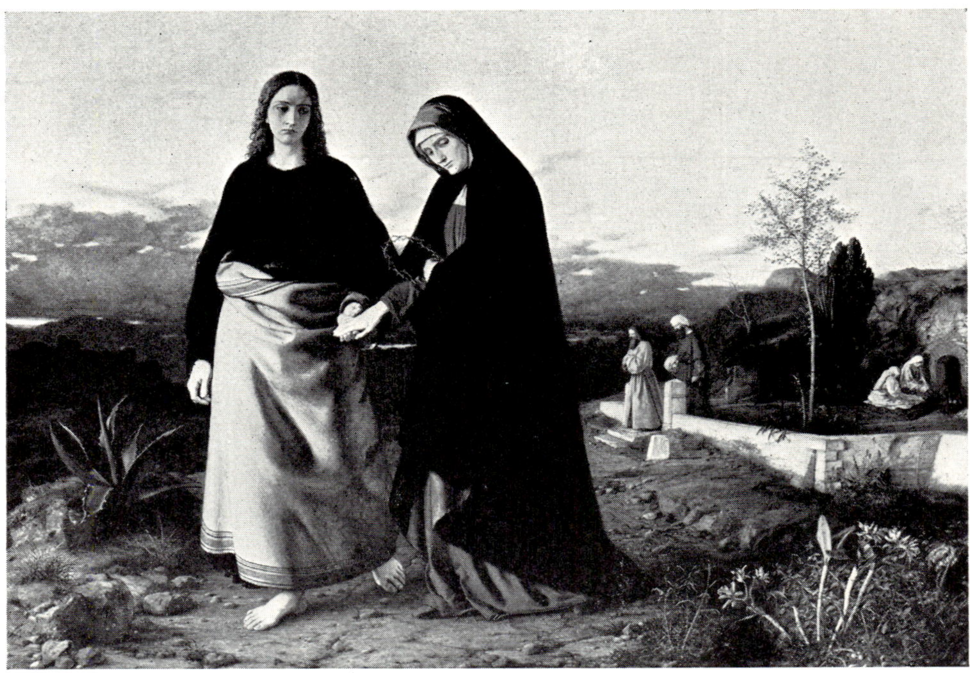

45. *Dyce: St. John Leading the Virgin from the Tomb.* 1844

The things which romantic art sought are themes more congenial to pictorial expression than to sculpture. But David d'Angers (1788–1856) worked from classicism toward a certain dramatic life, especially in his smaller works and his medallions. It was Rude (1784–1855), however, the creator of the group of the "Marseillaise" (Fig. 40) on the Arc de Triomphe, who broke away from the statuesque calm of the classicists and, in the clashing lines and rolling masses of that group, gave the best sculptural expression of romantic vehemence.

The great discovery of both the literary and the architectural romantics was Gothic architecture. The discovery had begun in the middle of the eighteenth century in England, with Gray and Walpole, as part of a fashionable taste for ruins and melancholy, and spread to France with the rise of romanticism. The great task of the restoration of Gothic buildings, dilapidated after the neglect and ill-considered additions of later centuries, was begun in the early nineteenth century. Viollet-le-Duc (1814–1879) is here the great name, not only for his restorations of Pierrefonds, Notre Dame, and the Sainte Chapelle, but for the

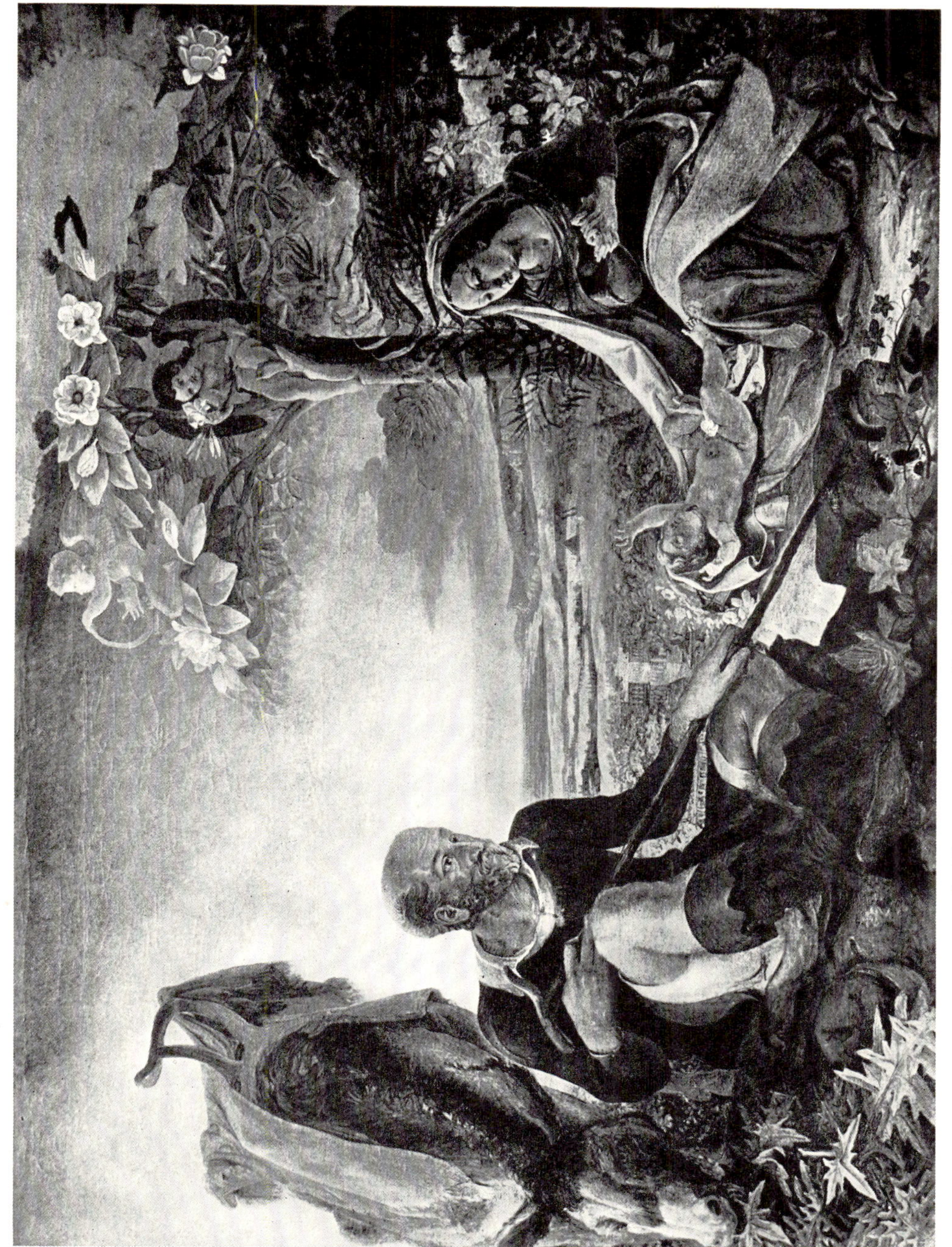

46. Runge: *Rest on the Flight into Egypt.* 1805–06

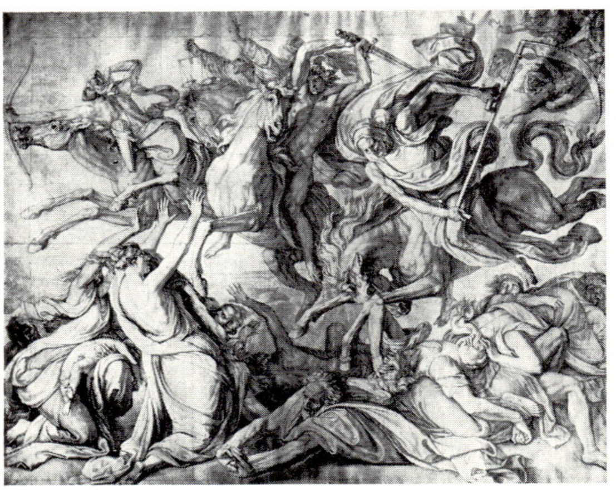

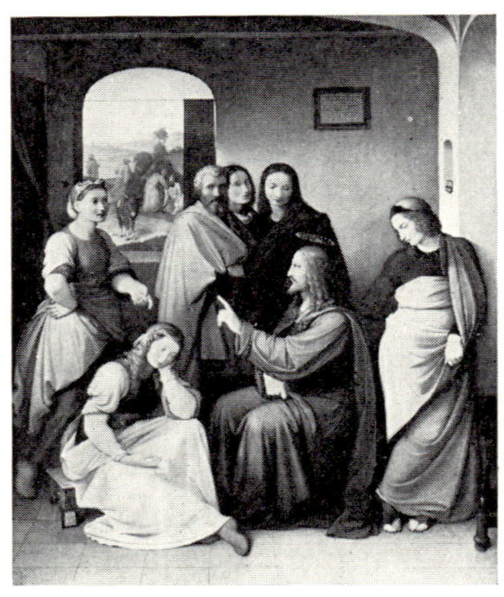

47. *Cornelius: Riders of the Apocalypse*
(cartoon). 1846

48. *Overbeck: Christ in the House*
of Mary and Martha. 1815

standard of scholarly knowledge set by his *Dictionnaire raisonné de l'architecture française.* Entirely new buildings, such as Gau's Sainte Clotilde in Paris (1846–1857), were rare because, at least in France, the need to build new churches was far less than the need to repair the old ones.

In England a revival of Gothic building began much earlier than in France. The repair and restoration of medieval buildings was active from 1780 onward, and, as Sir Kenneth Clark has pointed out, Windsor and most of the ducal castles had been done over in the Gothic style by 1830. Walpole's Strawberry Hill (1750–1783) was the first great new country house to be done in medieval style. Designed in a strange rococo Gothic, invented chiefly by Walpole himself, with the help of Chute and Richard Bentley, Strawberry Hill set up a theory of archaeological correctness and an actual practice of a kind of fantastic stage design. The real aim of the first phase of romantic architecture in England was not so much an imitation of existing medieval buildings as a search for the theatrically "sublime." James Wyatt, for example, in restoring Salisbury Cathedral, removed the choir screen and placed the medieval tombs, which were standing in their original medieval positions scattered through the nave, in a new position between the arches of the nave arcades. Archaeological correctness meant less to Wyatt than the romantic theatrical effect of his long vista. In Wyatt's designs for the famous Gothic country houses, Fonthill Abbey (begun 1796; Fig. 41) and Ashridge (begun 1806), dramatic vistas and rooms of knife-like narrowness and height expressed his theatrical ideal more freely, unhampered by the presence of actual medieval work.

The second generation of romantic architecture found its leaders in Gilbert Scott, notable for his rash restorations of medieval buildings, and Pugin, who allied the movement with the religious revival of the nineteenth century. But its chief figure was Charles Barry (1795–1860), whose Houses of Parliament (1840–1857) in London (Fig. 42) are the masterpiece of the English Gothic revival.

J. M. W. Turner (1775–1851) carried romantic theatricalism into painting. In his early work a strong influence of Dutch realism mingled with that of Claude Lorrain; but the realistic strain faded out, and by the 1820's he was no longer content even with the baroque grandeur

49. *Ferstel: Votivkirche, Vienna.*
1856–79

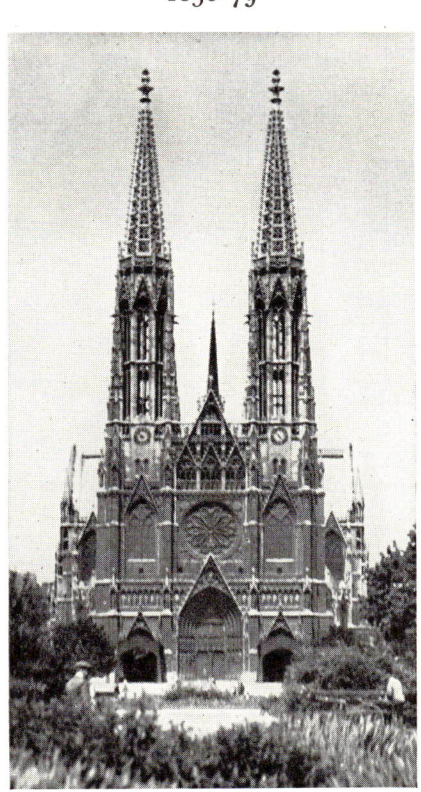

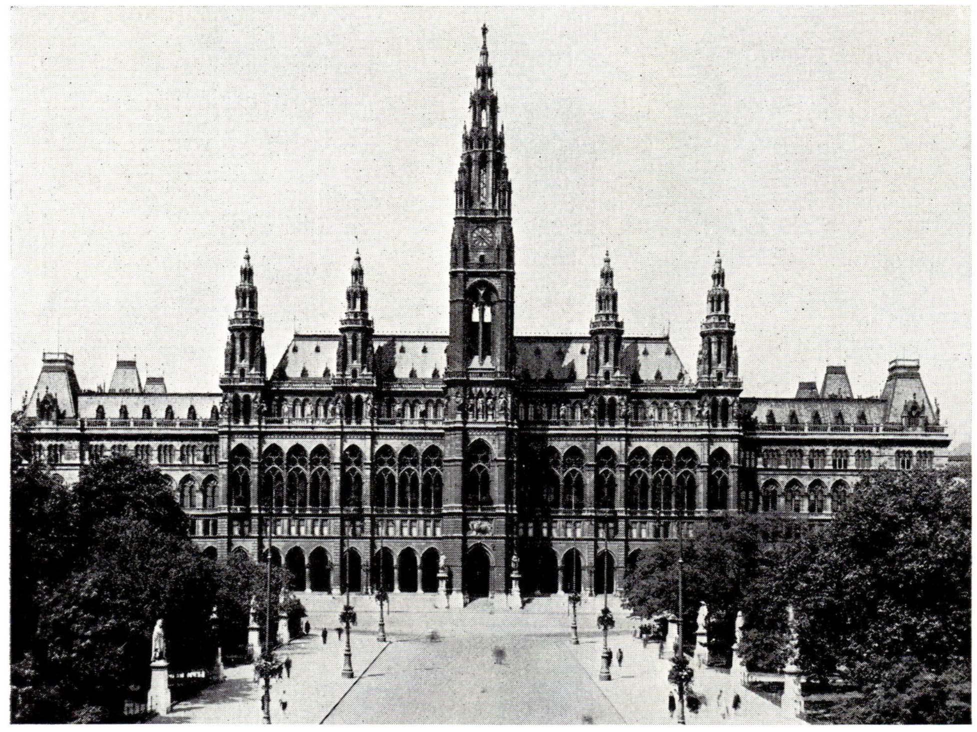

50. *Schmidt: Rathaus, Vienna.* 1872–82

inherited from Claude and launched himself, for the first instance in the nineteenth century, into an art of pure color. Turner's final glowing, confused, melodramatic canvases, filled with an ache for an unreal and unattainable sublimity, can hardly be thought of apart from their age, so perfectly do they represent the Byronic mood in painting (Fig. 43).

The brilliant, uneven Richard Parkes Bonington (1802–1828), one of the first discoverers of medieval subject matter, was a resident of the Continent and as much a part of the French as of the British romantic movement. His "Henri III and the English Ambassador" (Fig. 44) was done at the height of the mutual interchange of influence between him and Delacroix, at about 1828. The brilliant, painterlike style which he created and helped to establish as the idiom of romantic painting was largely based upon the Venetians of the eighteenth century, whom he had seen during a visit to Italy in 1826.

The style of the English historical painters evolved gradually through Leslie and Eastlake into Victorian sentimentalism. Dyce (1806–1864) was both a link with the German Nazarenes and an able historical painter (Fig. 45), who took part in the decoration of the Houses of Parliament. His work helped to pave the way for the literary and artistic movement of the Pre-Raphaelites, which came in 1849. It is hard to see now why the Pre-Raphaelites were considered revolutionaries, for with the exception of the doctrine of naturalistic accuracy of detail, which links them to a later period, they merely continued the tendencies of the romantic generation. They are, however, best included in another chapter.

Romanticism was so native to that union of idealism, sentiment, and acute racial self-consciousness which was the mental atmosphere of Germany in this period that it was the inevitable goal of the eclectic movement. In the first decade of the century two north-German painters,

51. *Allston: The Rising of a Thunderstorm at Sea*

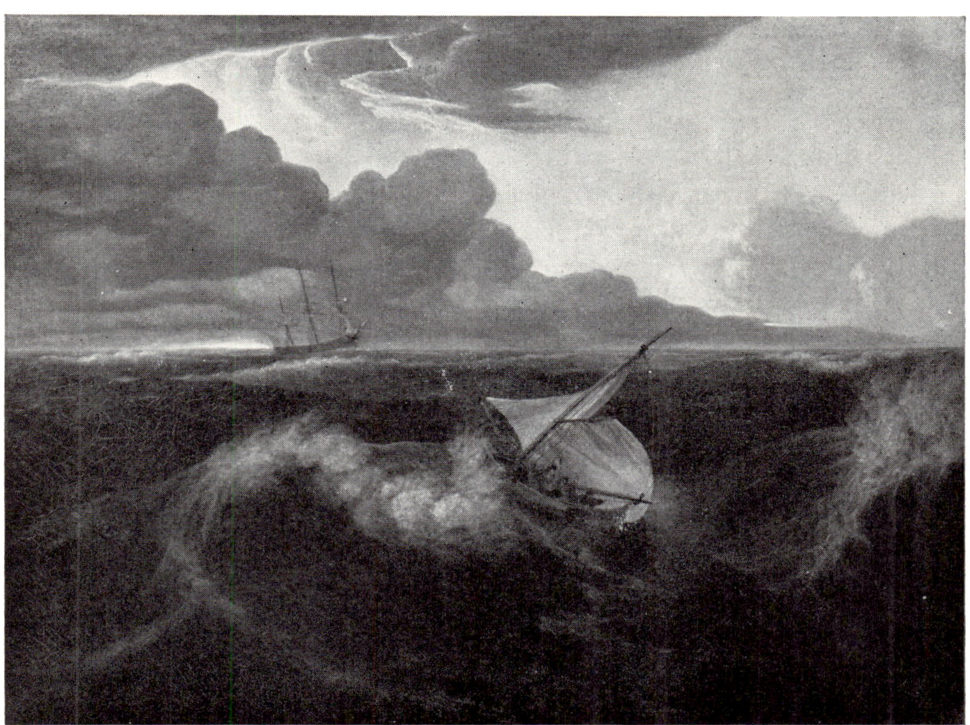

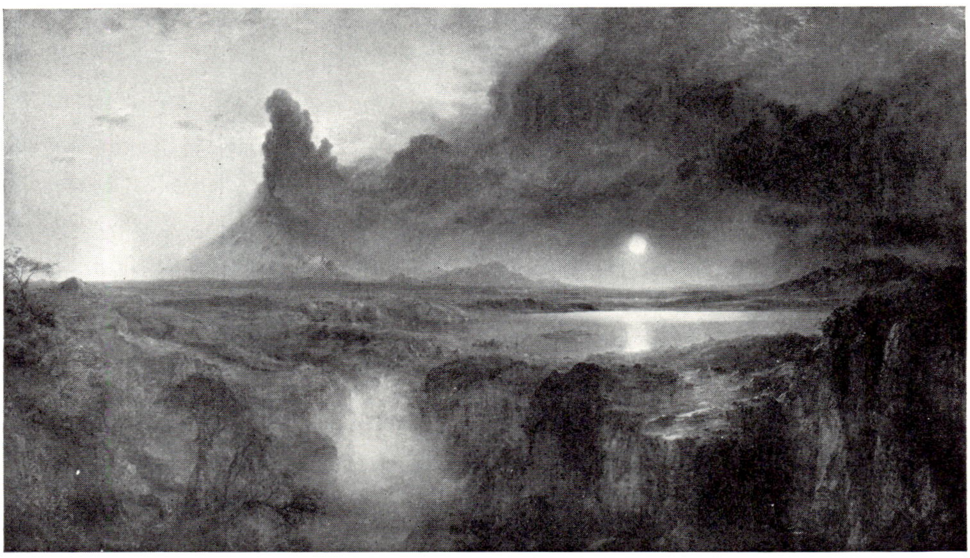

52. *Church: Cotopaxi.* 1862

Runge (1777–1810) and Caspar David Friedrich (1774–1840), both pupils of the Academy of Copenhagen, turned painting away from the Mediterranean to the misty and introspective North. Runge's tight, linear style and the hard naturalism of his portraits seem to promise only a cold north-German honesty, but his ideal subjects are filled with a strangely impressive mysticism (Fig. 46). Caspar David Friedrich, a landscape painter of Dresden, substituted for the idylls of the classic school a love of the mysterious and melancholy qualities of his own pine-fringed Saxon hills.

But a different romanticism, destined to dominate Germany from the South, was born in Rome among a group of enthusiasts who called themselves the Nazarenes: Overbeck, Cornelius, Schadow, Veit, Schnorr von Carolsfeld, Führich, Steinle. The Nazarenes were social and religious enthusiasts; they founded a semi-monastic community in an abandoned monastery near Rome and there, in an artistic brotherhood, tried to recapture both the spirit and the substance of the age of faith. Taking as their model Italian art of the Renaissance, they made the revival of the monumental fresco one of their chief aims. In 1819 Cornelius (1783–1867; Fig. 47) the strongest of the group, went into the service of the Crown Prince Ludwig, later the famous Ludwig I of

Bavaria, and in 1825 became head of the Munich Academy. Munich
became the center of an enthusiasm for grandiose mural cycles. Other
Nazarenes went to Düsseldorf, Frankfort, Vienna, Dresden. A great
wave of interest in German national lore and in the Middle Ages was
under way. The sentimental illustrative style propagated by the Nazarenes had enormous success (Fig. 48). The school had to the full the
official support which was denied to the American historical painters.
Yet, lacking both a strong sense of form and an understanding of color,
the Nazarenes had none of the essentials of monumental art, nor does
it appear now that the ideas of the time required epic treatment. It is
the black and white of Rethel (1816–1859) and the occasional small pictures of the Viennese Schwind (1804–1871), rather than the frescoes,
which alone seem to live out of all the work of the historico-romantic
school.

In German architecture an enthusiasm for "English" gardens and
for Horace Walpole's theatrical Gothic was the first phase of romantic
taste. The English Gardens in Munich and the fantastic play castle of
the Emperor Francis I at Laxenburg, outside Vienna, are among the
best examples of the genre. So complete was the mixture of classic and

53. *St. James's Church, Arlington, Vermont.* 1831–32

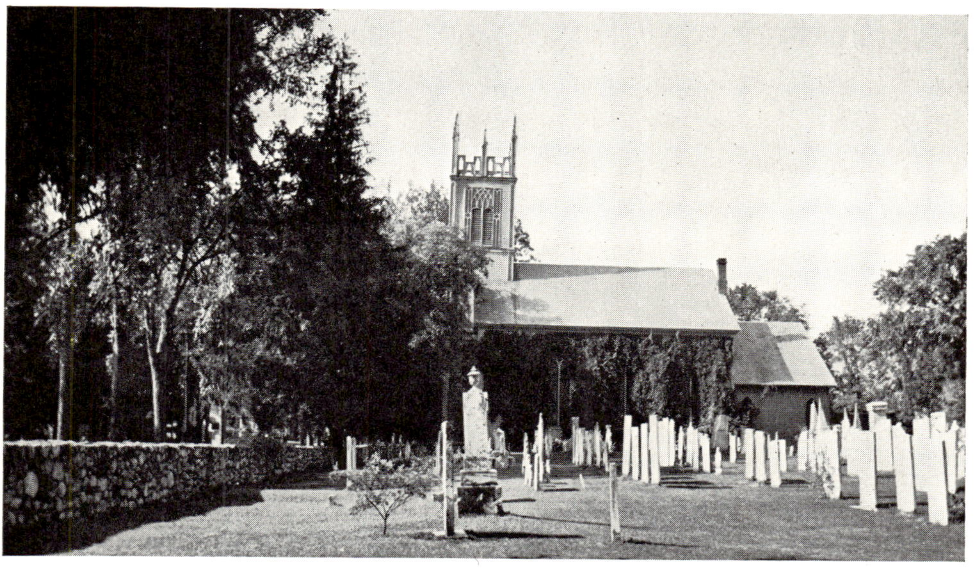

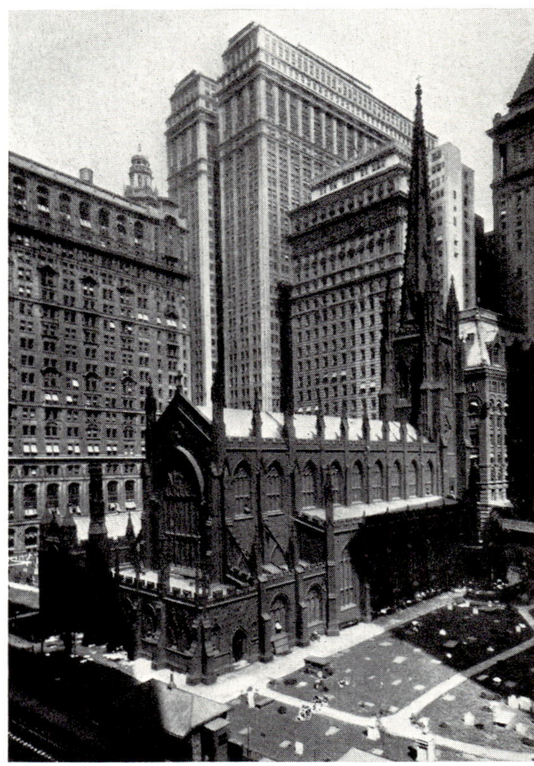

54. Upjohn: Trinity Church, New York.
1846

romantic feeling in Munich that, at the same time that Klenze's classic Walhalla was rising on the banks of the Danube, King Ludwig had the Basilica in Munich built in Italian Romanesque style and the Ludwigskirche in Tuscan Gothic.

The chief achievement of the later, more scholarly phase of the Gothic revival in Germany was the completion of Cologne Cathedral (1842–1880). In Vienna, Ferstel's noble Votivkirche (Fig. 49) and the great Rathaus by Friedrich Schmidt (Fig. 50), although they are not free from the unsubstantial look of nineteenth-century Gothic, warn one against the folly that condemns all nineteenth-century Gothic architecture indiscriminately.

American literature from 1820 onward was strongly stirred by English and German romanticism. Generations of Americans went abroad with

Byron's *Childe Harold* and Longfellow's *Hyperion* as guidebooks. But in spite of the enormous appeal exerted upon inhabitants of a new country by the old and the strange, suffused in the sunset tints of poetry, America made little contribution to romantic idealism except in literature. Only Upjohn's Trinity Church in New York can be considered as an authentic masterpiece of the Gothic revival. No painter, with the possible exception of Allston, even began to do what Irving and Hawthorne and Emerson did for their generation.

The historical style of painting grew steadily more emotional from the time of Allston's return in 1818. In the small canvases which were his chief output in this country Allston returned to the romantic qualities that were natural to him: deep atmospheric color, moods of revery, awe, or sweetness, and frequently to subjects drawn from contemporary blood-and-thunder literature that is now, happily, completely forgotten. The fantastic "Deluge" in the Metropolitan Museum, "Saul and the Witch of Endor," "Spalatro's Vision of the Bloody Hand" (an illustration of Mrs. Radcliffe's *The Italian*) were typical products of his return. His landscape of "The Rising of a Thunderstorm at Sea" (Fig. 51), grave and impressive in color, and haunted by the vast and awe-inspiring power of nature, is one of the most distinguished expressions of romantic sentiment in American art.

The vague yearnings and fleeting moods of romanticism, unless sustained by a powerful sense of form, could lead only to weak and sentimental painting. Happily for American art there was little encouragement for the young men around Allston to devote themselves to figure painting, which was the road toward those treacherous bogs of excess of sentiment and dearth of technique that swallowed their German and English contemporaries. The War of 1812 ended the habit of studying in London. Some art students wandered to Italy, and a few toward the middle of the century found their way to Düsseldorf, but in general the trips abroad of the next generation were vists of men already mature. Until the establishment of Eakins' atelier at the Pennsylvania Academy of the Fine Arts and of the Art Students' League in New York, in the seventies, there was no school in this country in which a painter could learn the command of the human figure necessary to imaginative composition. Landscape was, however, the great interest of American art, and in it the grandiose was rather left to one side, except in certain pictures by Thomas Cole (1801–1848) and F. E. Church (1826–1900), in whose famous "Niagara," "The Heart of the Andes," and "Coto-paxi" (Fig. 52) the taste for the sublime found a romantically imposing outlet.

The romantic revival of Gothic architecture was, on the whole, more fortunate than romantic idealism in painting. Gothic had never disappeared from church architecture, and Latrobe, in 1804, presented a scholarly English Gothic design as an alternative scheme for the Baltimore Cathedral. But the first phase of building came in the 1820's and 1830's, and was, as one might expect, a kind of pictorial Gothic, done usually with wooden rather than stone detail and designed often by men who had never studied a true Gothic structure. St. James' Church, Arlington, Vermont (1831–1832) is a good example of the unaffected dignity which was often achieved under these surprising circumstances (Fig. 53), while the wooden Gothic "villa" of the mid-century sometimes shows a charming fantasy. But the masterpiece of the romantic movement in America was Richard Upjohn's Trinity Church in New York (1846; Fig. 54). It is ostensibly an English Perpendicular design, but the narrow, slender proportions which Upjohn gave to his bays and piers are in the idiom characteristic of the nineteenth century. James Renwick, whose chief work was St. Patrick's Cathedral, New York City (1876), while slightly more correct in style, never equaled the feeling of life which Upjohn was able to communicate to his creation.

The idealistic movement was thus a common effort on the part of all western nations. Important as Rome was as a center of the classic theory, varying expressions of classical idealism arose independently in all parts of the western world. The classic revival began in architecture first in the United States, while the English tradition of painting became, as has been pointed out, the source of the future development of continental painting. The weaknesses of historical eclecticism — its destruction of tradition and its unfounded faith in the power of the artist to create a new world by merely wishing to — are only too apparent. In spite of many great achievements on the part of individual artists, the period as a whole left the western world by 1840 poorer in essential ways than it had been in 1780. The era had destroyed the craft tradition of art, which had passed down an accumulated technical skill from the earliest times to the end of the eighteenth century, so that the artists of 1840 were immeasurably inferior in technical knowledge to even minor figures of the seventeenth and eighteenth centuries. And the artist's grip upon the business of life had been weakened. He was no longer a craftsman who played a natural part in the work of the world but a self-constituted poet and seer with pretensions as much greater than those of his baroque predecessors as his technical powers were weaker. The task of the great artists of the rest of the century, as they themselves said over and over again, was to rebuild the craft of their ancestors. But if the idealistic artist lived in isolation from the craftsman it was a self-sought isolation, which is in its way an exact expression of nineteenth-century society. The claim of the idealist artist to being prophet and seer, his exaggerated reliance upon his own inspiration, his contempt for accepted forms and yearning for the remote ideal are only the moral idealism, the individualism, and the impatience of his age in their purest form. The weaknesses of historical eclecticism are more commonly seen, perhaps, than its representative character. But whatever his failures, the idealistic artist did not fail to create the living image of his world.

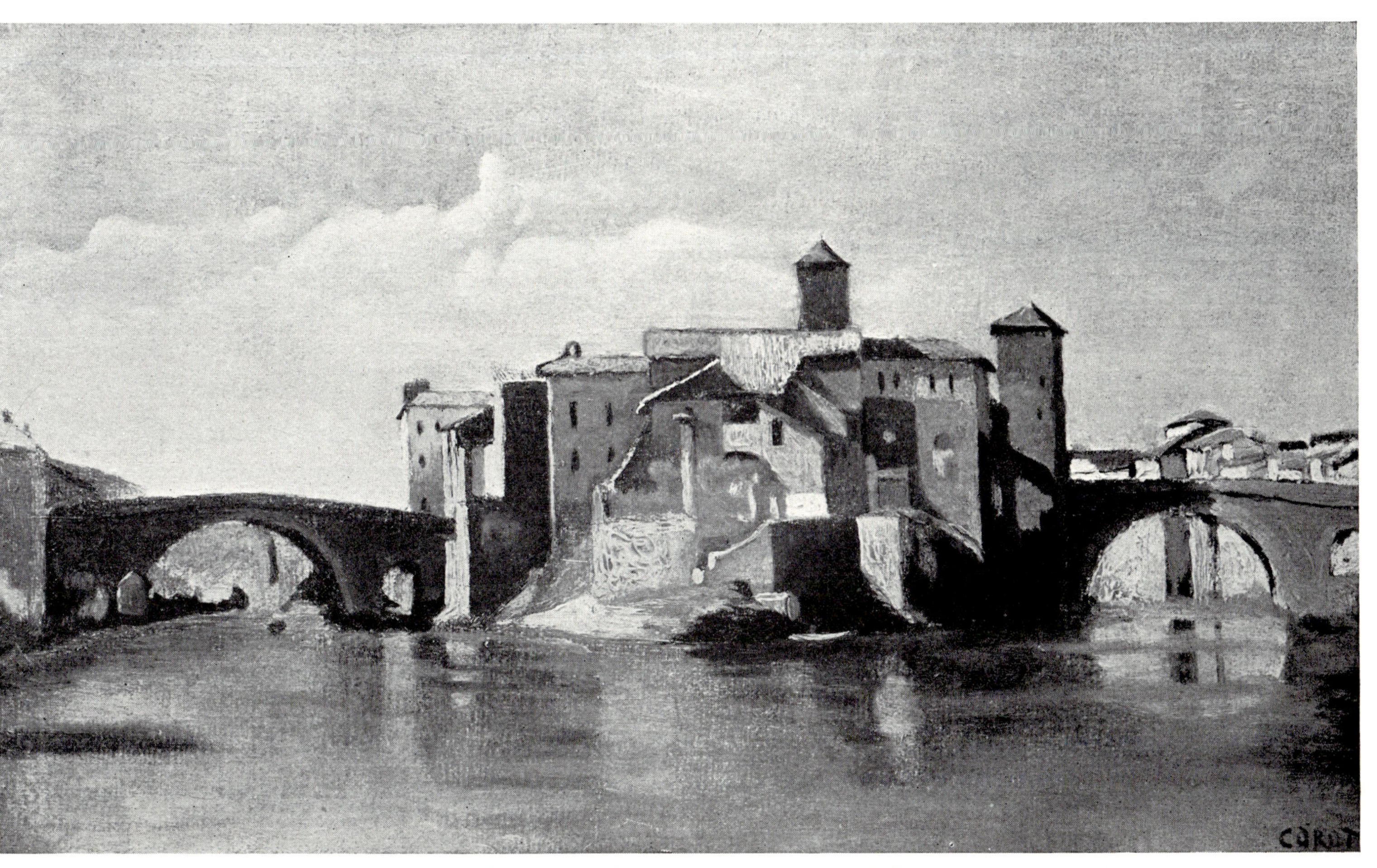

55. *Corot: Island of San Bartolomeo.* 1826–27

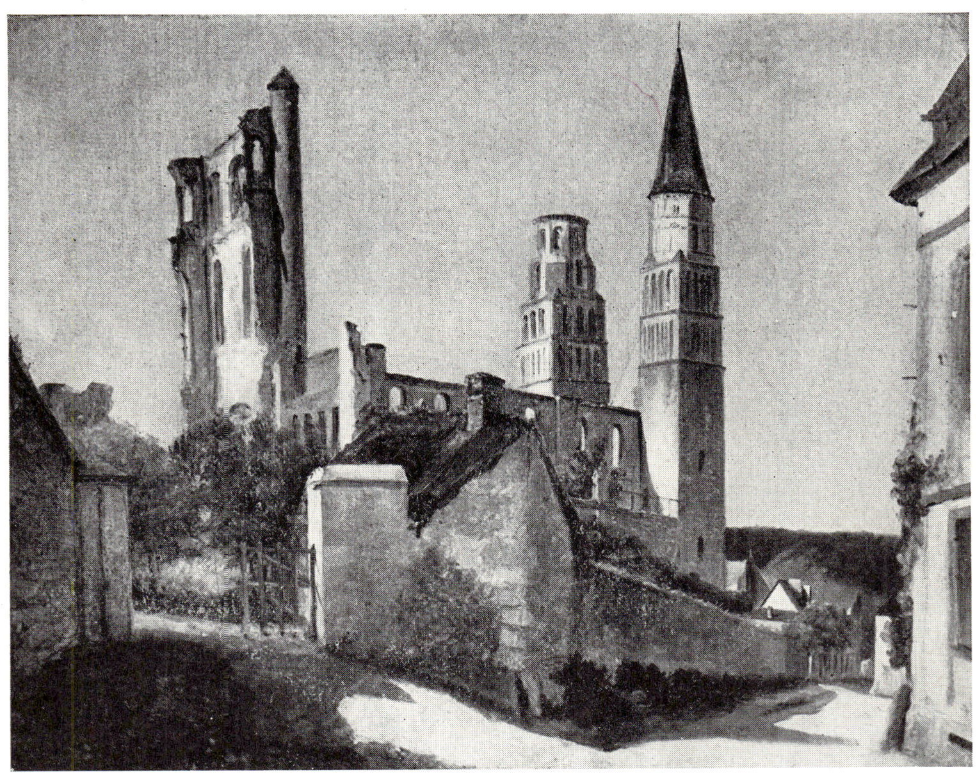

56. Corot: Jumièges. 1829–30

CHAPTER III

ROMANTIC REALISM

THERE WAS an important difference in thought between the two halves
of the romantic movement. The romantic idealists, such as Delacroix,
Allston, and Cornelius, created an ideal world in their imagination
and strove to embody it in their pictures. As we have seen, they shared
with the classicists the detachment from contemporary life which made
Ingres exclaim, "Let me hear no more of this absurd maxim: we must
have the new, we must follow our country. . . . There was once on
the globe a little corner of the earth called Greece, where, under the
most beautiful of skies and among inhabitants gifted with unique intellectual organization, literature and the arts shed, *for all peoples and all
succeeding generations,* as it were, a second light upon the things of

nature." [1]   Although some artists professing this theory created living art by the strength of their inner life or the richness of their style, much of the work of the period, being rooted only in a passing theory, has died with that theory.

But there was another tendency of romantic thought, to turn in simple trust to the face of nature. The literary type of this side of the movement was Wordsworth, as the type of romantic idealism was Byron. And while the romantic idealists, in their endeavor to create a world of passionate free emotion at some moment of imagined perfection in the past, developed a dramatic and grandiose style, the romantic realists sought only to contemplate nature and to make their expression of its beauty simple, direct, and transparent.

In the world upon which they looked, society was being remade under the new driving force of the middle class, liberal in politics, commercial in outlook, domestic in its habits, and profoundly certain of itself and its own way of life. This faith came to a crisis in the political revolts of 1828–1832, the election of Andrew Jackson, the Orleanist revolution, and the English Reform Bill, which ended the rule of the landed gentleman. These popular movements, by destroying the power of blood and tradition, added to the power of wealth and so to the importance of the towns. And two themes dominate in romantic realism: the worship of nature, on the one hand, and, on the other, the interest in popular life, especially the life of the great new cities that were spreading, smoking and dirty, over the landscape.

There was little room in this world for monumental or idealistic art: men were building neither palaces nor cathedrals but houses. The tradition of classic taste lingered, however, long after the reality had disappeared. Both the Orleans government in France and King Ludwig I in Bavaria made great efforts to encourage historical murals, but Delacroix's decorations for the Hall of Battles and the Chamber of Deputies remain as perhaps the solitary results of any promise of permanence from that vast expenditure of official patronage. The nineteenth century required small pictures to decorate its homes and to express its domestic taste. That this taste was in great part untrained and senti-

---

[1] Quoted by Jacques Fouquet, in *Formes*, March 1931, p. 44. The italics are mine.

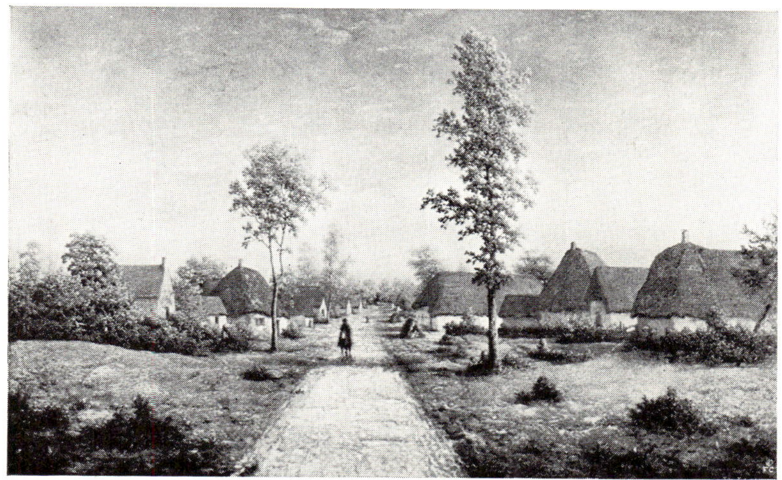

57. *Rousseau: Village Street of Becquigny.* 1864

mental, that it was pleased by much that has not outlived its time, is natural; for humanity achieves rare discernment as seldom as any other great ability. But romantic realism — that is to say, landscape, genre, and portrait painting — at least attempted to direct the artist's imagination toward life itself, and nineteenth-century art made its most notable and characteristic achievements in small paintings for houses.

A second field for romantic realism was opened by the great increase in the reading public and the rise of the popular novel and the illustrated periodical. The graphic techniques were transformed and enlarged. Wood engraving was given an entirely fresh form; copper engraving gave place to steel; and lithography appeared. The cartoonist and the illustrator produced some of the most vivid and lasting work of the period.

The landscape and genre of romantic realism were nonetheless not accepted without a struggle. The popular opinion upon art, which had for three generations been based upon abstractions — the superlative value of the past and the contemptible nature of the present — gave way very slowly to the new taste. If in France by 1850 Delacroix, who had been exhibiting for nearly thirty years, was still suspect, and if the taste of the French public was devoted to such sentimental academic painters as Delaroche, Ary Scheffer, and Couture, it is easy to understand why Daumier and Corot had their difficulties. In other countries the historical tradition was a powerful habit to be overcome, but not an active and persecuting prejudice such as existed in France. When the French realists were at last accepted by French critics, a natural revulsion of taste made the later nineteenth century greatly over-value the Barbizon painters. But though we again have revised, some-what downward, our opinions of the school, the early nineteenth century still remains one of the major periods of landscape painting, if only because of two men, Corot and Constable.

Three great forms of landscape were at hand as examples to the artists who were to make the nineteenth-century landscape. The heroic land-scape of Claude and Salvator Rosa, a formal baroque harmony of light and space, had been continued through the eighteenth century by certain of the best landscapists (Wilson, Hubert Robert, and Piranesi, for example) and was still the current, accepted pictorial language on the Continent and in the United States. The seventeenth-century Dutch, more natural in detail, set the example of an equally formal harmony of tone and color. The eighteenth-century Venetians on the other hand — Canaletto, Guardi, and Bellotto — had attained, with the traditional Venetian freedom of stroke and luminosity of color, a deli-cious freshness of light and air that the nineteenth century was long in equaling.

58. Daubigny: Mills at Dordrecht. 1872

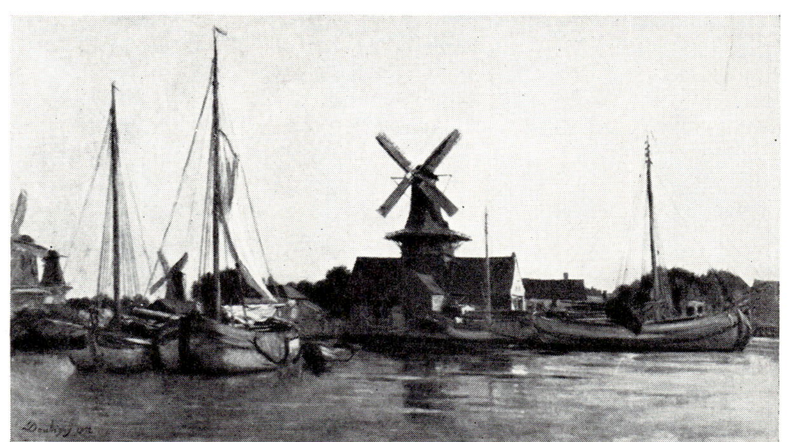

The landscapes of Corot (1796–1875) must be divided into two periods. From his first visit to Italy in 1825 until his third visit in 1843–1845 he shows in his work the self-surrender to nature which was the romantic vision at its best. His art consisted then of an exquisite freshness of eye combined with the delicate French gift of style. In this early period he painted direct from nature, altering little in the studio. "The Island of San Bartolomeo" (Fig. 55) and "Jumièges" (Fig. 56) are little masterpieces of a new sort in the history of landscapes. In this straightforward romantic realism, the grand, tranquil vista of the baroque landscape composition disappeared. Corot was led by his romantic conception of the largeness and freedom of nature to another, and more sunny, grandeur of space: the horizon is small in these pictures, but the light is infinite. His method of creating space was also new. The eye is led inward from foreground to sky by a sequence of planes in cool, luminous color. The sturdy geometry of their construction is saved from harshness by the delicate color and also by the indefinable grace which is the bouquet of Corot's personality.

A less spacious conception of nature marked the other Barbizon painters — Rousseau, Diaz, Dupré, Daubigny, all younger men than Corot. Théodore Rousseau (1812–1867) adopted an approach close to that of the Dutch (Fig. 57); when he and Corot are hung side by side, Corot seems as formal as Poussin. Rousseau was the more naturalistic in detail, warmer in color, and through his preoccupation with the middle ground (to which he gave the greatest accuracy of detail) more limited and intimate in suggestion of space. Daubigny (1817–1878) made the important innovation of painting entirely before nature, rather than in the studio (Fig. 58). The simplicity of his river scenes, painted from a houseboat on which he traveled the waterways of northern France and Holland, gives a certain monotony to his lesser work, but the grave and imposing command of light and space of his best work gives him a high place among nineteenth-century landscapists.

If romantic realism discovered a new vision of nature and made landscape the study of the character of simple scenes, it discovered likewise a new vision of humanity. This was the great age of the realistic illustrator. Daumier, it is unnecessary to stress further, was a great

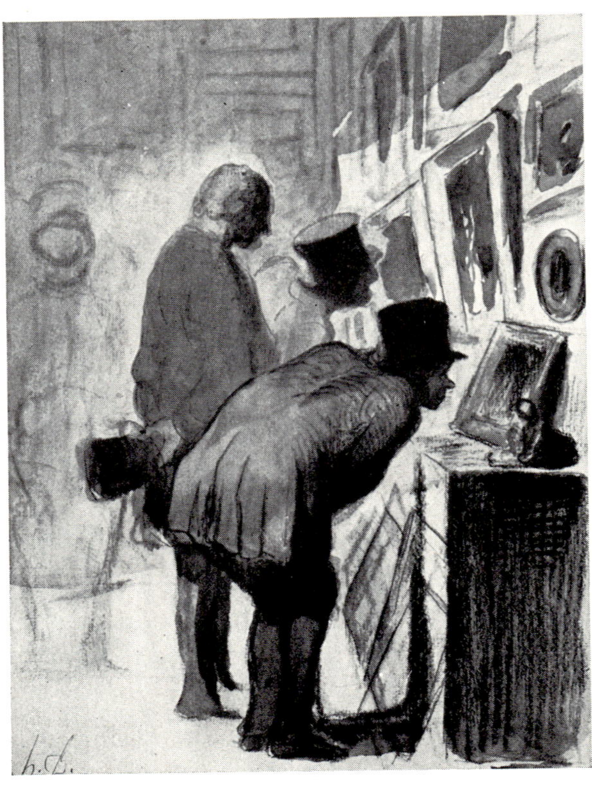

59. *Daumier: The Connoisseurs*

painter, but he was also one of the most penetrating and humorous of the French illustrators. The religion of liberty and the crusading ardor of the humanitarianism of his time give depth and force to his characterizations beyond that of any of his contemporaries. He was a master of street life and the movement of crowds (Fig. 59), while the inner nobility of the human being that shows through the mystery and pathos of life in his conception of humanity places him spiritually in the first rank of nineteenth-century art. He was one of the earliest masters of the new medium of lithography, in which he executed most of his youthful work. His political caricatures were ended by the *coup d'état* of Napoleon III, and thereafter his peculiarly pungent and timeless humor was used only in his illustrations of Parisian life.

The more urbane Gavarni (1804–1866) was likewise an illustrator and master of lithography, but Daumier's deep-seated passion is replaced in Gavarni's art by a quiet, ironic humor (Fig. 60). Constantin

Guys, the third of the great illustrators of this time, had a narrow though skillful gift for the fashionable parade of Paris.

The old technique of etching was transformed by Méryon (1821–1868), the greatest of those romantic artists for whom the living presence of the past, in the Gothic cathedrals or in the old houses of Paris, afforded an intense excitement. In his late, mad period he filled his etchings with strange visions, but in his early period facts were exciting enough to him. His direct natural vision, his feeling for the character of inanimate objects, and the airy luminosity of his style are a prelude to the great development of Impressionist graphic art (Fig. 61).

The new nineteenth-century technique of wood-block reproduction found its master in Gustave Doré (1832–1883), whose art bears out Aldous Huxley's observation that romanticism is essentially best adapted to comedy and in its moments of tragic intensity is always on the verge of the ludicrous. His rhetorical oils and his illustrations for Dante no longer retain any tragic power, but his comic illustrations to Balzac and Rabelais, of great pith and fancy, warm with the soft richness of the wood-block process, and vividly atmospheric in technique, are still thoroughly alive.

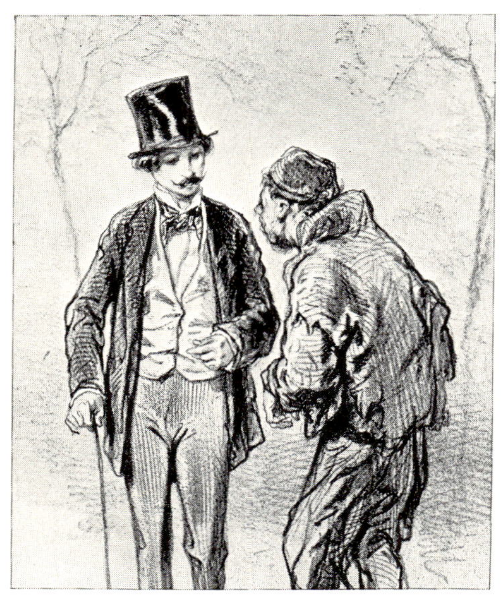

60. *Gavarni: A moustache and no regiment! But still you'd buy an old soldier a drink, eh, Colonel?*

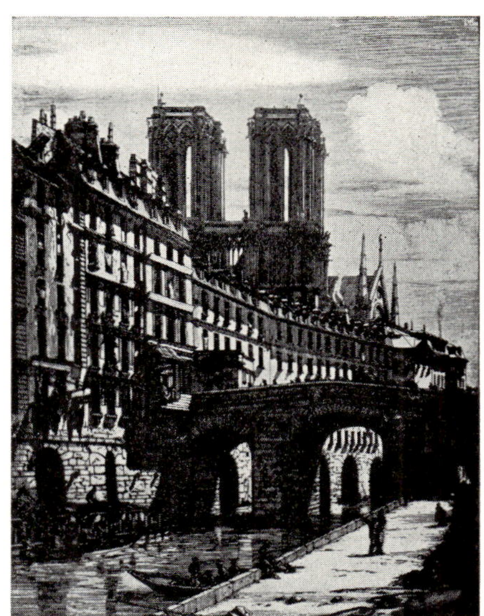

61. *Méryon: Le Petit Pont, Paris (etching)*

Romanticism brought back into France a style of light and color in place of the severe linear style of the classicists, and some of the men of 1830 advanced so far in their search for atmospheric and chromatic effect that they are hardly to be distinguished from the Impressionists. But the moral and ethical bent which made Daumier more than a realist made Millet (1814–1875) also more. Millet may be defined as a genuine peasant, of primitive and deeply Christian origin, who read Virgil. His subjects were so transparently simple that no one in France had before bothered to record them; yet they are illuminated by the sensitive and melancholy dignity of Virgil's *Eclogues*. Millet in one aspect represents the humanitarian sentiment which was so strong an element of nineteenth-century thought; yet he had the quality of classic generalization which distinguishes French realism from all others. The curve of a farmer's back as he leans over to his child has written in it not only all his life but all of a phase of life as well (Fig. 62). Such an ability to raise the individual fact to the level of a type is the power of generalization in the Latin mind (I use mind, not blood) penetrating the fortuitous events of life with the sense of order and permanence.

62. *Millet: The First Step* (*drawing*)

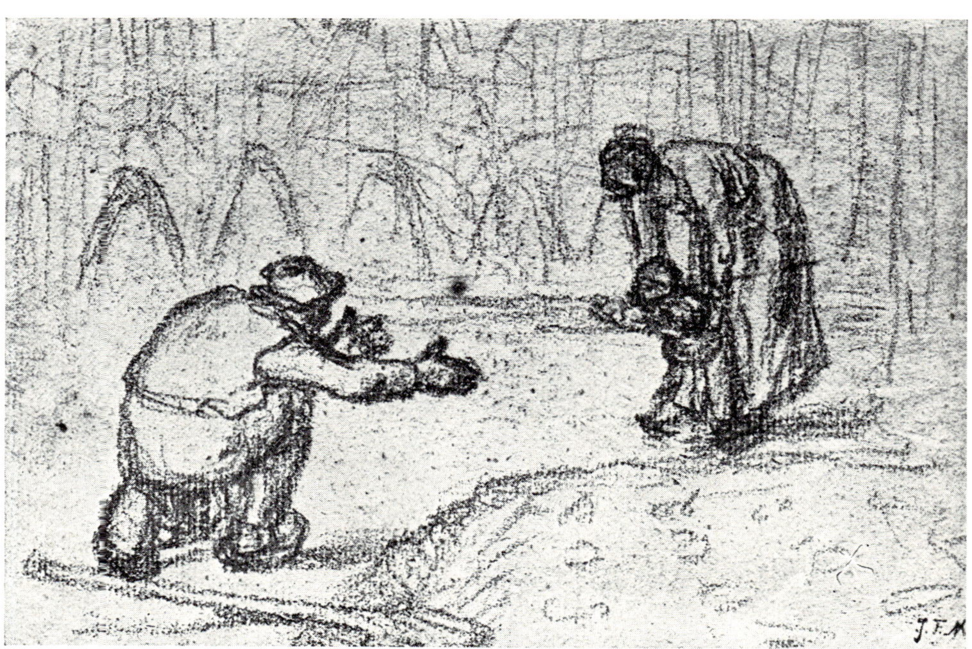

Corot, Daumier, Millet, all have this quality, which appears sometimes even through the naturalism of Barye (1796–1875), the sculptor of the movement.

Animals, which furnished Barye with his chief interest, were one of the enthusiasms of the romanticists. Géricault and Delacroix loved to represent animals. Landseer's name leaps to mind, familiar through the once ubiquitous prints of his sentimental paintings. But Morland, Ward, Stubbs, and Bewick in England, and in America the gifted and forgotten Alexander Wilson, as well as Audubon, were all at work to make the early nineteenth century a remarkable period of animal art.

In the appeal from eighteenth-century reason to romantic sentiment in English art, English literature played a leading part. It fostered the sympathy with the common man, the love of nature, the pride in English ways which found expression from 1800 onward in a remarkable group of landscape, genre, and animal painters: Constable, Crome, Wilkie, Leslie, Stubbs, Ward, Bonington. When in 1821 Géricault exhibited his "Raft of the Medusa" in London he was much impressed by the character of English painting. The heroic pathos of his earlier work was modified by the experiences of this visit toward a more quiet poetry of simple, undramatic scenes, in which he becomes the ancestor of the French realists.

The great figure of this school in England was Constable (1776–1837). There is no better example than he of that almost religious love of nature which animated the romantic realist. Almost completely self-taught, he was the son of a miller in Suffolk who began to paint as an outlet for his delight in his native countryside. He was encouraged by Sir George Beaumont, who lent him some water colors by Girtin and Claude's "Landscape with Hagar" (now in the National Gallery). In spite of his admiration for the great baroque landscapist, he had found his way, by 1810, to a completely direct, unclassical vision. It was not until about 1815, however, that he began to achieve the technique with which, from 1825 onward in increasing measure, he created a new chapter in landscape painting. It is well known how the free, rich paint of his landscapes, exhibited in Paris at the Salon of 1824, caused Dela-

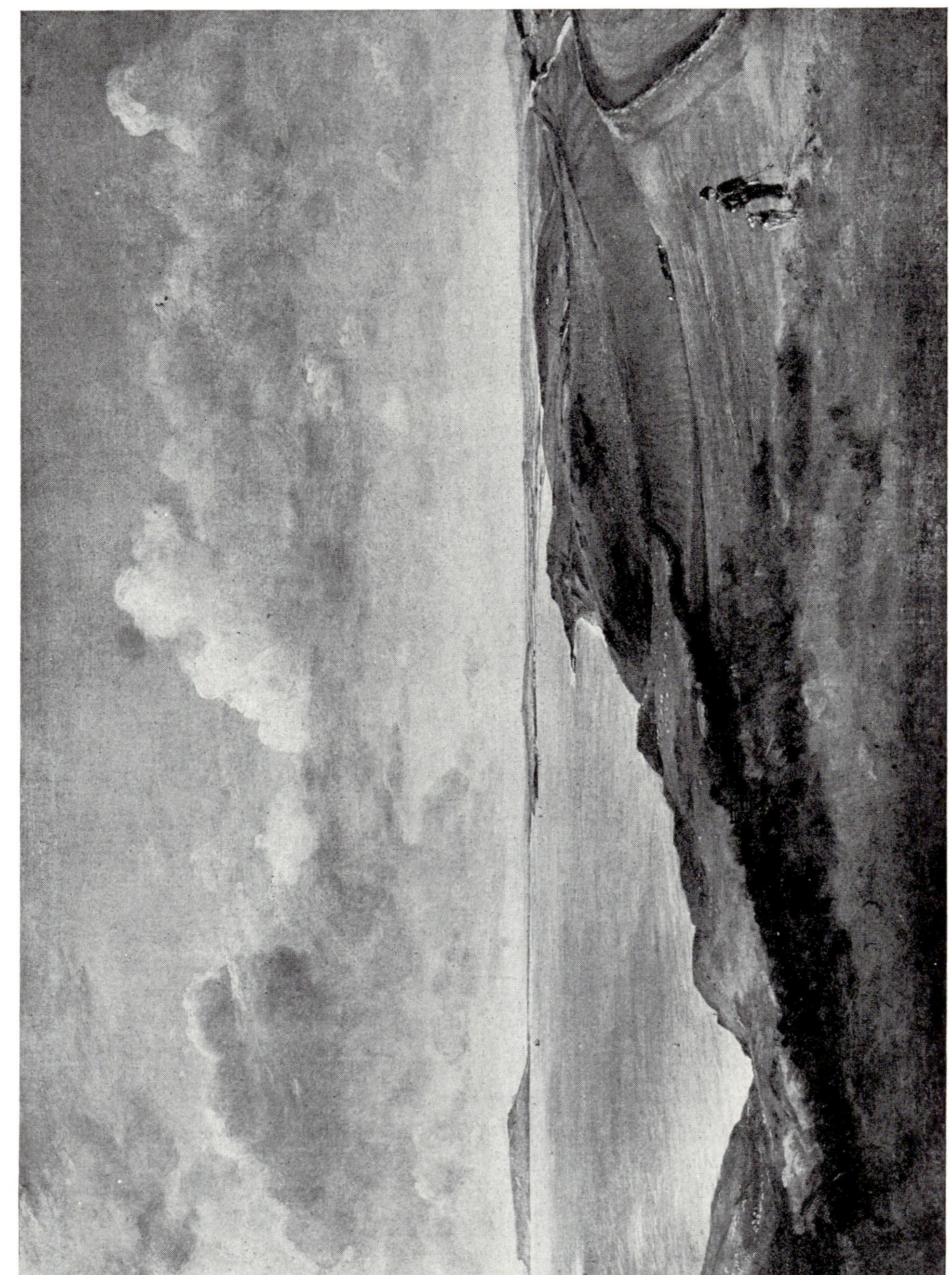

63. *Constable: Weymouth Bay, c. 1815*

croix to repaint entirely the land and sky in his "Massacre at Scio."
It is the more remarkable that Constable's sumptuous use of paint was
developed to catch fleeting effects of solitude and wandering clouds,
the pale English sunlight breaking through clouds after rain, or the
ripple of wind in trees, which are effects that no one before him had
painted. The conventionalized imitation of Dutch color, which still
prevailed in the fine water-colorists working around him, Girtin (1775–
1802) and John Sell Cotman (1782–1842), gave place in Constable to
an exact perception of the soft silver of English light. It is characteristic of English painting that this awareness came first and the magnificent painterlike technique afterward; that form, in other words, followed
sentiment (Figs. 63 and 65).

John Crome (1768–1821), the leader of the Norwich school, was also
a landscapist of fine quality. Chiefly self-taught from the examples of
Hobbema and Richard Wilson, he attained in his best work a broad
simplicity and a transparence of light that make him one of the most
pleasing figures in this golden age of landscape (Fig. 64). Turner also,
in his early oils and water colors, from about 1805 to 1812–1814, worked
with a direct realism inspired by the Dutch, but in the second decade
of the century his ambition to surpass Claude began to lead him into
his later rhetorical style.

The Scot, Sir David Wilkie (1785–1841; Fig. 66) was the best of the
nineteenth-century genre painters who represent the English tradition
of moralistic realism founded by Hogarth. Wilkie, though a shrewd
observer, was far from Hogarth's equal as an artist, and Victorian genre
fell off rapidly from the eighteenth-century standard. The rich vein of
social satire was worked more successfully by the less pretentious graphic
artists. Hogarth's satire, as it came down through Rowlandson, Cruik-
shank, and H. K. Browne, well-known as the illustrator of Dickens,
passed through the same change from savage caricature to quiet comedy
of manners as did the literary tradition from Swift, through Fielding,
to Dickens and Thackeray. *Punch*, founded in 1841, became the meet-
ing ground of a new generation of illustrators who finally abandoned
caricature for realism. Their medium was the new process of wood-
block reproduction from pen-and-ink drawing, their métier the humors

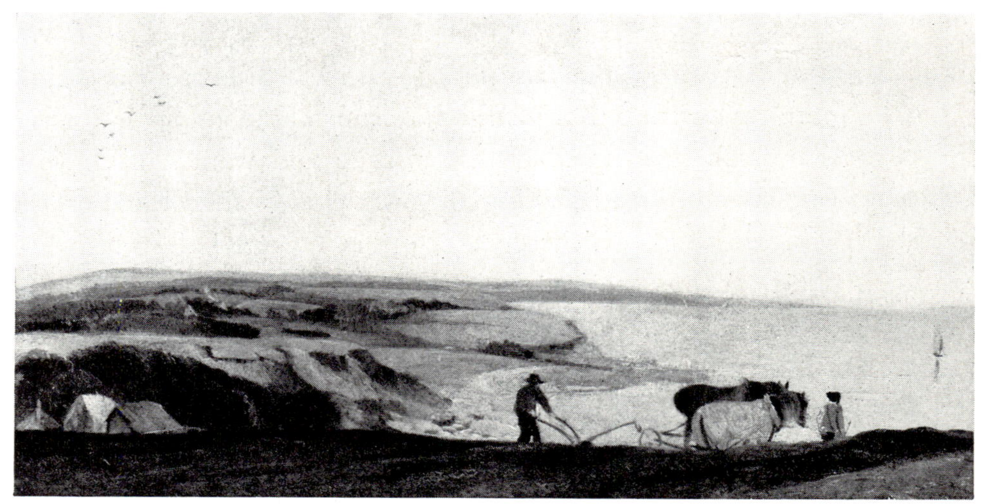

64. *Crome: View of the Solent, c.* 1805

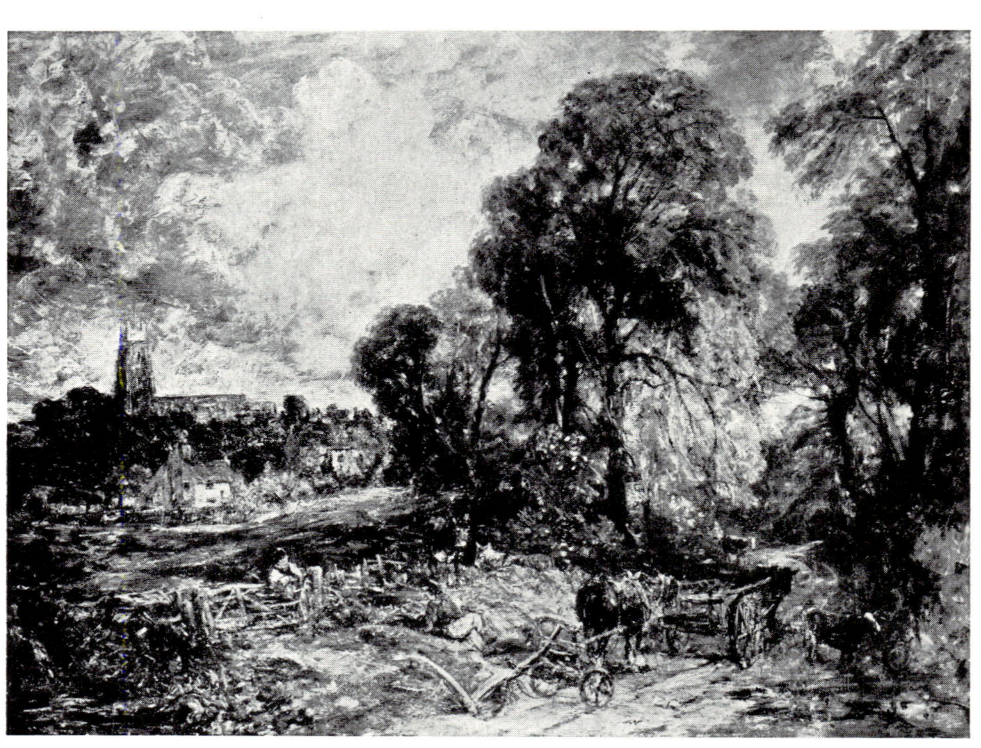

65. *Constable: Stoke-by-Nayland*

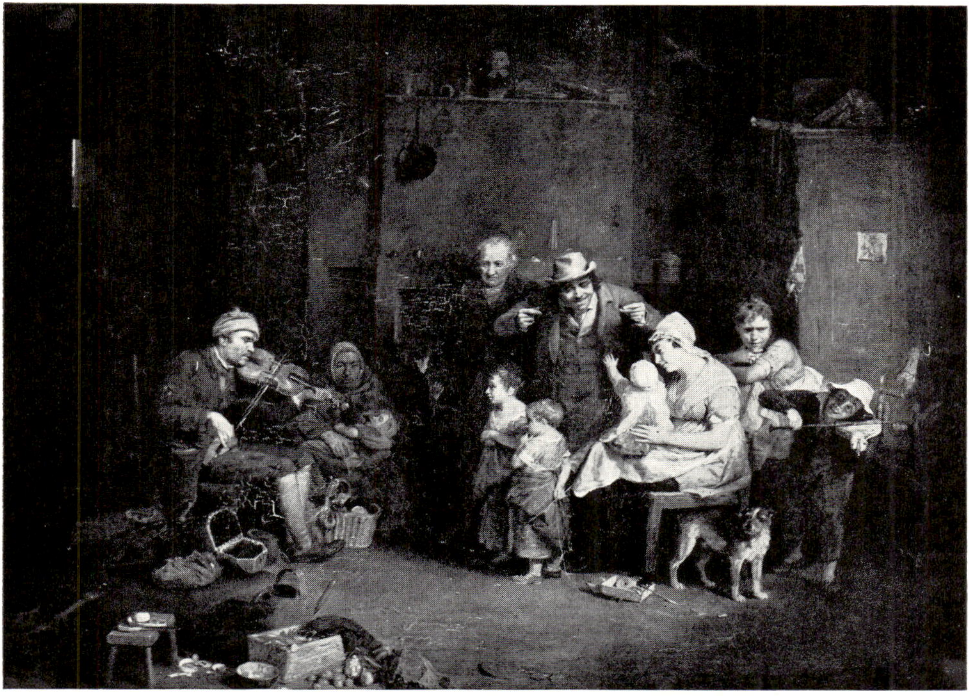

66. *Wilkie: The Blind Fiddler.* 1807

of English family and social life. John Leech (1817–1864), the friend of Thackeray and a famous *Punch* artist; Charles Keene (1823–1891; Fig. 67), who worked for *Punch* and for another new illustrated weekly news magazine, the *Illustrated London News* (another characteristic creation of the time); George Du Maurier (1834–1896; Fig. 68), who worked for *Punch* and other periodicals — all dealt with the everyday life of middle-class England. Their shrewd power of observation and deftly real atmospheric technique was something new, and achieved such success that they created a national tradition still living today. The wood-block process, which made these men possible, owed its origin to Bewick (1753–1828), the great Scottish illustrator, engraver, and naturalist. The clear lights and rich contrasts of tone of this technique lend a characteristic charm to Victorian book production.

The reversal of opinion which has taken place in the past generation or two upon German romanticism is astonishing. The great names of

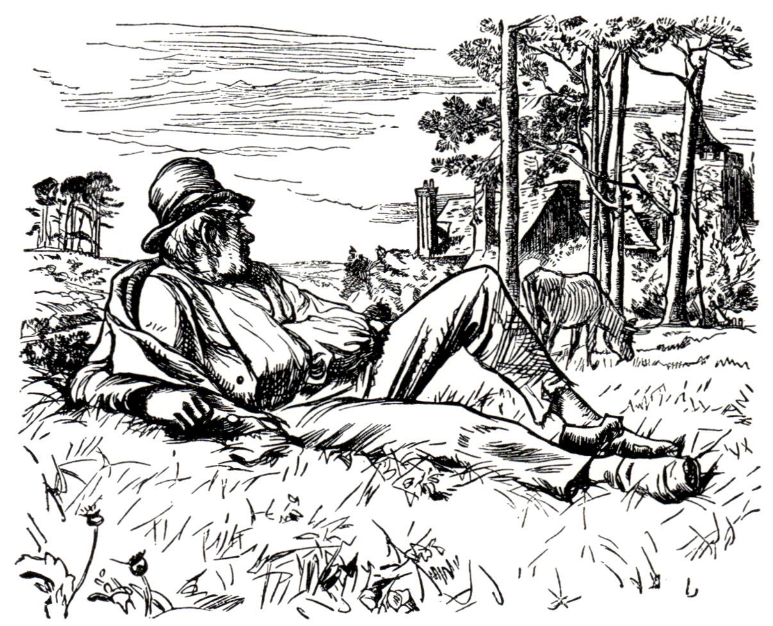

67. Keene: The Beggar's Soliloquy. 1861

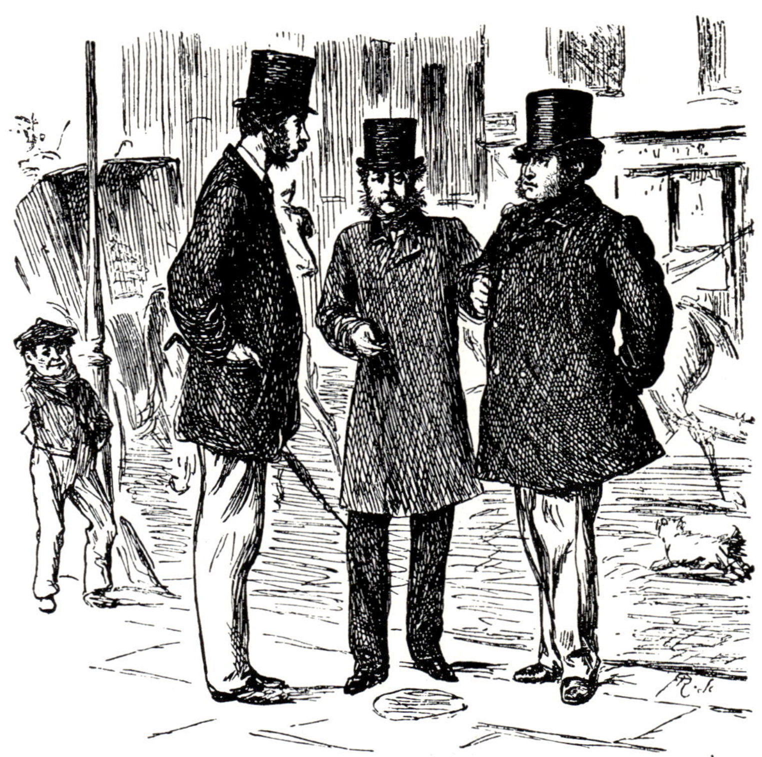

68. Du Maurier: The Little Moment before the Introduction.
1865

the nineteenth-century histories were the Nazarenes, who now seem to point only too plainly to a vast self-flattery in those German critics who believed that German *Tiefstimmung* (depth of feeling) had of itself created a great art. The painters whom we now enjoy are the little masters of Biedermeier painting, almost forgotten in the later nineteenth century, who made no pretense to grandeur or soul but with modest affection painted the life about them.

The first half of the century saw in Germany, as in other countries, the rise of an educated, home-loving, patriotic middle class. Unlike the same class elsewhere, however, it failed to gain control of its destiny in the revolution of 1848 (a failure which G. M. Trevelyan considers the great defeat of European history), and its liberal culture was dissipated by the power-politics of Bismarck. To the era of its rise belongs the development of Biedermeier painting, in which German sentiment, controlled and disciplined by a sturdy realism, left a charm-legacy.

It was a period of many local centers in German life. Berlin was not so important in painting as in architecture and sculpture. Hamburg and Dresden had their Biedermeier schools of painting. But the more important centers were in the south, in Munich and, especially, Vienna.

The Biedermeier style falls naturally into two divisions. The earlier painters, like Runge and Caspar David Friedrich (already mentioned in the chapter on romanticism) worked in the classicist period and in the tight linear style of their generation. Runge (1777–1810), in Hamburg, painted portraits and family groups with a cold exactitude of detail in which one can feel the new worship of nature fiercely setting aside the easy generalizations of the rococo (Fig. 69). Runge was a mystic, even in his devotion to fact. The Berliners, on the other hand, Schick, a portrait painter and pupil of Jacques Louis David, and Füger, the painter of military and sporting scenes, showed a kind of hard, dry naturalism that is honest but uninspiring. The directness of the north-German eye was more interesting when Blechen (1798–1840), a pleasing landscapist of the next generation, began to paint with a more fluid and atmospheric brush (Fig. 70). In Dresden Friedrich (1774–1840) and Kersting (1785–1847), the latter attached to the Meissen porcelain

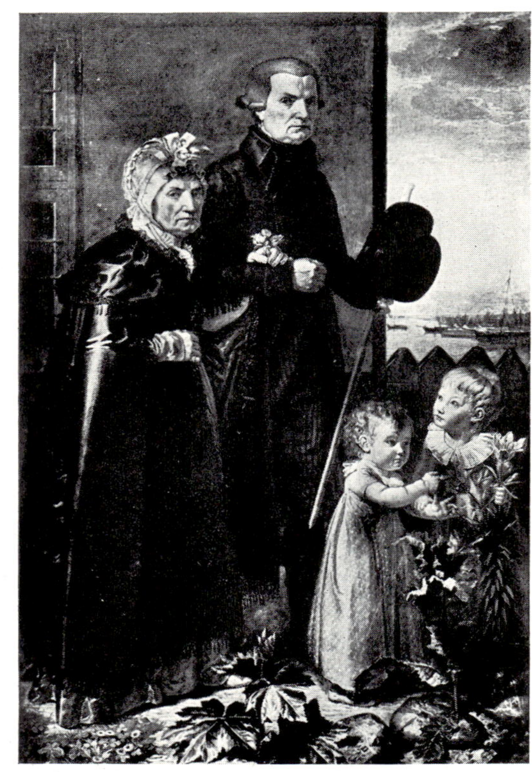

69. *Runge: Family of the Artist.* 1806

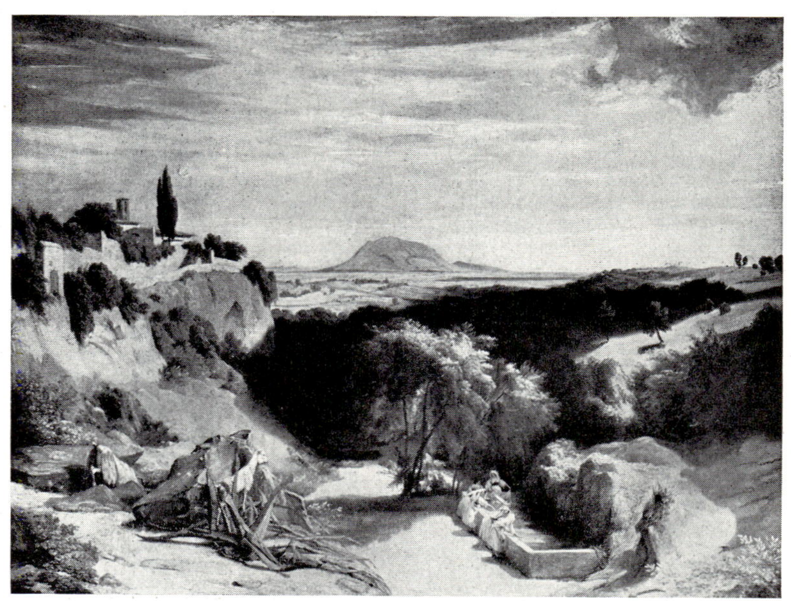

70. *Blechen: View of Soracte from Civita Castellana.* 1829

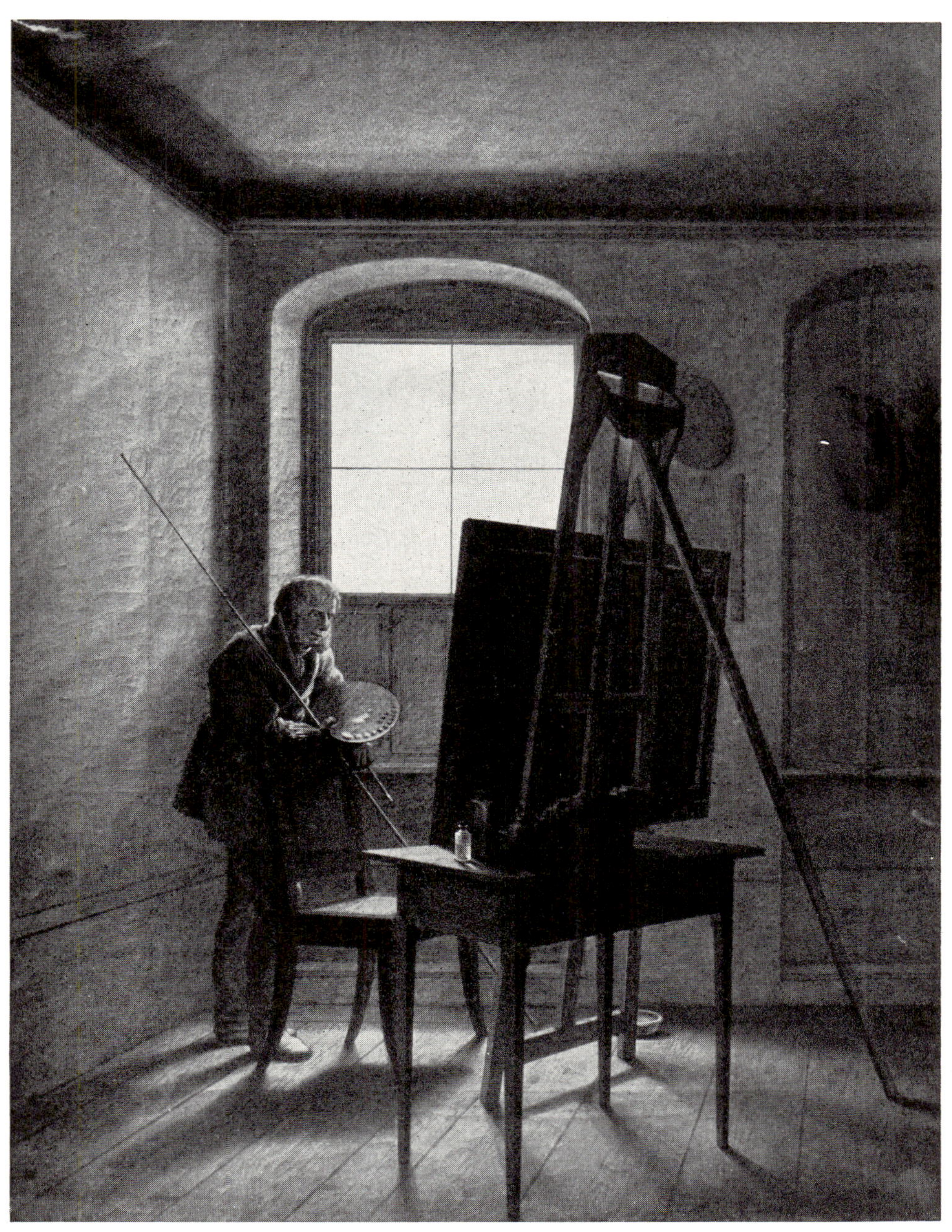

71. *Kersting: Caspar David Friedrich in His Studio.* 1811

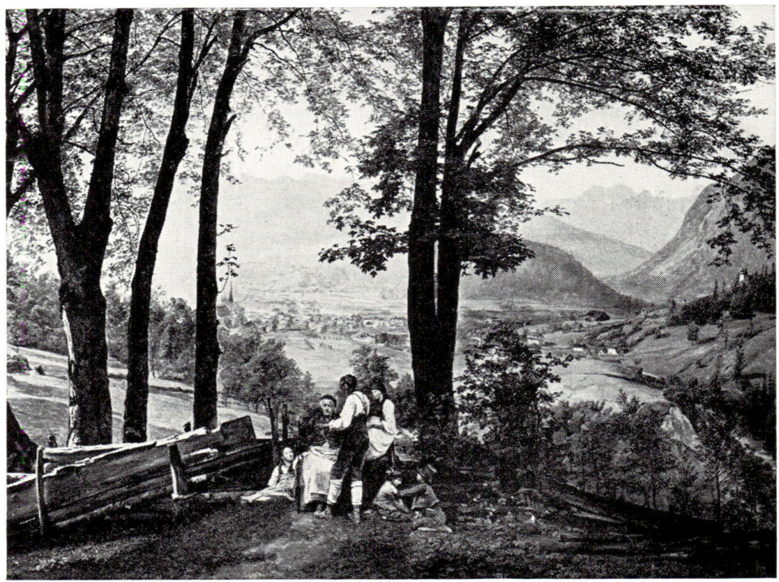

72. *Waldmüller: View of Ischl.* 1838

factory, also worked in the early linear style. Friedrich is an excellent example of the cold romantic revery of the north-German romantics. "Listen intently to your inner voices. You must hold sacred every pure emotion of your soul; for in the hour of inspiration, it is incarnate in a plastic form." [2] Unfortunately his handling of oil paint is timid and mean. Kersting, like Friedrich and Runge a product of the Academy in Copenhagen, was a charming painter of interiors (Fig. 71) in a precise linear style.

The quality of *Gemütlichkeit,* which was the real subject of Biedermeier painting, was at its best among the warmer and more genial south Germans. Vienna, a flourishing and aristocratic capital, had emerged from the Napoleonic Wars the political center of the Continent. The great musical and artistic flowering of Viennese life, which carried over from the eighteenth century through the first half of the nineteenth century, created an atmosphere in which the academic abstractions of the classicists and Nazarenes did not take hold; the Viennese temperament was too warm and spontaneous. A fortunate influence

[2] Quoted by Louis Reau in Michel, *Histoire de l'art* (Paris, 1905–1929), vol. VIII, pt. I, p. 241.

was exerted upon painting by the presence, at the Congress of Vienna
in 1814, of Lawrence, the English portrait painter, and Isabey, the
French miniaturist. Lawrence's influence upon the development of
Delacroix's painterlike style has already been mentioned; he was felt
also in Vienna. Wilkie likewise had an influence, widespread on the
Continent, through prints of his pictures.

Ferdinand Waldmüller (1793–1865), the chief figure of the early
linear style, painted humorous and sentimental scenes of peasant life
that are like Wilkie in their charm and in a certain obviousness of
thought. With his careful, exact portraits and his landscapes of the
Wienerwald and the Salzkammergut, he is important in every phase
of Biedermeier painting (Fig. 72), but his hard touch and his over-
exact and rather airless technique are less pleasing than the fresher,
more painterlike technique of certain less famous contemporaries. One
can find these charming, modest painters in Vienna in the Belvedere,
the Rathaus, and the Liechtenstein Gallery. The landscape of Jakob

73. *Danhauser: Mother Love*

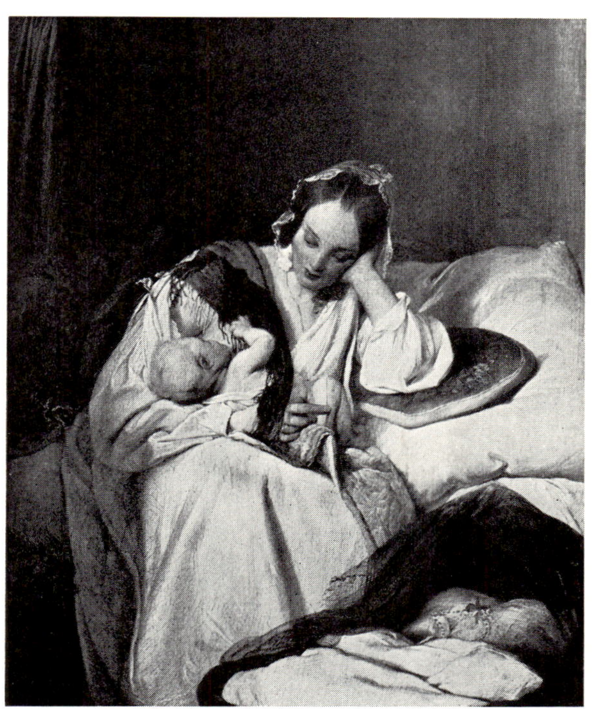

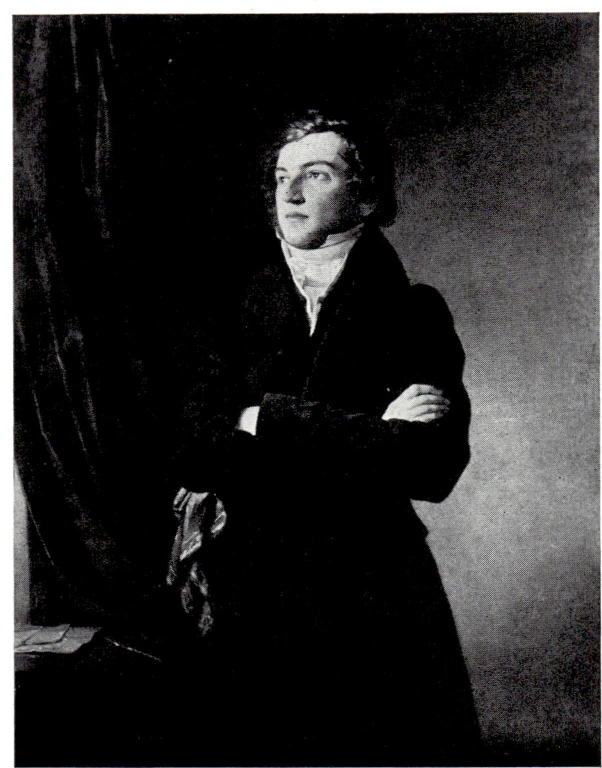

74. *Amerling: The Painter, Robert Theer.* 1831

Alt, Rudolf Alt, and Friedrich Gauermann, the humorous and sentimental genre of Stöber and Danhauser (Fig. 73), the sensitive romantic
portraiture of Amerling (Fig. 74), the illustrations of Austria's countless
white-coated military campaigns by Pettenkofen and Michalowski — all
are genial and delicate in sentiment, and form a delightful expression
of the Vienna of Schubert and Grillparzer.

The culture of Vienna was old, urbane, and polished; Munich was
just emerging as a capital in the early nineteenth century. More provincial in tone than Vienna, it was the capital of a distinctly peasant prov-
ince, and its good-humored but somewhat coarse atmosphere clung to
its art. Wilhelm Kobell (1766–1855) very early in the century made
studies of peasant life and military campaigns which in their own
precise, hard way are full of light. Rottmann, in his landscapes of
Greece, was also feeling his way toward a concentration upon light.
But it was Karl Spitzweg (1808–1885; Fig. 75), a self-taught artist, who

had the best gift for painting. He was a humorist of a delicate, fanciful
sort, a teller of diverting anecdotes in pictures which are as enjoyable
for their delicate realism and fine mastery of light as for their story.
Like Daumier, he was both artist and satirist, the difference being that
Spitzweg's art was rooted in *Gemütlichkeit* and Daumier's in liberal
humanitarianism.

In America, from 1800 onwards, there was a lively production of
landscape and genre painting which expressed the rise of the same new
culture and new attitude toward nature we have seen in Europe. Romantic idealism was a late and feeble growth here but romantic realism
was the natural expression of nineteenth-century American life. It began
early and was in full flower by 1830, while a second generation pro-
longed its life through the 1870's before it was swept away at last by
new ideas.

75. *Spitzweg: English Tourists on the Campagna*

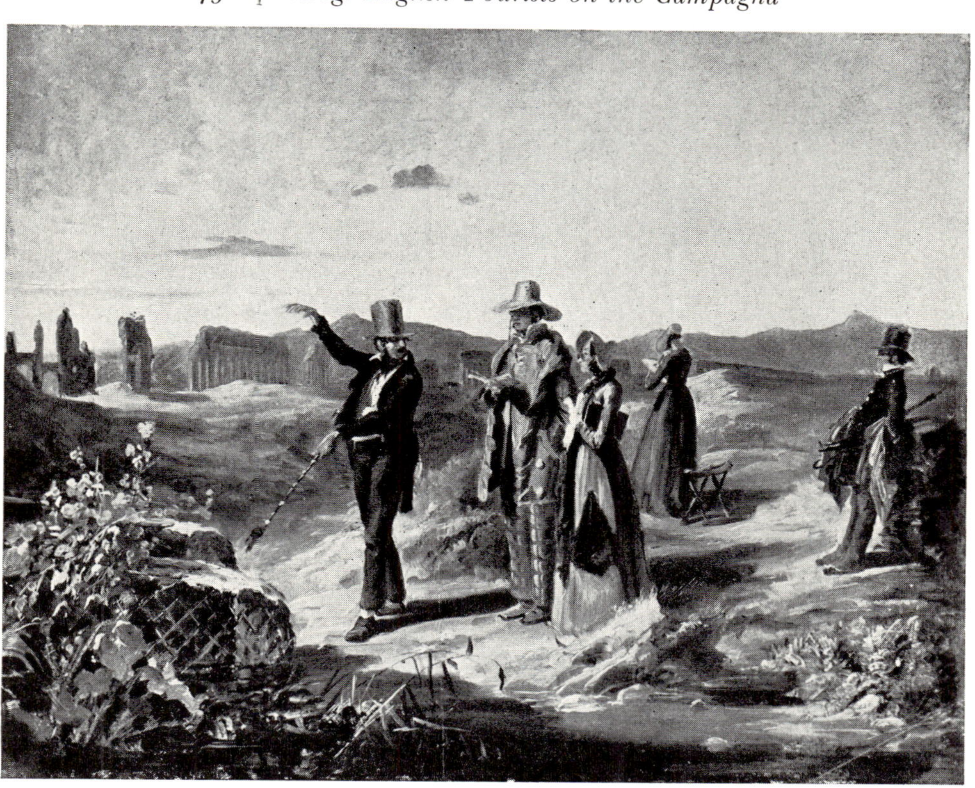

In America all the forces of the early nineteenth century seemed to combine to favor a realistic romanticism. The culture of the eighteenth century had faded away, leaving a new world which had an intense faith in the theory of democracy and in the values of democratic life which were believed to be peculiar to America. This was the great period of westward expansion, and the stupendous task of settling the continent turned the attention of the country inward upon itself and away from Europe. Moreover, the draining of population westward tended to detach people from the more stable communities of the east, thus weakening the force of tradition and throwing people back upon nature.

The pictorial style of the first half-century in the United States was linear and precise. The London-trained painters, such as Stuart and Allston, failed to pass on their painterlike technique to the generation of the twenties and thirties. The romantic realists were very largely trained upon engravings: some of them were steel engravers who developed into painters, while few of them had the experience of Sully in the English coloristic technique that Lawrence and Constable practiced.

76. Doughty: Nature's Wonderland. 1836

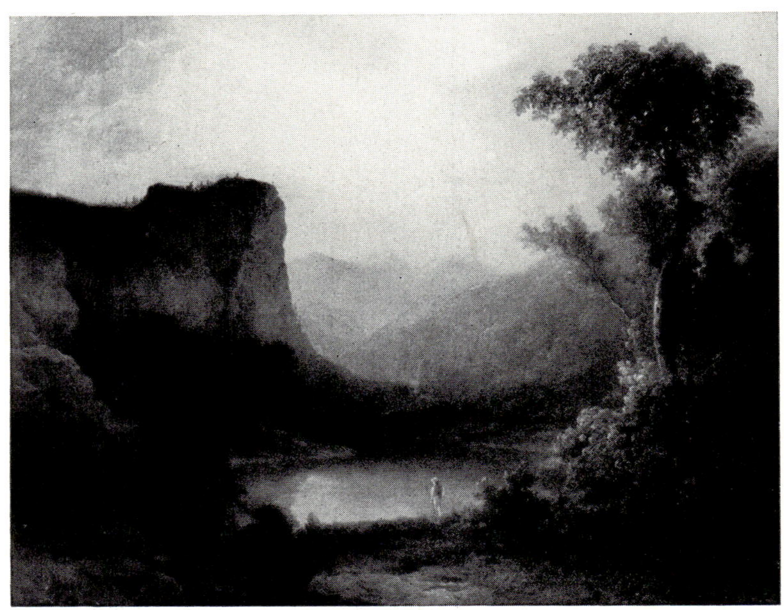

The frontier also made itself felt upon the style of the age in a curiously unexpected manner. The westward migrations across the Alleghenies contained a very high percentage of educated men, but the population, thinly spread through the wild interior, was cut off from all the arts except literature and music. Artists continued to be born in this population, but they were separated by their environment from the tradition of the plastic arts. Western painting from the time of Van Eyck and Masaccio had been three-dimensional, concerned, that is, with creating imaginative images of solid forms within the deep space of their pictures. Among the artists cut off from tradition there was a marked tendency to relapse into a two-dimensional style. It was not a simple failure to achieve a three-dimensional form but in some cases a positive development in the opposite direction, toward a map-like, decorative pattern. Strangely enough, this can be found even in artists

77. *Durand: In the Woods.* 1855

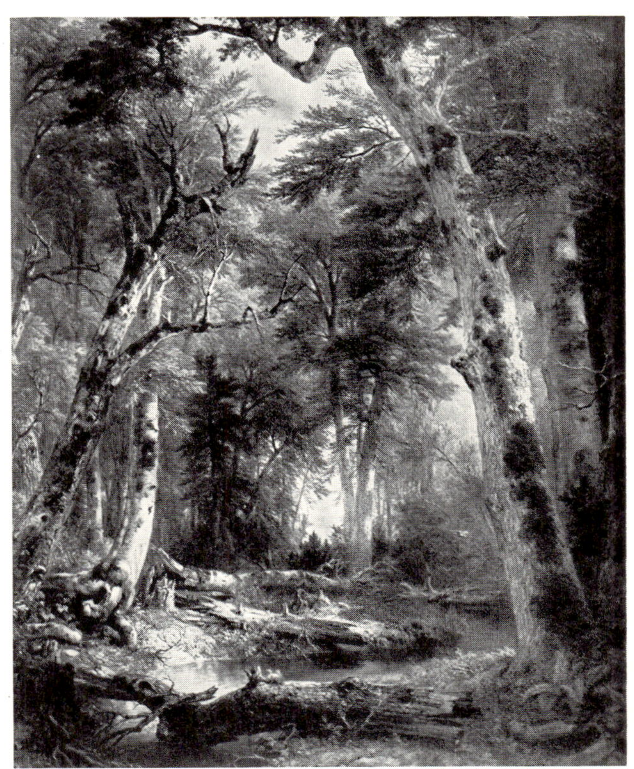

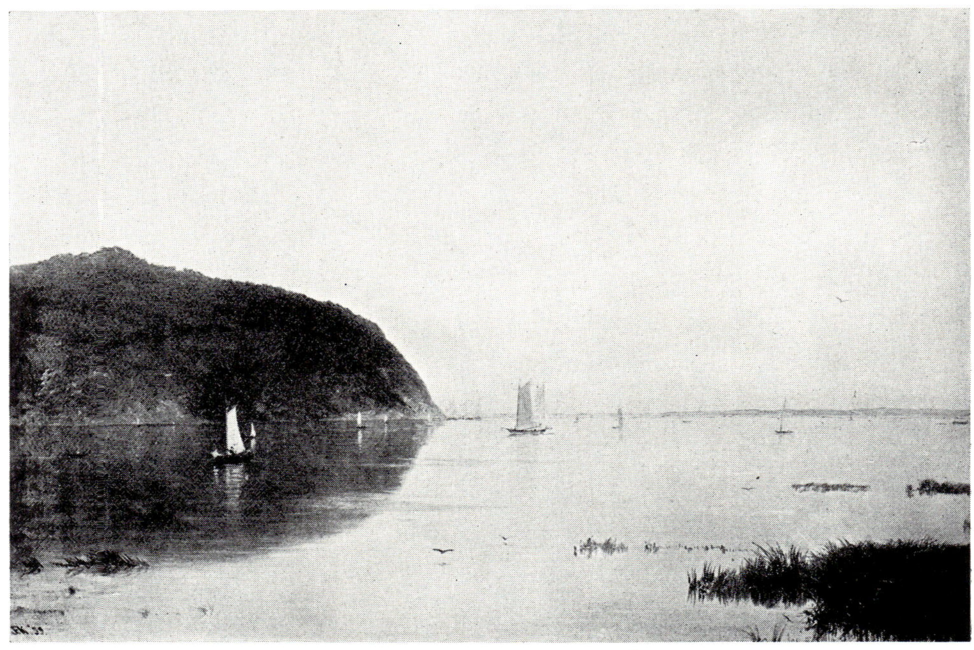

78. *Kensett: Shrewsbury River.* 1859

trained abroad. Ralph Earl (1751–1801), a pupil of West, learned the solid English style well enough to do the very creditable full-length "Portrait of a Man in a Landscape Setting" at Worcester. Yet later in life, wandering about in the little towns of the Connecticut Valley to which the dearth of sitters and his irregular habits condemned him, he developed a picture-making faculty of an entirely different sort. The Ellsworth double portrait in Hartford shows a growth toward a two-dimensional style, composed in flat color areas rather than volumes. What Earl did, many folk artists did also, led by the obscure instinct that runs in primitives and children beneath the conscious levels of our tradition.

Nonetheless, anyone who has read the biographies of these romantic artists, and has seen not only how slowly they developed but how often their achievement seems fragmentary and incomplete in comparison with the character of the man, can fail to feel that circumstances placed a crushing load upon the artist. Chester Harding (1792–1866), for example, was twenty years old before he knew of another kind of painting than house painting. There is no better illustration of the value of tradition — craft tradition and social tradition — in art than the history of the nineteenth century in America.

The same century throughout all of western culture is equally illuminating in the light it throws upon the independence of art from external or material circumstance. Patronage was lavished upon the wrong people — upon the Nazarenes in Germany and the Academicians in France and England — while almost without exception some crushing weight of popular opinion or social circumstance weighed upon the true creative talents. Yet living art continued to spring up, whether among European artists who had to fight the critics and their fellowmen in order to develop, or among boys born in lonely clearings upon the American frontier. Can we ask a clearer proof of the impossibility of either controlling or destroying art, which goes like a wind of the spirit, where it will?

Ralph Earl was the first American to break away from the eighteenth-century landscape tradition which derived from Claude and Salvator Rosa, to try to make a faithful portrait of the character of the landscape he saw before him. In 1800, almost exactly contemporary with the appearance of the two great heralds of English and German romanticism, the *Lyrical Ballads* of Wordsworth and Coleridge (1798) and the *Athenaeum* of the brothers Schlegel (1799) Earl painted the "View of Worcester, Looking East from the Leicester Hills" (Worcester) which is the first extant landscape in America painted in the mood of a disciple rather than master of nature. From that time onward a broadening stream of landscape and genre led into the nineteenth century in America, amplifying the old portrait tradition, which, even with the addition of historical painting, had offered little outlet to American sentiment.

The change of taste had as its first result a reversal of the eighteenth century's dislike for the wilderness. The vast, shaggy, untamed continent into which the Americans were beginning to penetrate offered an intoxicating theme for the romantic artist. Harriet Martineau wrote in her *Travels* (1834–1836):

The valley of the Connecticut is the most fertile valley in New England; and it is scarcely possible that any should be more beautiful. The river, full,

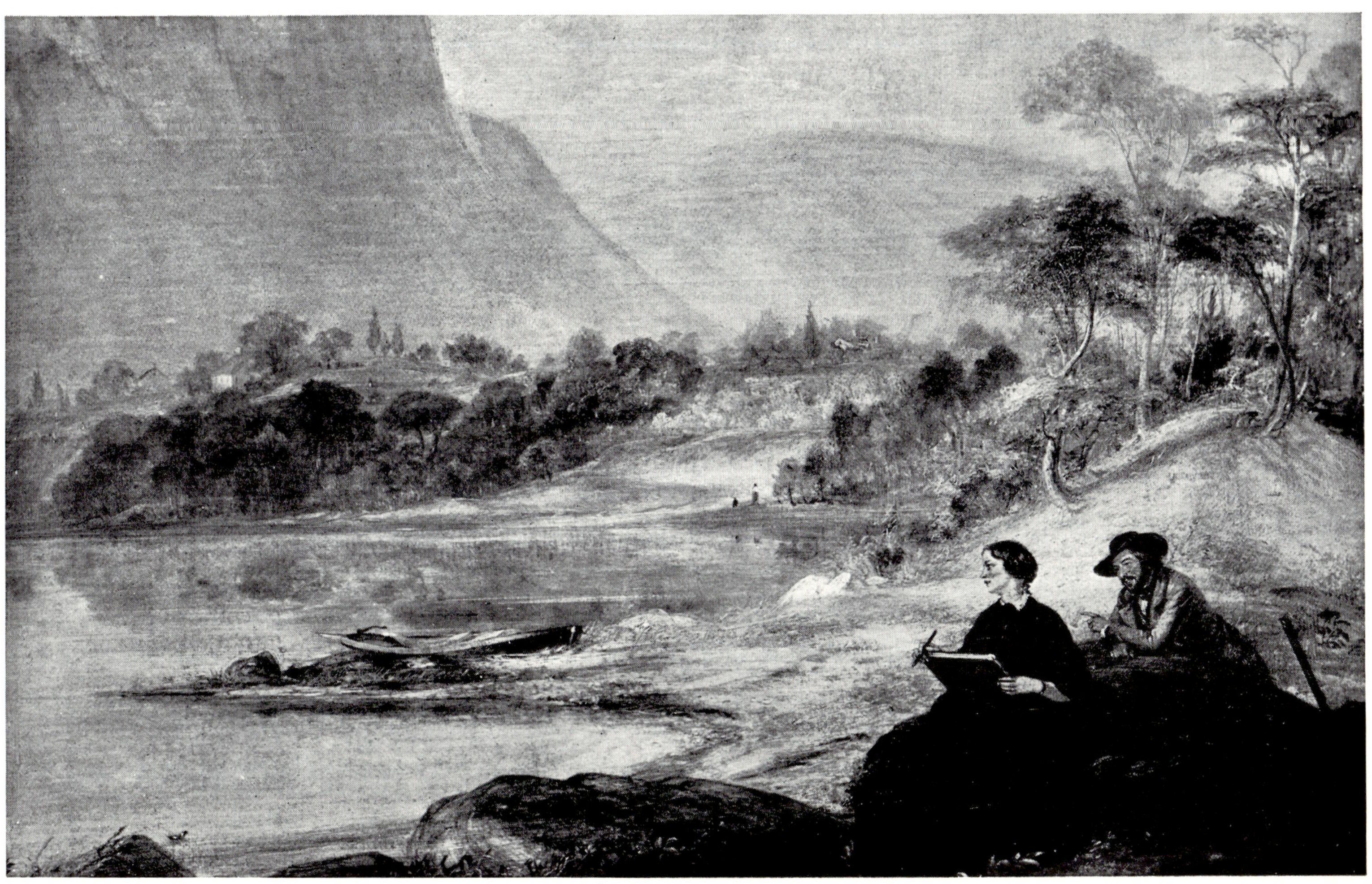

79. *Mount: The Artist and His Wife Sketching*

broad and tranquil as the summer sky, winds through meadows, green with pasture, or golden with corn. Clumps of forest trees afford retreat for the cattle in the summer heats; and the magnificent New England elm, the most graceful of trees, is dropped singly, here and there, and casts its broad shade upon the meadow. Hills of various height and declivity bound the now widening, now contracting valley. To these hills, the forest has retired; the everlasting forest, from which, in America, we cannot fly. I cannot remember that, except in some parts of the prairies, I was ever out of sight of the forest in the United States; and I am sure I never wished to be so. It was like "The verdurous wall of Paradise," confining the mighty southern and western rivers to their channels. We were, as it appeared, imprisoned in it for many days together, as we traversed the southeastern states. We threaded it in Michigan; we skirted it in New York and Pennsylvania; and through New England it bounded every landscape. It looked down upon us from the hill-tops; it advanced into notice from every gap and notch in the chain. To the native it must appear as indispensable in the picture gallery of nature as the sky. To the English traveler it is a special boon, an added grace. . . . Next to the solemn and various beauty of the sea and sky, comes that of the wilderness. I doubt whether the sublimity of the vastest mountain range can exceed that of the all-pervading forest, when the imagination becomes able to realize the conception of what it is.

One can feel this sense of the wonder and beauty of the wilderness in the naïve landscape of Doughty (1793–1856), who gave up a trade in his late twenties to devote himself to landscape painting (Fig. 76). Thomas Cole (1801–1848) discovered the Hudson Valley and the Cats-kills, and painted them with a cool palette and linear touch of considerable charm; unfortunately the melodramatic taste of the day led him also into unpictorial, theatrical epics like "The Course of Empire."

It was characteristic of this school to strive for an impression of vastness; a view from a hillside clearing or rock ledge over a panorama of river, valley, and lake, and range upon range of mountains, was their favorite subject. The influence of steel engraving upon their technique has already been mentioned. Two of the best of the school, Durand (1796–1886; Fig. 77) and Kensett (1818–1872; Fig. 78), were engravers before they became painters. Cropsey, Casilear, F. E. Church, Weir, James MacDougal Hart, and many others did excellent work in a delicately linear style. Their means were simple; a palette of cool greens and blues and a warm brown, space suggested by a diagonal vista, and

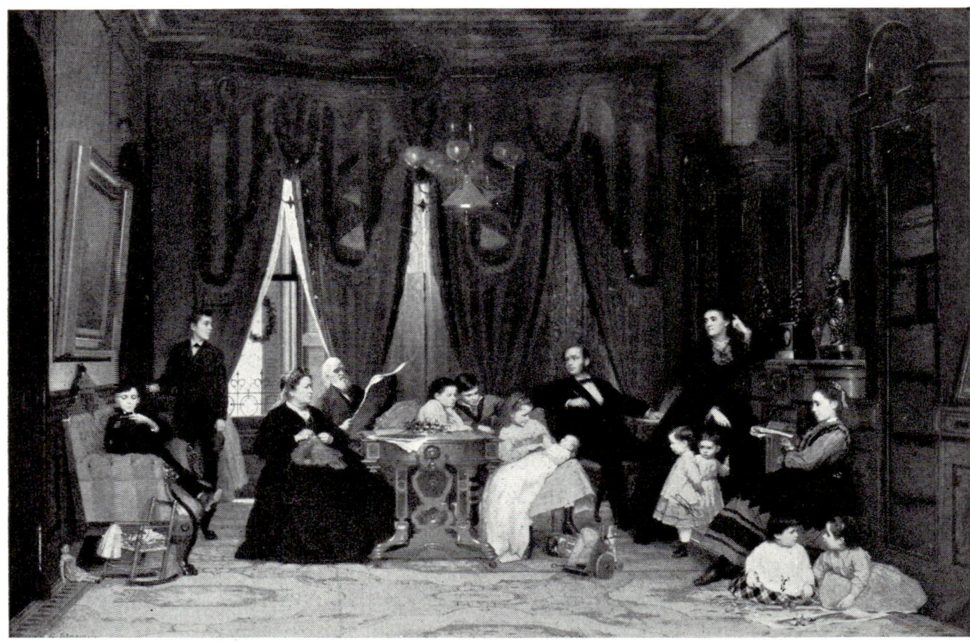

80. *Johnson: Family Group.* 1871

a simple tonal progression from dark foreground to a silvery sky were the mechanics of the school. Their technical means were adequate to the self-subordinating poetry of their love of nature. The Paris- and Munich-trained men who brought back an atmospheric, painterlike style in the seventies heaped ridicule upon this meticulous manner, but it is hard to see now that the later manner created space or air or the poetry of nature with greater felicity, or with a more transparent reality, than did that of the Hudson River painters. A change in the conception of space, from vastness to the intimate and restricted view of the Barbizon manner, more clearly divides the romantic realists from the later men. Inness, Wyant, Whittredge, and Homer Martin span both periods, and the change can be seen in their work.

Henry Sargent (1770–1845) of Boston was the earliest of the genre painters. His rare pictures show a truer eye for the pictorial, rather than the anecdotal, value of contemporary society than one would expect in such a pioneer. William Sidney Mount (Fig. 79) and Eastman Johnson (Fig. 80) were the two best painters of the life of the farms and cities in the east. Mount (1807–1868) was a portrait and still-life

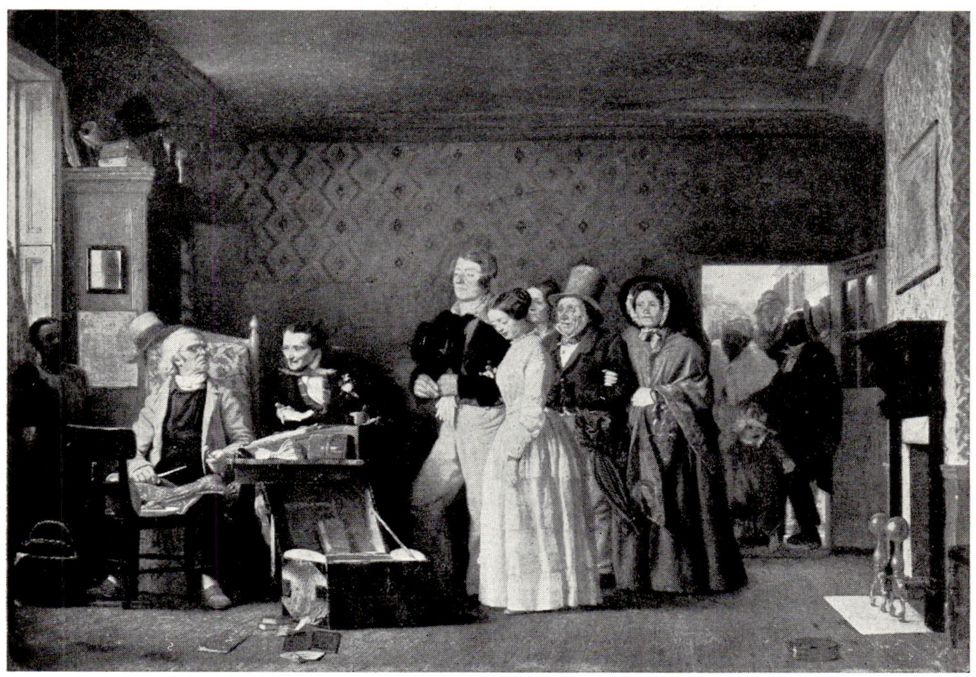

81. *Woodville: The Sailor's Wedding.* 1852

painter in New York before the example of Dutch painting turned
him to genre. Ill-health took him home to rural Long Island, where he
discovered the humors of country life, then at its most racy and distinctive stage. Mount's humor was of the order of Washington Irving's,
genial and quietly sentimental. His fault was a tendency to dryness and
over-finish in his technique, but he was capable at times of a fluid
delicacy of touch, as in "The Artist and His Wife Sketching," a charming image of the romantic artist. Among his contemporaries, Richard
Caton Woodville (Fig. 81) and T. P. Rossiter were the best. Woodville,
a Baltimore painter, studied at Düsseldorf and caught something of
the overstatement which makes that school so tedious; yet his fresh,
delicate style shows the gifts of a true painter. Rossiter was likewise an
excellent painter, though marred occasionally by the excessive senti-
mentality of his age. Eastman Johnson (1824–1906) was the chief of
the second generation. He, too, studied at Düsseldorf, but shook off
that unfortunate beginning by copying and studying at The Hague.
His best genre was done within the first twenty years after his return

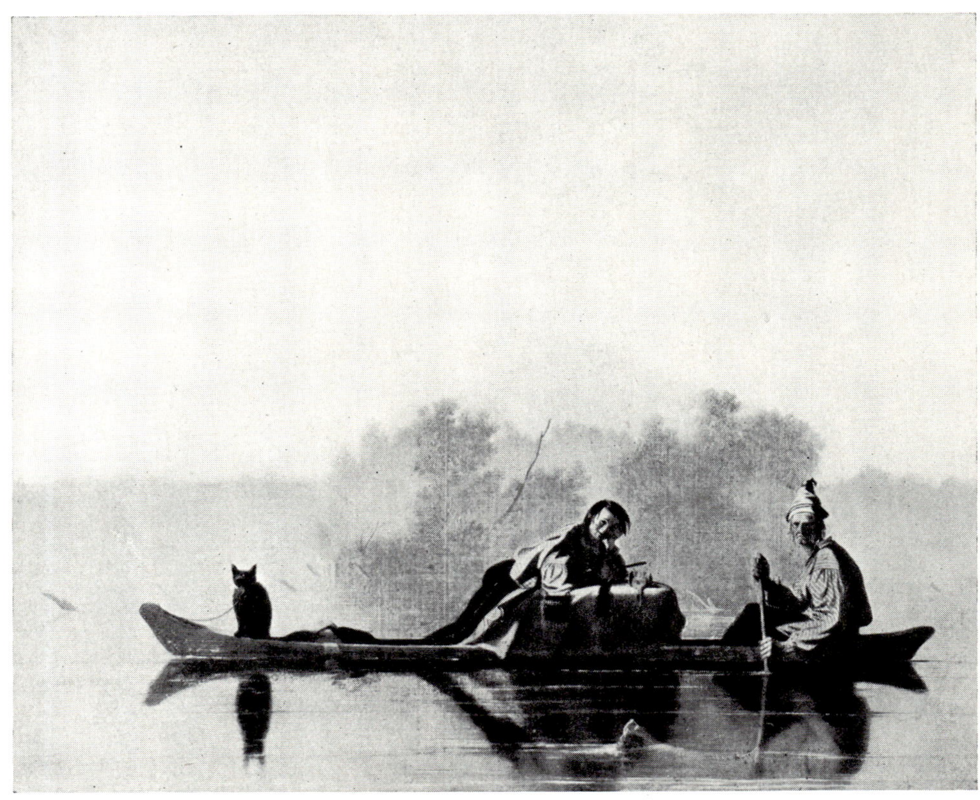

82. *Bingham: Fur Traders Descending the Missouri, c.* 1845

to the United States in 1855; later, under the influence of the Munich school, he changed to an atmospheric style in which his genuine gifts for genre were lost, although he continued to be one of the few really distinguished portrait painters of his age.

The life of the frontier also had its recorders. George Catlin (1796–1872) was a portrait painter in Philadelphia until he saw a deputation of Plains Indians, in buckskins and feathers, passing through to Washington. The splendid physique and the fierce, free air of the Indians persuaded him that only on the Great Plains could an artist find, in the nineteenth century, human beings of that physical and mental perfection which the world worshipped in ancient Greece. In 1832 he left Philadelphia for the upper Missouri, which was then more than two months' journey from the outposts of civilization at St. Louis. His paintings and drawings of the Indian life he found there, and subsequently in other parts of the Americas, show a genuine sensibility struggling with an inadequate technique. Catlin left, nonetheless, a fascinating and irreplaceable mass of work. Audubon also left a record of the wilderness. But the most interesting of the genre painters of the frontier was George Caleb Bingham (1811–1879). At the age of eight Bingham was taken by his family to the remote edge of settlement in Missouri. His introduction to art was a brief contact with Chester Harding (then almost equally untrained), who had gone to Missouri in order to paint a portrait of the aged Daniel Boone. A year of study in Philadelphia, where he knew the solid, competent Neagle, was his only formal training at the time he did his best work. Between 1844 and 1856 he did a series of pictures of the buffalo hunters, half-breeds, trappers, and flatboatmen of the Missouri frontier which show an astonishingly sensitive technique and an ability to deal with this unprecedented material in the best tradition of romantic realism (Fig. 82).

83. *Mount: The Studious Boy (wood engraving by Adams).* 1834

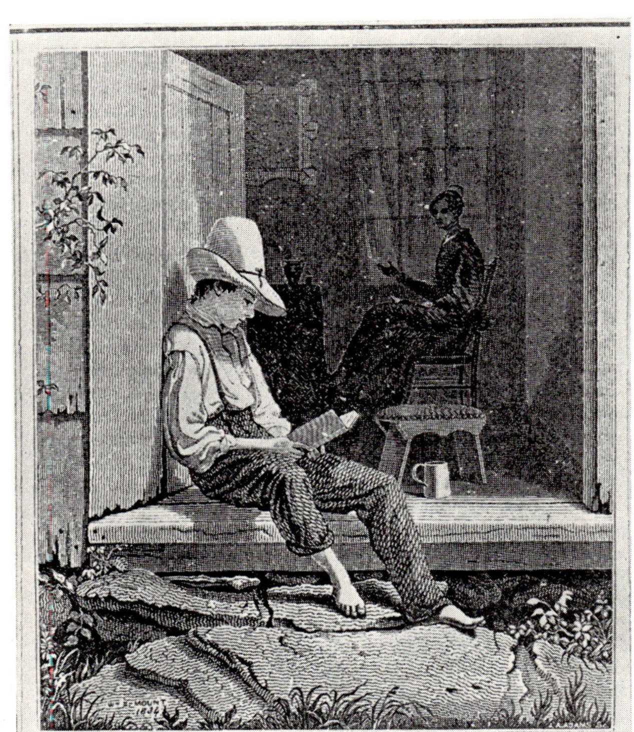

Further study at Düsseldorf taught him to overpaint and oversentimentalize, so that it is no great waste that he gave up art later to take part in the fierce political struggles of a border state before and during the Civil War.

Meanwhile black-and-white illustration took its own course. Steel engraving developed early in the century. The flowering of that style under the Smillies, the two Durands, and Kensett founded a national tradition which still exists in the unique work of the Bureau of Engraving and Printing in Washington. Woodcut reproduction developed more slowly (Fig. 83); the usual technique was coarse and repellent until the 1870's. F. O. C. Darley (1822–1888) was the first romantic illustrator to emerge above the crudity of the process. Darley's facile but spirited pen-and-ink illustrations for Irving, Cooper, Longfellow, and other romantic authors, were almost the only wood-block illustrations of this period to retain an interest today. The next generation was more fortunate.

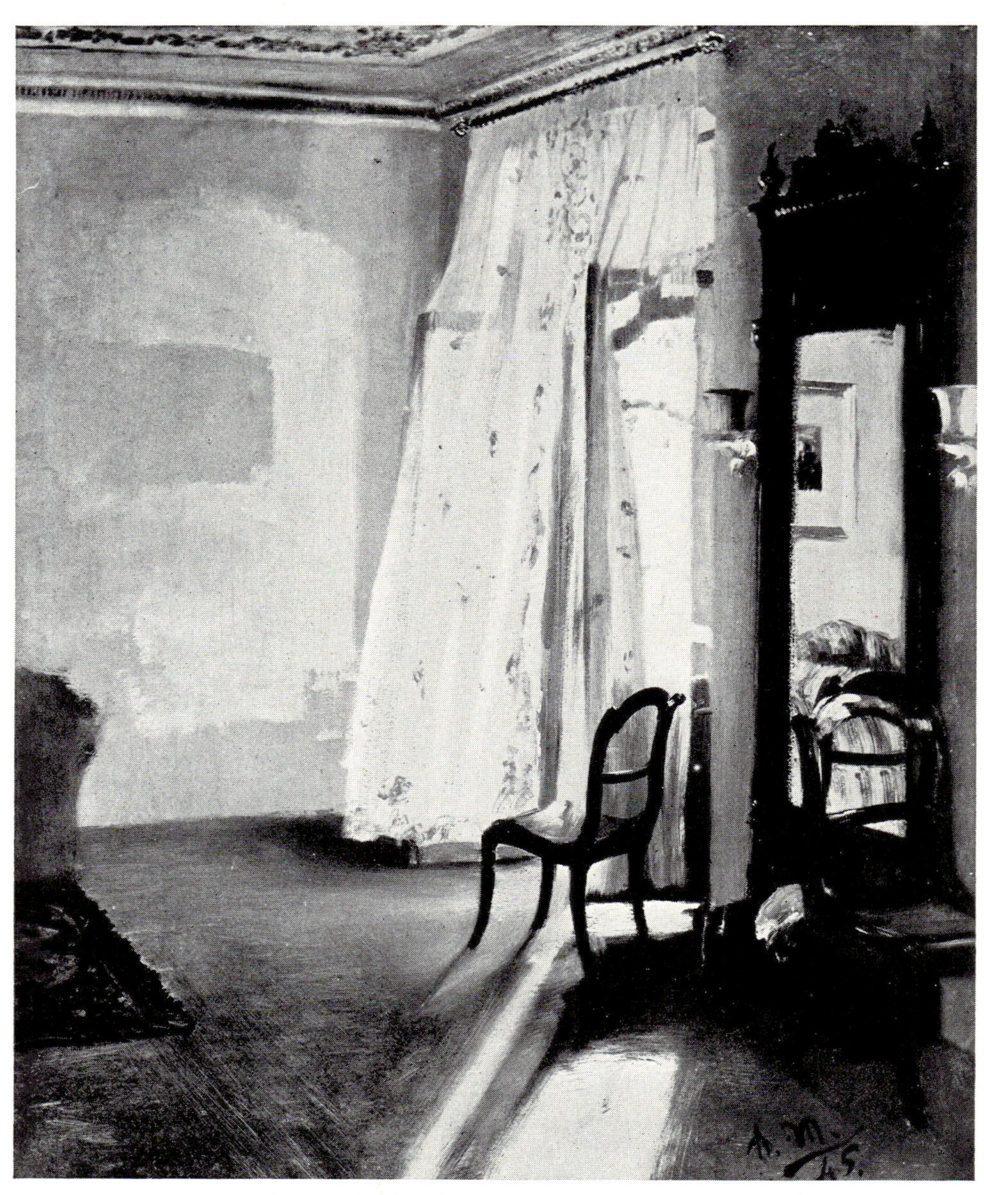

84. Menzel: The Balcony Room. 1845

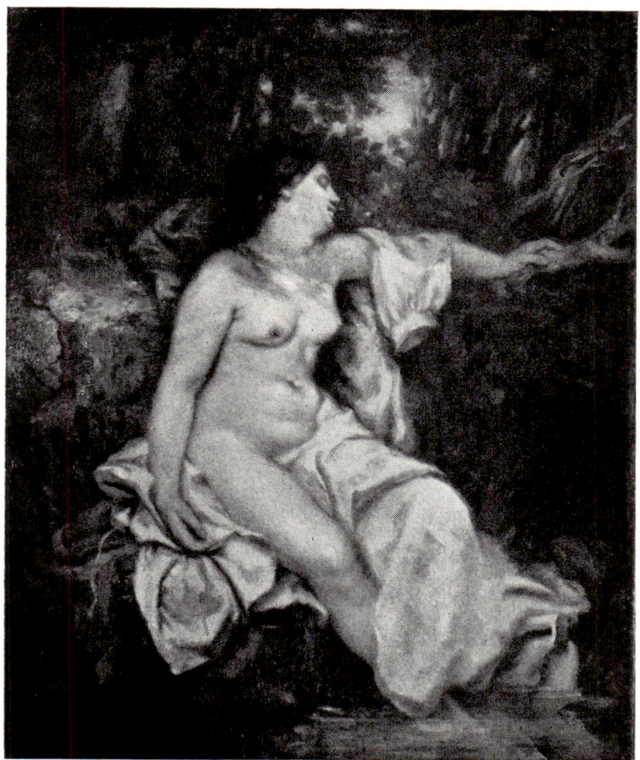

85. *Courbet: Midday Dream.* 1845

CHAPTER IV

OBJECTIVE REALISM AND IMPRESSIONISM

THE TEMPER of the succeeding age, which began about 1850, was bitterly
hostile toward romanticism's historical, literary, and ethical qualities.
The historical and philosophical methods of thought which had characterized the romantic period began to be displaced by the methods of
science. The era of idealistic thought was over, and Herbert Spencer's
mechanistic explanations of the universe lay just beyond the horizon.
Ethically, also, the world was changing. In place of the religion of liberty
that animated the liberals of the early nineteenth century came a new
line of prophets — Comte, Owen, Proudhon, Marx — who promised to
redeem the world by economics. Into the arts also came a new spirit of
objective, realistic thought, analytical rather than synthetical in nature.
A painting by David or Delacroix had appealed not only to the observer's

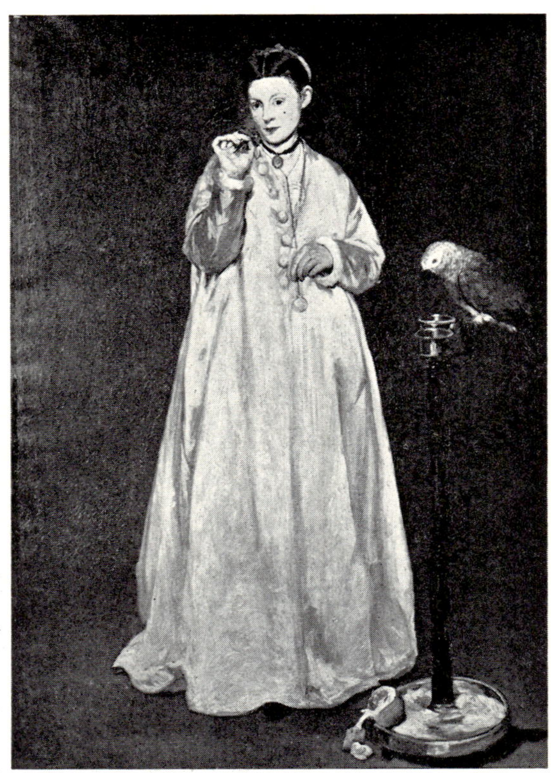

86. Manet: Woman with Parrot. 1868

eye but to his memory and his powers of thought; the process of understanding it involved his knowledge of history and of literature, his ethical theory of what life should mean, his share in that dream of human freedom and perfection that haunted the earlier generations of the century. The problem of creation for the next thirty to fifty years was to rid the mind of all these preconceived ideas and sentiments, and to use the faculty of sight alone, to achieve an objective vision into which neither forethought nor afterthought was allowed to enter.

If one can compress into a phrase the distinction between the realism of the romantics and the objective realism of the age of science, it is that in the later realism the bouquet of tenderness is gone. The romantic realists, however transparent and self-effacing in style, were moved by sentiment. For the new men, facts were exciting enough: they gave themselves to the excitement of discovery of the world but not to the excitement of interpretation; they were anti-idealistic.

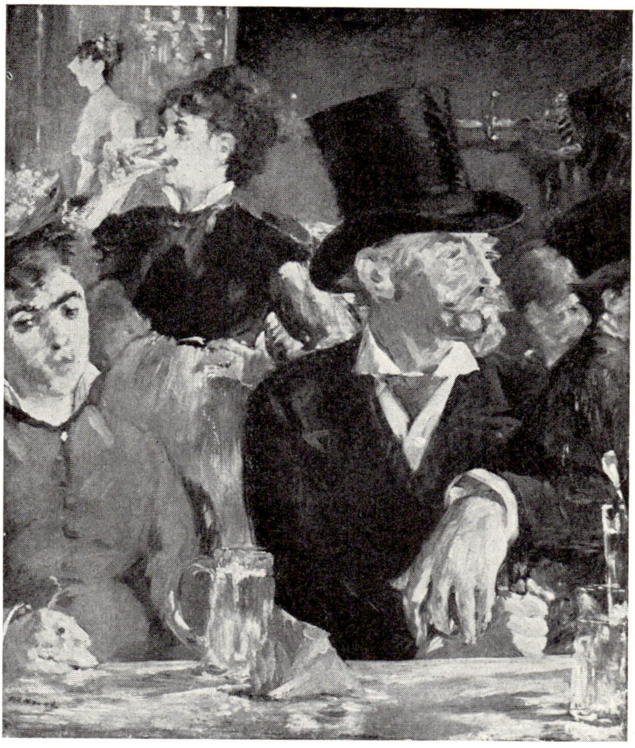

87. Manet: In the Café

In 1845 there were painted two pictures by two unheralded young men, one in France, one in Germany, which may be taken as the starting point of the new era. Menzel's "Balcony Room" (Fig. 84) in Berlin and Courbet's "Midday Dream" (Fig. 85), now in Detroit, are simultaneous creations of a wholly dispassionate eye. Menzel painted an empty room in a middle-class home, with a sunlit curtain blowing gently inward on the summer wind. The Frenchman's more formal instincts made themselves felt in the other picture: Courbet painted a sleeping nude, warmed with sunlight and glowing against a bank of glossy green foliage. But this nude has nothing to do with Ingres's search for ideal grace and ideal beauty: she is a robust peasant girl whose flagrant reality must have seemed a little shocking at the time. The subject that is no "subject" but merely the discovery of plain reality, the interest in sunlight, the painterlike touch, the absence of any scheme of ideas other than the pure exercise of sight — all the charac-

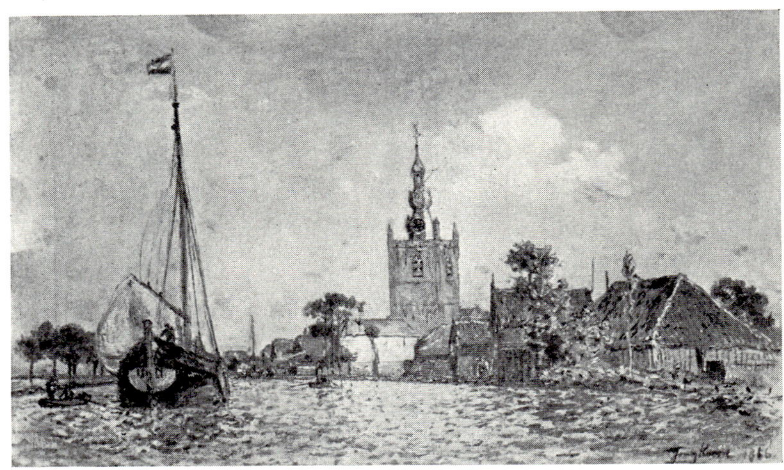

88. *Jongkind: Canal in Holland.* 1866

teristics of the art of the seventies were already there in these two pictures.

Courbet (1819–1877) was symbolic of the new attitude of mind. Contemptuous of historical and religious imagination or, indeed, of anything in art but facts; gifted, but vulgar and lacking in a marked degree the power of intellectual construction, so that he too often created superb studies rather than works of art; aggressive, imposing himself upon the world with the showmanship of a Barnum; the friend of Proudhon, whose influence made him a political malcontent, and a Communard — he was the incarnation of many of the century's most distinctive and some of its most unattractive traits. Nonetheless, he was an artist of power. He was not an innovator in style, except in the massive, painterlike richness of his pigment. It is his complete objectivity of mind that makes one realize he does not belong among the idealists.

But to objectivity of thought was joined a new pictorial style by another man who was to give French painting a complete and decisive change of direction. Édouard Manet (1832–1883) came of the upper level of the permanent civil servants who had for centuries, through all its changes, administered and governed France. Possessed of the capacity for intelligent enjoyment of social life which marks his race, Manet was by birth placed in a position to enjoy the life of the most urbane capital of the world. He received his artistic training

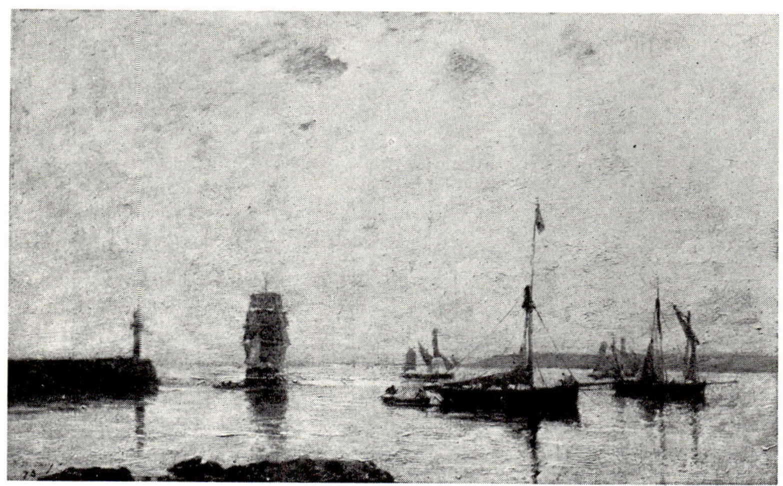

89. *Boudin: Marine, Bordeaux.* 1873

from Couture, famous for elaborate and wholly factitious reconstructions of the past like "Romans of the Decadence," but he took as his
models in painting first Giorgione, then the great Dutch and Spanish
realists of the seventeenth century. It was Manet's great achievement,
as it had been of his models, to shatter an outworn idealistic tradition
by a fresh return to nature and a new conception of beauty. That conception — the charm of everyday reality done in painterlike manner
with a new luminous palette — was received with bitter hostility by
the older artists and by the public at large, but it captured the imagination of a group of younger artists, who rallied loyally and affectionately
about him. Manet's mind was like a clear lens, free from any coloring
of the academic studio vision. Through that lens, at once colorless and
intensifying, one looks at whatever was pleasant to the eye in his be-
loved Paris; the pretty women and well-dressed men, the little parties and
pleasant houses, the races at Longchamps, the theaters and *cafés* of that
age of elegance and leisure are all preserved in his work, with a novel
freshness that comes from the objective quality of this new vision. To
enjoy a picture of this new sort no knowledge of the past, no memories,
no ideals are necessary; it requires no interpretation, no stirring within
the mind of associations implanted by education or reading, as does a
work of historical idealism. All that one needs is a pair of eyes to see

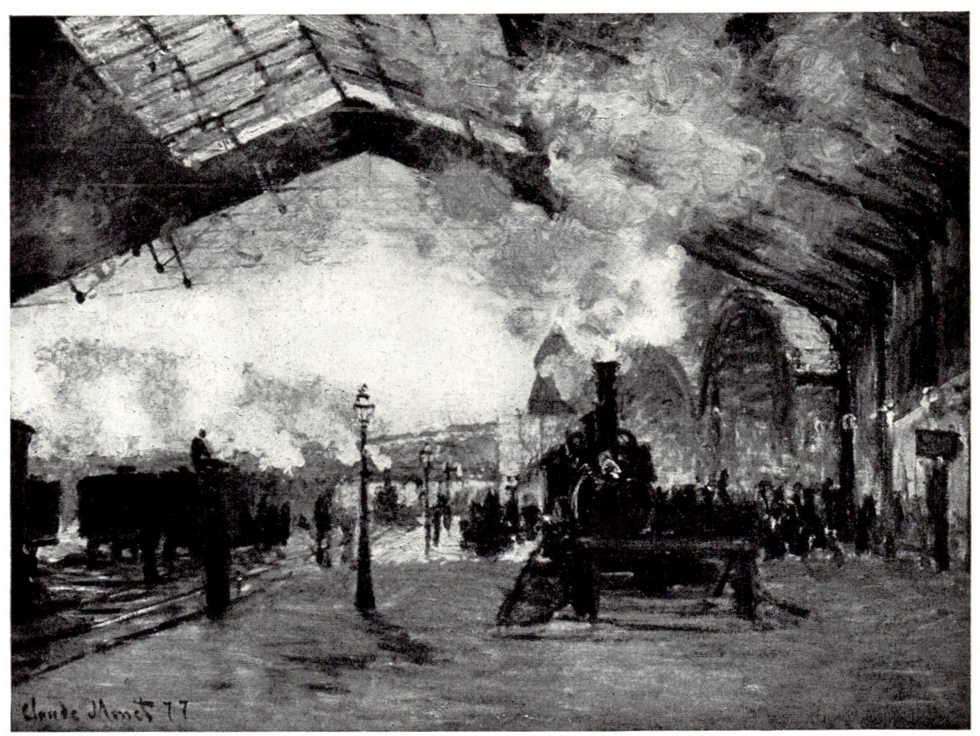

90. *Monet: The Old Saint-Lazare Station; The Train for Normandy.* 1877

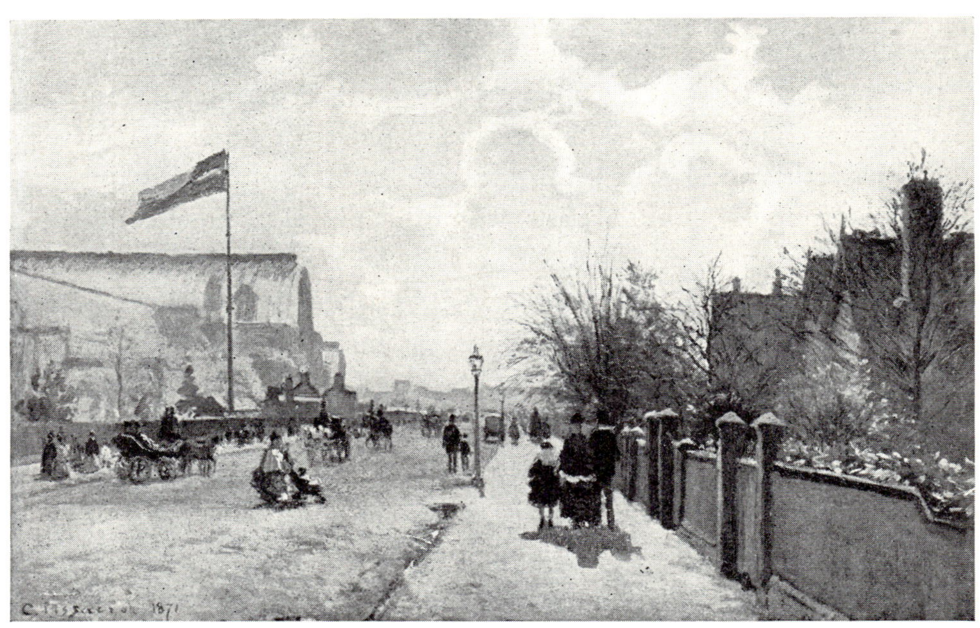

91. *Pissarro: The Crystal Palace, London.* 1871

what Manet saw and a readiness to enjoy the pleasant pageant of life as Manet was ready to enjoy it. And in spite of political disasters Paris at this time offered a supremely enjoyable spectacle. Its cosmopolitan period had not yet begun. During Manet's lifetime Paris replaced Rome as the capital of art students, but it was as yet a purely French city whose gaiety and social charm is forever distilled in Manet's canvases.

Manet's early style, under the influence of the Venetians and the Spanish realists, is warm and dark, and shows strong contrasts of tone (Fig. 86). In his second phase he began the great effort of his generation to capture the luminous colors of sunlight (Fig. 87). He began to simplify the idiom of painting; to substitute color for tone, light for shadow; to eliminate shadows from flesh tones and to model his figures by changes of color and by outline. In place of changes of tone (from light to dark) he used changes of hue (red to blue). Details disappeared, until his figures count simply as big areas of luminous color against contrasting backgrounds. To his older contemporaries his figures seemed raw and ugly, but to the eager young men about him Manet revealed an enchanting new world to be explored.

Larger and more important than the work of any one man, the whole

92. *Monet: Nymphaea.* 1907

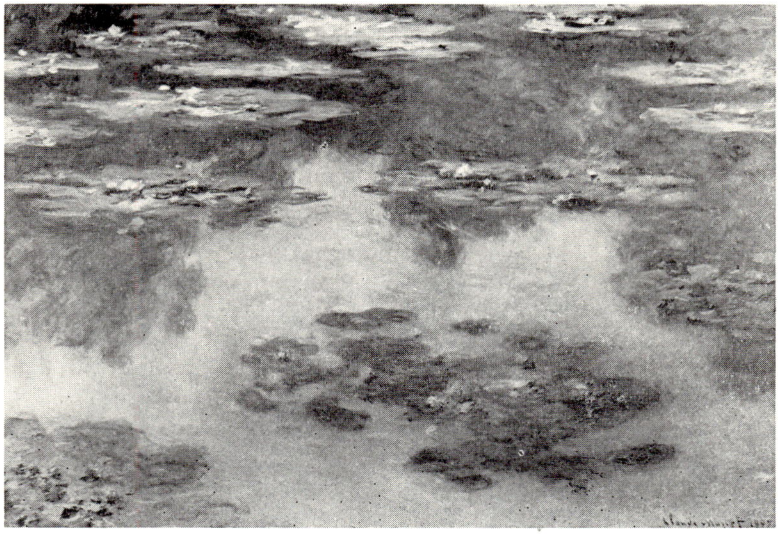

drift of European painting was, by 1850, toward luminous, atmospheric color. Delacroix and Corot, among the older generation, show this clearly in their later work; and the presence in the south of France of a school of painters (of whom Monticelli is the most conspicuous) who used a heavy, gorgeous massing of paint is evidence of the same trend. In the third quarter of the century landscape painting was especially important in bringing a complete change of palette. Corot had already developed it toward a cool grey tonality. Two younger landscapists, Jongkind (1819–1891; Fig. 88), a Dutchman acclimatized in France, and Boudin (1824–1898; Fig. 89), had by the sixties advanced to still freer touches of color and bolder vibrations of light. They also, unlike Corot, applied the new objective vision to landscape, making exact studies of the character of a day or a phase of light in a particular spot. Both were, as landscapists, happiest in small canvases of subjects, such as a harbor or canal scene, which enabled them to study the light of the sky reflected in water. Boudin, in particular, had also the felicity of touch and creamy richness of paint which at this period distinguished the best of the French from all other painters.

In the seventies the suggestion made in the delicate canvases of these painters was developed into the blaze of a new style by the Impressionists, Monet (1840–1926; Fig. 90), Pissarro (1830–1903; Fig. 91), and Sisley (1839–1899). The technique of separate strokes of pure color ("broken color," or white light broken into its prismatic elements) which was the Impressionists' medium for the study of light and air is regularly attributed to the influence of the experiments in light made by contemporary physicists, but one wonders if as much credit should not be given to another science, chemistry, which had transformed the painter's palette by the creation of the cadmiums and chromes and kindred pigments, that introduced a hitherto unknown brilliance of hue. Impressionist color is a step in a development of trying out the potentialities of these new pigments that came to a climax forty years later with the Fauves.

The first group exhibition of Impressionism was held in 1874. It included Pissarro, Monet, Sisley, Renoir, Berthe Morisot, Cézanne, Guillaumin, and some others who, like Degas, did not use broken color but

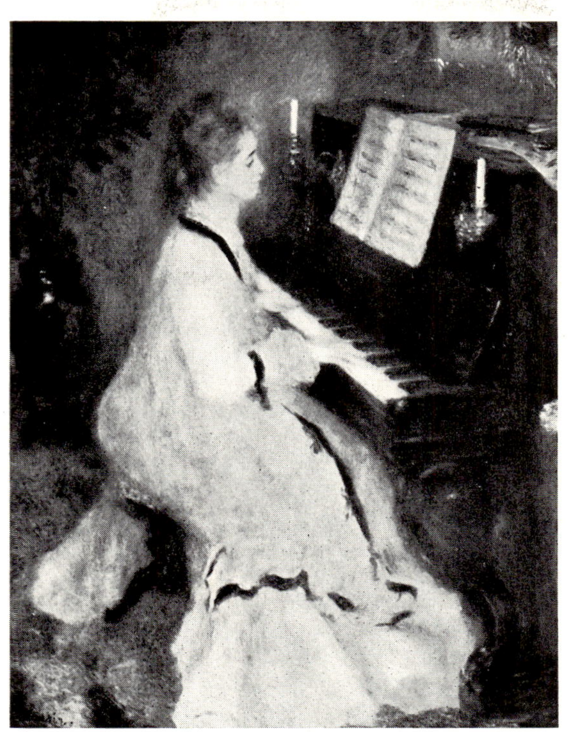

93. *Renoir: At the Piano*

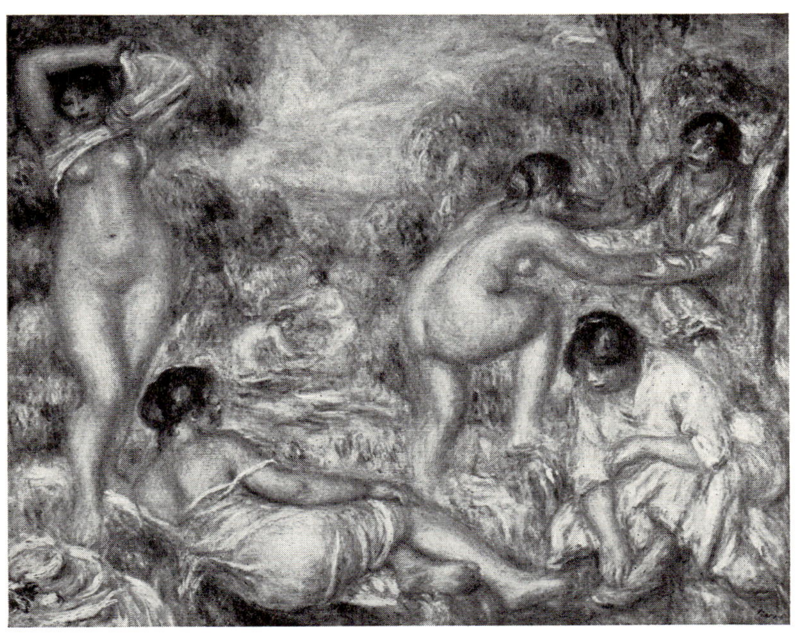

94. *Renoir: The Bathers*

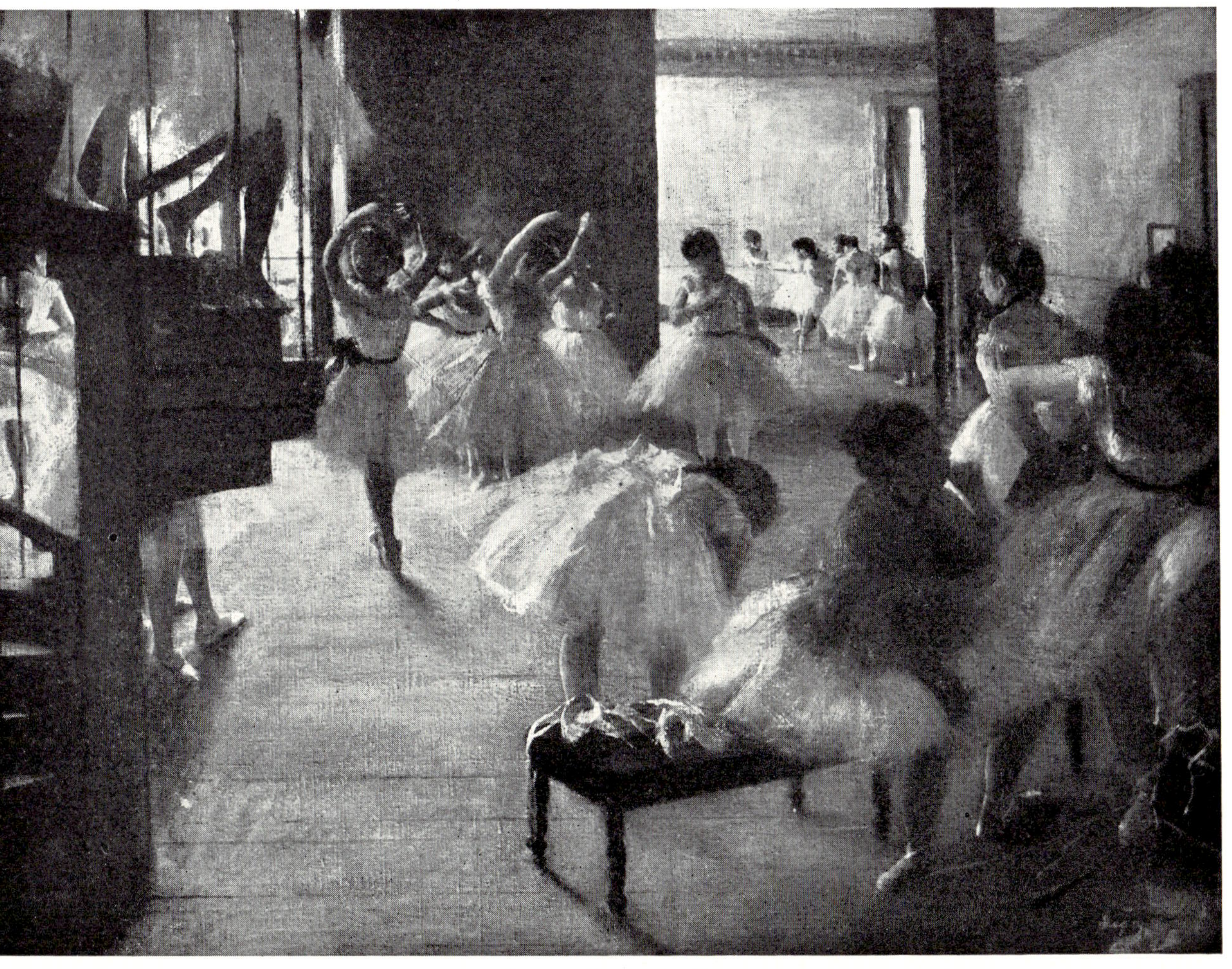

95. *Degas: École de Danse*

were allied by a common spirit of independence. Monet has been pushed by popular renown into the leadership of this group. He was not, perhaps, its strongest painter, but he carried the technique to its logical conclusion. His high-keyed transparent harmony of color, his manner of hatching with brush strokes of pure color in order to catch the vibration of sunlight, his absorption in the problem of air and light were to exert a world-wide influence in the next forty years. The same style was characteristic of the other landscapists, but Monet explored the technique so far that in his water lilies series he sacrificed all other qualities — of outline, form, even space — to color nuances (Fig. 92). He was also completely the objective realist, unable to work except in front of his subject; and his subjects seem well called "impressions," for they have the nature of quick glances at the casual face of nature, like an unforeseen glimpse out a window.

In this respect Monet violated the instinct for form and order which was the taproot of French art. There was a reaction from such formlessness in the work of Renoir (1841–1919). Renoir was primarily a painter of human beings, although to his singularly happy temperament all things good to look at — whether pretty women, children, flowers, animals, or sunny landscapes — were good to paint (Fig. 93). In his early period he was as eager an explorer as Manet of the cheerful life and stir of Paris. The early canvases of the blue and ivory period form one of the most delightful chapters in the story of the objective realist's discovery of everyday reality. Later his color took on a warm glow of Provençal sunlight. But as Monet's impressionism sacrificed more and more of art to nature, Renoir drew closer and closer to the formal classic French tradition, until his late compositions make one think of nudes by Boucher or Poussin, or even Titian, represented in the opulent shimmer of Impressionist color (Fig. 94).

Degas (1834–1917), although he exhibited for a time with the Impressionists, was a far more complex artistic personality than any other of that group. Like Manet and Renoir he was a superb painter-illustrator. With a talent like Manet's for enjoying the spectacle of life in an entertaining metropolis, and a more roving and inquiring mind than Renoir's, he distilled the whole life of Paris into a series of un-

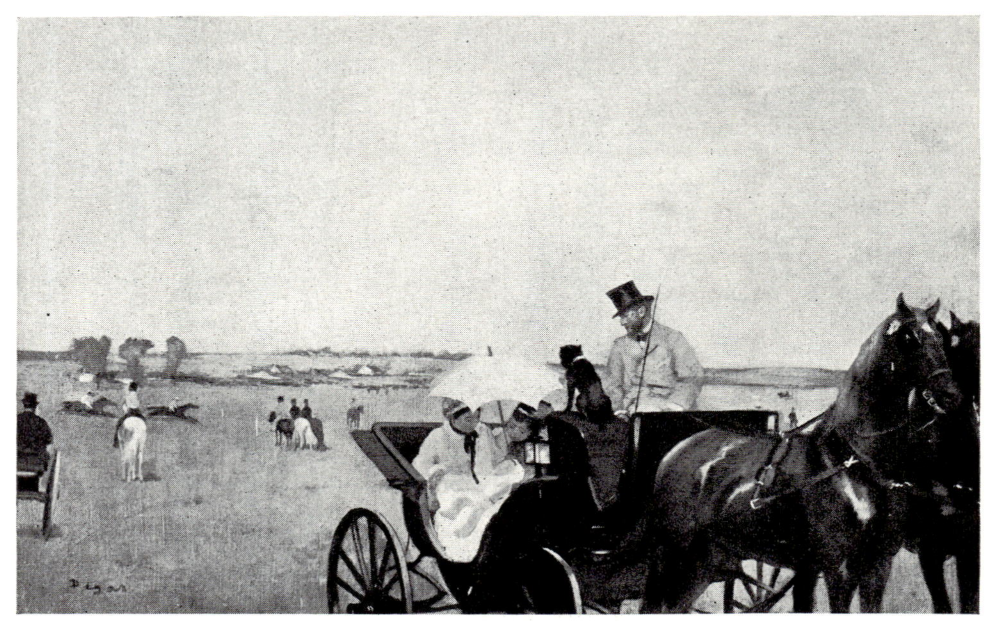

96. *Degas: Carriages at the Races*

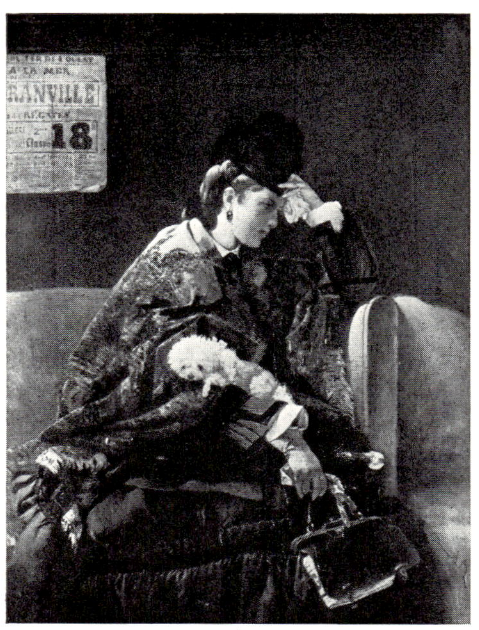

97. *Stevens: At the Railway Station*

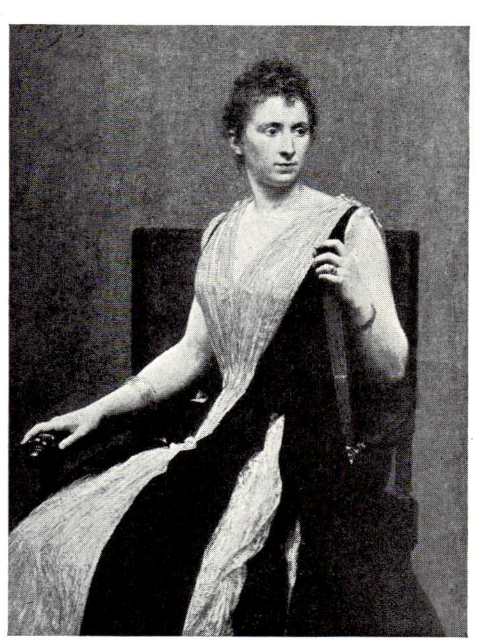

98. *Fantin-Latour:*
Mme Leopold Gravier. 1889

forgettably vivid images: its aristocrats and its Bohemians, its crowds at the races (Fig. 96) and strollers on the boulevards, dancers and milliners and laundresses at work. In its totality his work has an effect like that of Boswell's *Life of Johnson*: it preserves in all its freshness, like a fly in amber, the charm of life at a favored moment in time; and indeed, as the life of Johnson's London was truly English life at its best, so Degas's Paris was the best of an old, somewhat narrow, but delightful French culture, which Degas always insisted was ruined by the internationalism of the next century.

Degas's originality of technique is very great. He was a draughtsman of the school of Ingres who was able to absorb into that tradition the luminous, atmospheric color of Impressionism. He was, moreover, one of the first to study Japanese prints (the discovery in the sixties of the Japanese print was one of the decisive turns of the century) and to absorb their novel qualities of two-dimensional pattern. But while Whistler, his contemporary, sacrificed the solidity of objects and toned down his oil paint in order to catch the cool, fragile flatness of the print, Degas was able to assimilate the Japanese qualities of pattern into a style which retained the three great qualities of deep space, solid form, and the rich gloss of oil paint in which the greatest force of western painting has always lain (Fig. 95).

By temperament he was a classicist; he hated outdoor painting and the objective realist's dependence upon nature. Painting was for him a language of the mind. It was the central point of his achievement to discard all the old, tired conventions by which academic artists selected what was thought worthy of representation, and to renew the source of classic inspiration; for he, like the Greeks or the fifteenth-century Italians, created his serenely harmonious and ordered images out of the living material of the world about him.

A less imaginative use of the realistic technique produced the illustrations of Parisian life of Alfred Stevens (1828–1906; Fig. 97) and the portrait naturalism of Fantin-Latour (1836–1904), in whose grave, stiff pictures one feels the influence of the camera's exactness (Fig. 98).

The great sculptor of the Impressionist age was Rodin (1840–1917),

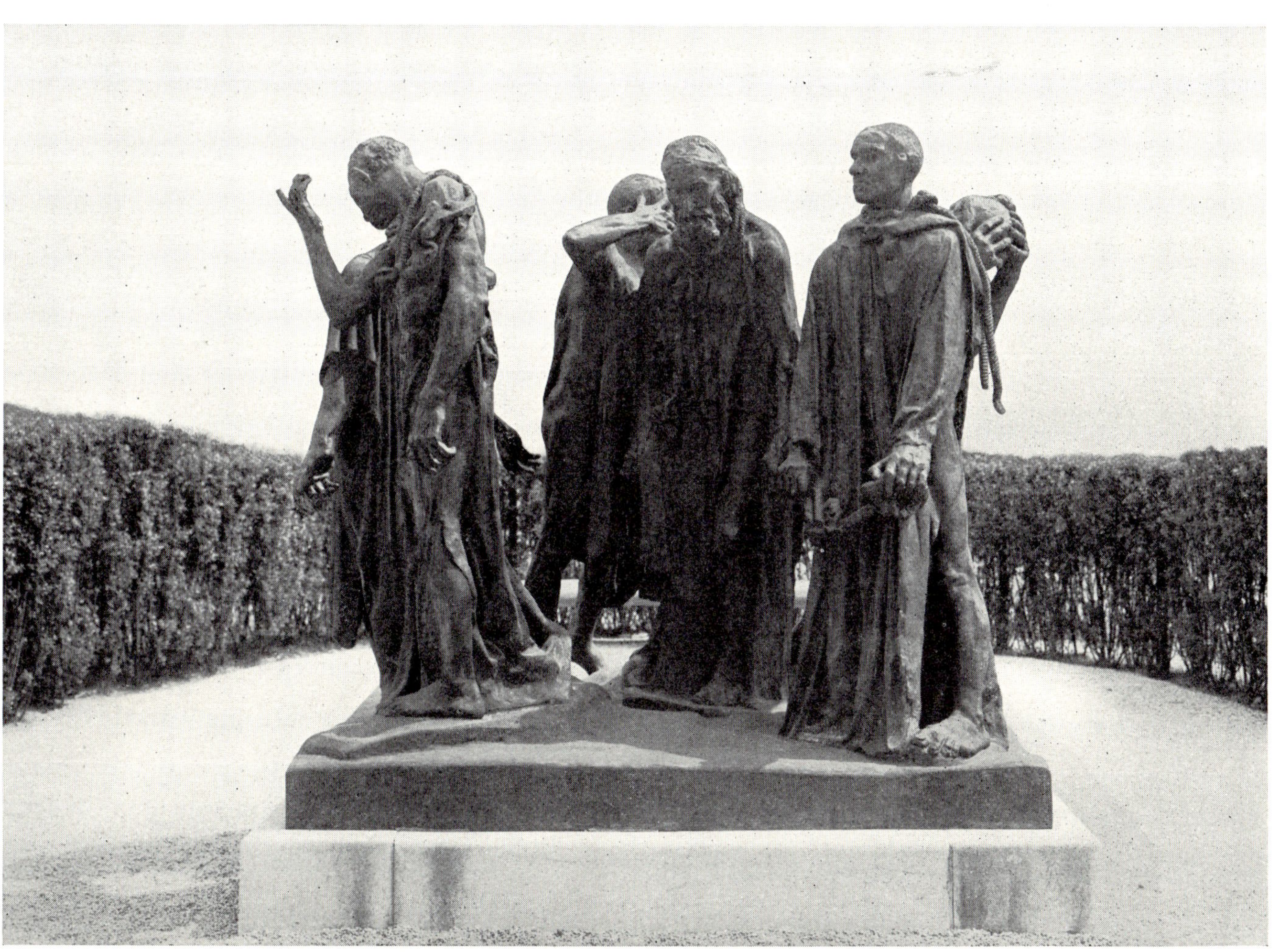

99. *Rodin: The Burghers of Calais.* 1884–88

to whom must be allowed the almost single-handed revival of sculpture on the scale of a great plastic and expressive medium. In his early work his way of escape from the dying idealistic style was through objective realism. The naturalism of his "Age of Brass" (which he worked on from 1875 to 1877) caused the lawsuit that made his fame, a lawsuit arising from the charge of certain fellow sculptors that the statue was a plaster cast of the model. In his mature work, however, Rodin made two great advances — an Impressionism of surface which rescued sculpture from the deadly cold surfaces of idealism and from the banal accuracy of the stonecutter; and the expression of dramatic emotion. In his masterpiece, the "Burghers of Calais" (1884–1888), his naturalism and his Impressionist forms, broken into a continuous ripple of light and dark, were the vehicle for the inner drama of seven souls facing the thought of death (Fig. 99). Rodin thus stands apart in his expressive purpose from the objective practice of the painters. Although the next generation of sculptors revolted against the fleeting, transitory quality of his forms, especially of his late work, Rodin's achievement in breathing the breath of life again into plastic art was one of the great accomplishments of the century.

In the sixties and seventies Paris came to assume the position which Rome had so long filled as the goal of all artists' dreams. The objective realism which was the "modern art" of the day, together with the intelligent urbanity of French life, began then first to exert the attraction upon all other countries which is written in the subsequent world-wide influence of French art. The years from 1860 to 1900, during which this influence gathered force, seem the golden age of the nineteenth century, when the western world enjoyed such peace and prosperity as it had never known; and, in spite of France's loss of the continental hegemony to Prussia in 1871, an extraordinary flowering of artistic genius made France the unquestioned center of artistic life. There remains the question why the artists who reflect the charm of life in those halcyon days and represent its culture with, as it seems to us, such sensitive distinction were received by their contemporaries with a hostility as unprecedented as it is shocking. Delacroix had lived in a certain

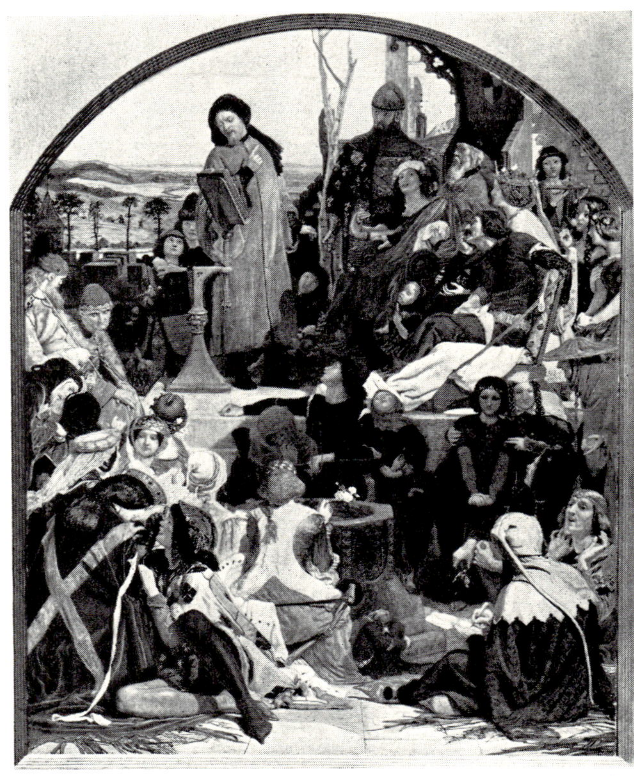

100. *F. M. Brown: Chaucer at the Court of Edward III.* 1856

isolation among the classicists, and Courbet had had his difficulties, which were, however, largely self-engendered and of a political nature. But the genial and urbane Manet, whose only desire was to give pleasure to himself and his contemporaries, was first received with abuse so coarse and savage as to appal one who reads the journals of the day. The war between the artists and the public, which embitters their relations to this day, began with Manet's "Déjeuner sur l'herbe" (1863) and "Olympia" (1865). Today these seem like academic set pieces in which Manet made use of groups of draped and undraped figures — familiar compositions for three hundred years — as the theme of two exercises in his brilliant new technique. Manet and all the Impressionists, and even Cézanne, wished sincerely to win the approval of the public and the official hierarchy of painters. The abuse heaped upon them provoked a certain degree of defense that hardened gradually in their suc-

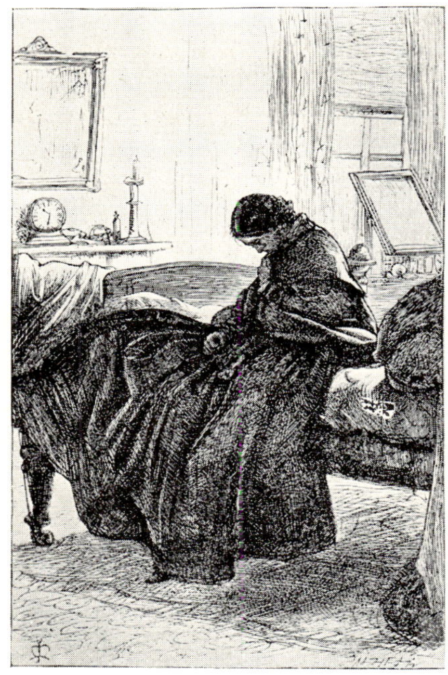

101. *Millais: Lady Mason after Her Confession.* 1862

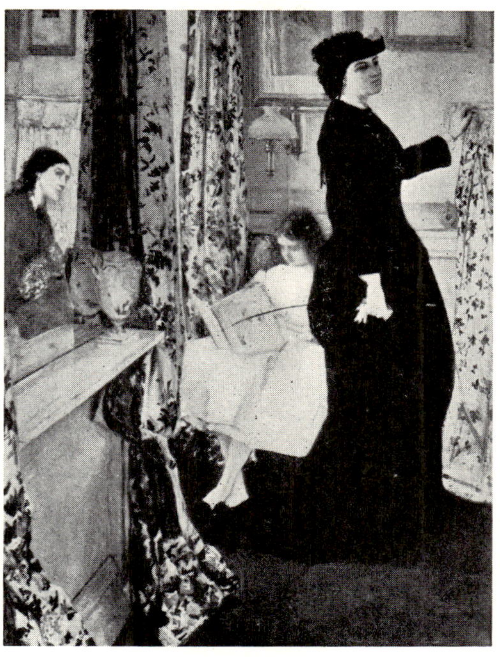

102. *Whistler: The Music Room*

cessors into a pride in not pleasing which has been one of the follies of artists down to our time.

But why did the war between artist and public arise? The most plausible explanation attributes it to the rise of mass civilization. So long as painting was the concern of a few who were by education or instinct the natural patrons of art, there was no rift between the artist and his public. The Salon was a small affair, held in a gallery of the Louvre and attended only by those whom a genuine interest brought there. But in 1865 the Salon was moved to a large building left from the International Fair of 1855; a far greater number of artists were allowed to exhibit; and the annual showing became a popular event. The arts became the concern of a great public determined to assert itself and to enjoy the pleasures of the aristocracy but in no way aware that esthetic judgments (especially of unfamiliar things) require great knowledge and highly trained perceptions. The new public turned for its ideas and opinions to the journalists, who were no better fitted to deal with the subject and who resented rather than welcomed the artist's

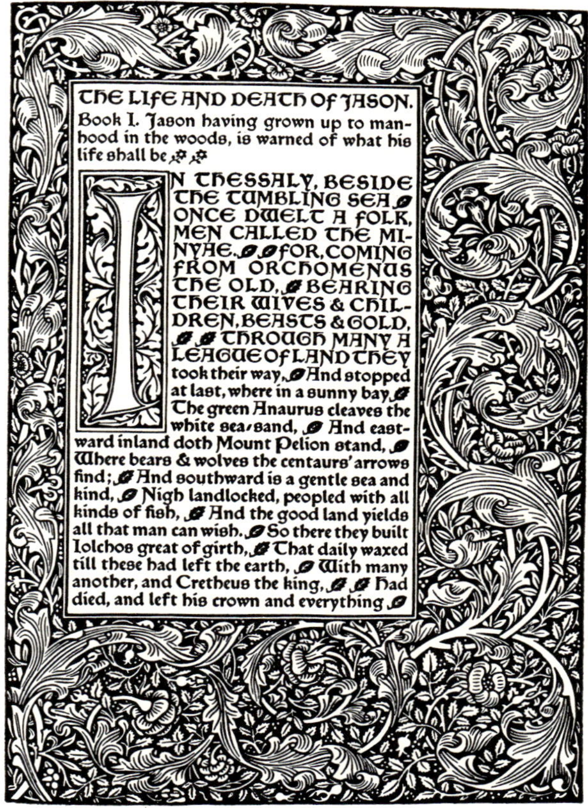

103. Morris: Page from the Kelmscott Jason.
1895

attempt to treat old subjects with a new technique and to see the world
through new eyes. The development of a better attitude was a long,
slow process.

Ford Madox Brown (1821–1893), trained in Antwerp in the naturalistic school of genre painting, introduced naturalism and a sharp, high-
keyed palette into the English historical school on his return to London
in 1846 (Fig. 100). Three years later the Pre-Raphaelite Brotherhood
was founded by his pupils. This movement has become so associated
in our minds with the later work of Rossetti that one must emphasize
the fact that its first and most essential doctrine in the early years, when
its best work was done, was an absolute fidelity to nature. It came into

existence, and spread to America,[1] as a doctrine of strict objective realism. The doctrine was reinforced by Ruskin, who in his devotion to nature preached a faithfulness of detail that existed, in the contradictory web of his esthetic doctrine, side by side with an advocacy of Italian Gothic art. It is enough to remember that Ford Madox Brown worked for eleven years upon one picture. In the Brotherhood Holman Hunt (1827–1910) is the obvious representative of Brown's naturalism, but Millais, especially in his book illustrations, shows the doctrine at its best (Fig. 101).

Whistler (1834–1903), on the other hand, brought to England the objective realism of Paris. His first, and best, work was done under the influence of Courbet (Fig. 102), but he rapidly developed into the phase of decorative Impressionism which was to flourish in England. In graphic art Whistler made soft gradations of atmosphere the source of a new technique, perfected in his Venetian etchings of 1881–1882. Seymour Haden (1818–1910), his brother-in-law, was one of the great English masters of black-and-white Impressionism. Decorative Impressionism developed also in England a series of charming minor masters, like Sickert and McBey, but the most interesting development came in the work of William Morris (1834–1896) and his reaction from the art for art's sake attitude, which in turn was one of the most important aspects of the later nineteenth century.

Paris, as has been said, became the magnetic pole of the world of art in the sixties and seventies. The imitation of French art, which has been the academicism of all other countries since that time, is one obvious result of this tremendous shift of center, but it was not the only result. The studio life of Murger's *Scènes de la vie de Bohème* or Du Maurier's *Trilby* was most unlike the actual existence of the best French artists, but among the crowds of foreign students who swarmed into Paris Bohemianism became a religion. Duret, the historian of the Impressionists, has spoken of the tendency of Parisian studio life to foster that attitude of contempt for all who were not artists, that desire

---

[1] The now forgotten but pleasant landscapist, W. T. Richards, of Philadelphia, is an example of this American Pre-Raphaelitism, which outdid the most exact of the Hudson River painters in its minute naturalism.

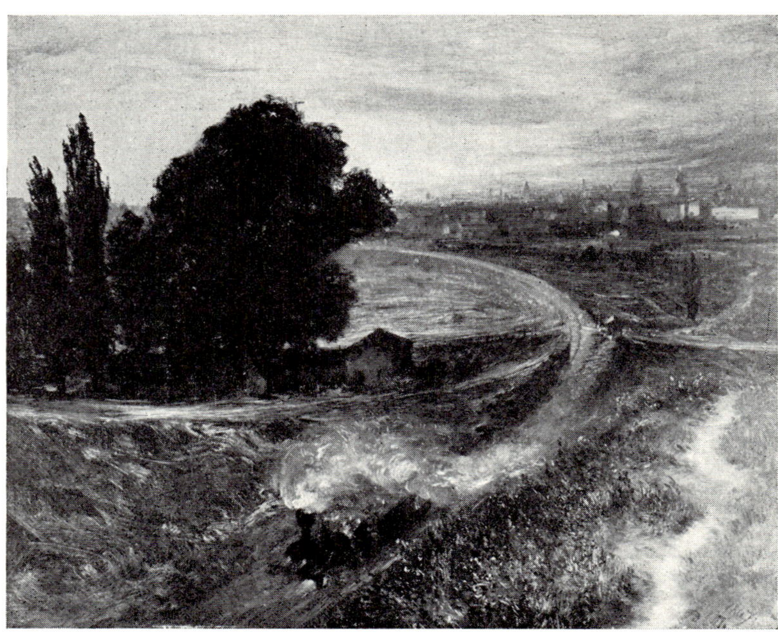

104. *Menzel: The Berlin–Potsdam Train.* 1847

to *épater le bourgeois,* of which Whistler became the great example. Degas, who despised this new cosmopolitan Paris, once said to him, "Whistler, you behave as though you had no talent." [2] One must be careful, in fact, to distinguish between the sanity and seriousness which marked the French artists and the exhibitionism of the Paris Bohemians. Nevertheless the Bohemian movement is important, because it created the atmosphere of art for art's sake — the tendency to make art a closed circle, within which one performed solely for the benefit of one's fellow initiates — which ran through the final third of the nineteenth century.

The extreme development of art for art's sake, as well as the most effective reaction against it, took place in England. Important as was the part played by Englishmen in the creation of scientific materialism, there were strong forces working in the opposite direction. The whole force of the great Victorian literary movement, together with the religious revival of the Oxford Tractarians and the activity of Ruskin, undoubtedly one of the most important of nineteenth-century critics, combined to reinforce the native social and ethical trend of the English

[2] Rothenstein, *Men and Memories,* I (New York, 1935), 101.

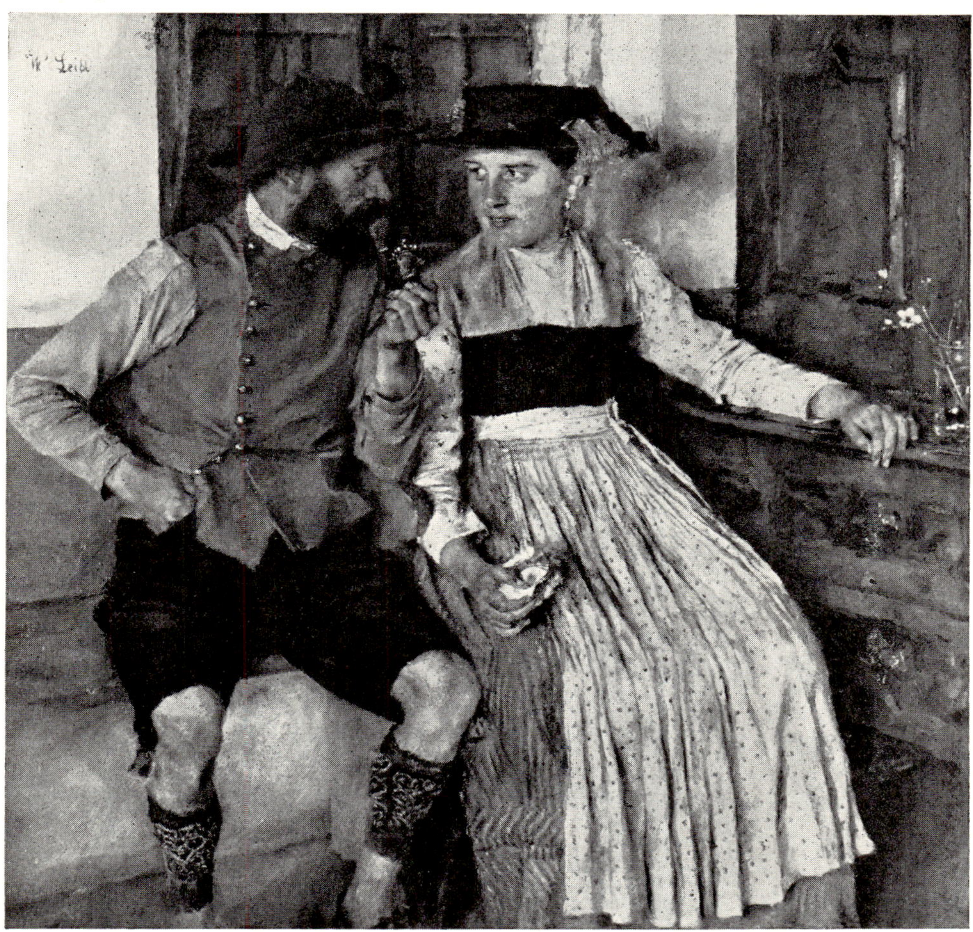

105. *Leibl: Man and Woman in a Farm Interior.* 1890

mind. England's deepest artistic traditions ran in contradiction to the notion of art for art's sake. William Morris was the man who best translated the native attitude into a program of life. A talented designer, craftsman, poet, and social reformer, he fought vigorously for the concept of art as a vital function of society and for the place of the artist as a man among men. His concern with art as an essential function of society led him into the practical applications of art and the foundation of the arts and crafts movement, to revive the social arts which the industrial era had reduced to sterile hackwork. His vigorous designs for textiles, wallpaper, furniture, and typography were of great importance. In his black-and-white designs for the Kelmscott Press, especially, he carried the Impressionist quality of vibration of light and dark into the decorative arts; and by giving to the lesser arts roots in the style of their own time, he created the first notable step toward the reëmerging unity of the arts in the twentieth century. It is fair to consider Morris' books of the Kelmscott Press as the most original contribution of England to the Impressionist period, even though the intense Impressionism of his printed pages is not our taste today (Fig. 103). His concern also with the humanity of the workman, which must give expression to itself in some creative effort, led Morris and Walter Crane to found an English form of Socialism which seems singularly civilized and humane, compared with the materialistic and mechanistic theories of the Continent, which were concerned only with the distribution of wealth and power.

Germany produced one of the great pioneers of objective realism in Menzel (1815–1905). In contrast to Courbet, who absorbed in spite of himself the formal Parisian tradition of painting, Menzel was a good *bürgerliche* German of the simple, old-fashioned sort, whose provincial milieu bred in him no elaborate theories. The great development of German factual thought which succeeded idealism has no stronger representative than he. His work falls into two periods. Before 1850 it was almost like Biedermeier painting in a rich painterlike technique, except that it was the expression of a mind completely clear of sentiment or preconceived ideas. The belief of the objective realists that anything is of esthetic interest if well observed is nowhere better illustrated than in these early studies of Menzel's, which range from a cart-horse waiting beneath a window to the lamplight on a row of casts hanging upon a studio wall, or a train speeding along the new Potsdam railroad line (Fig. 104). It is hard for us today to realize that it was a spiritual triumph in 1847 to discover esthetic value in a railroad train, but by such discoveries the world of art was enlarged, freed from the mixture of false sentiment and sentimental history which dominated the Nazarenes, and restored to its root experience — the direct intuitive exercise of sight — without which it dies. After 1850 Menzel began to devote himself to the analysis of light effects, and developed in his own

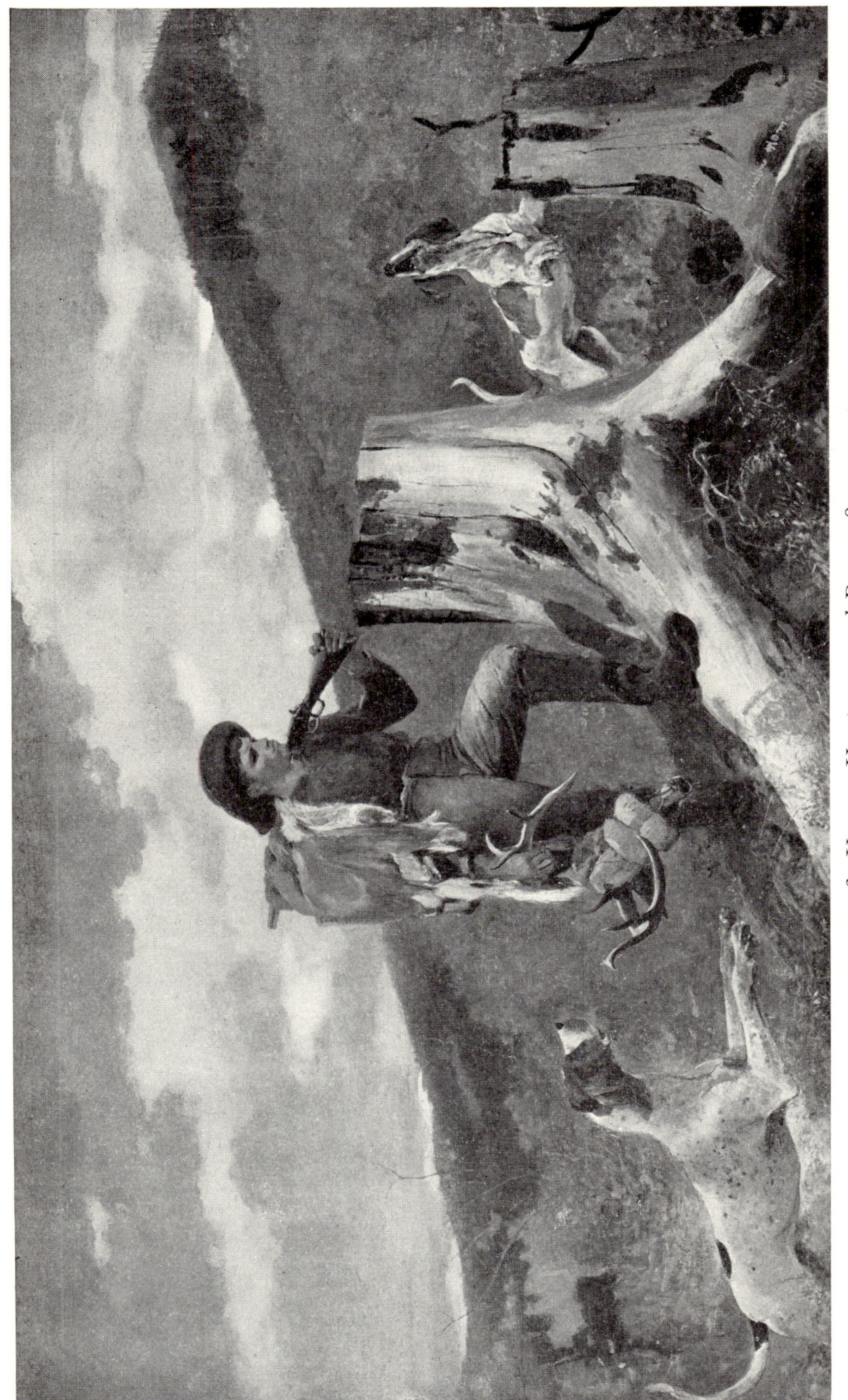

106. Homer: *Huntsman and Dogs.* 1891

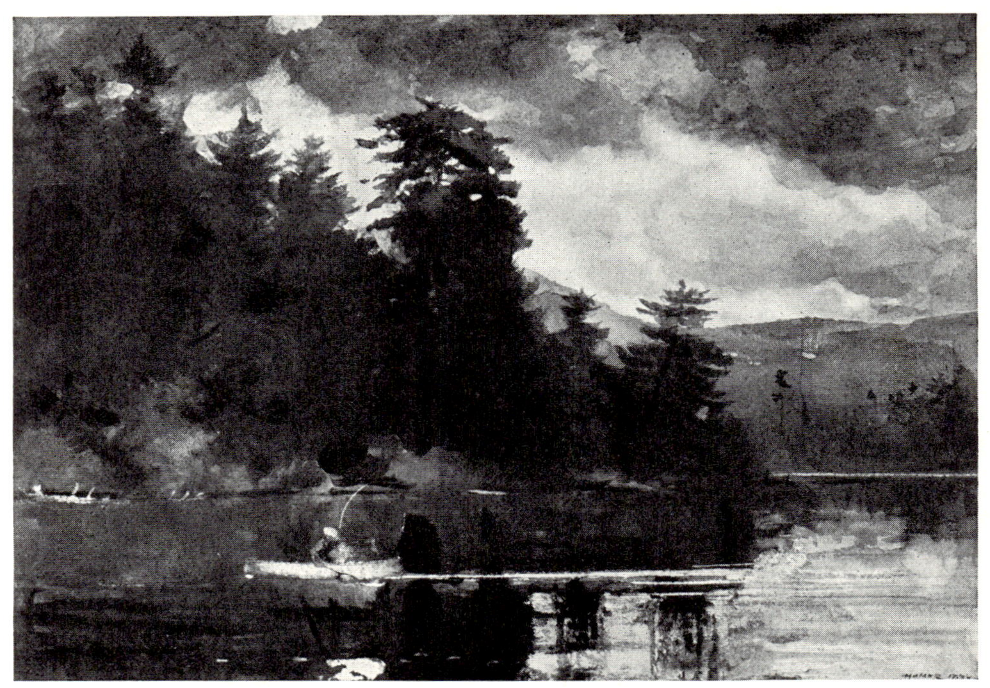

107. *Homer: Adirondack Lake.* 1889

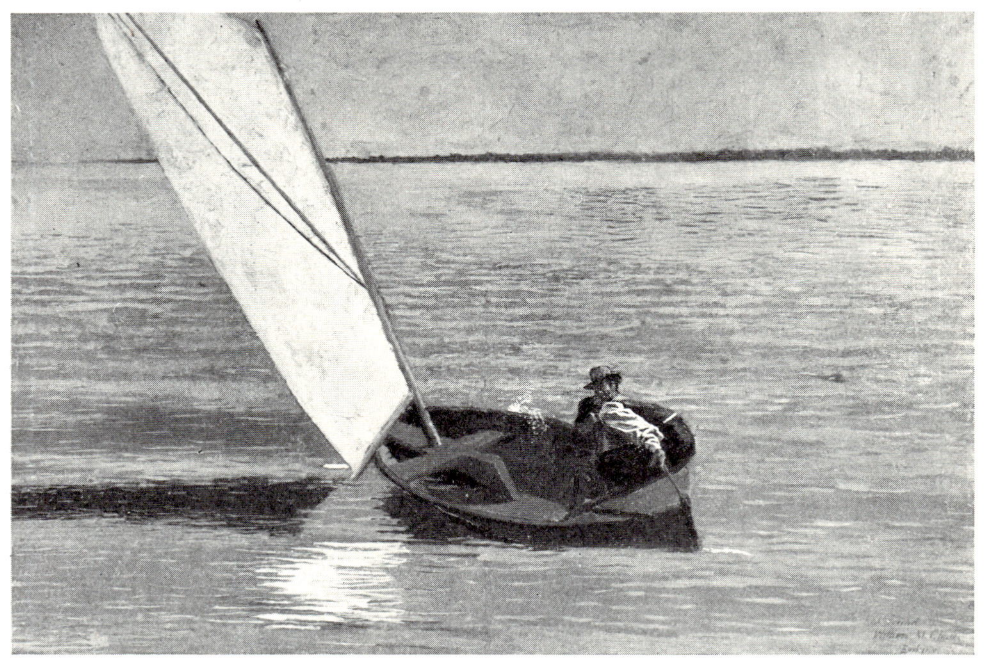

108. *Eakins: Sailing*

low-keyed color harmonies the same kind of study of the vibration of light which the Impressionists were carrying out in France after a different fashion. He also began his series of illustrations of the life of Frederick the Great, which show him as one of the great Impressionist masters of black-and-white, but which add little to his unique contribution of observation of nature.

Menzel represents an approach to the problems of light and of objective vision made by German art independently of the French school. Thoma, in Frankfort, felt the direct influence of Courbet and Manet, and absorbed the tonality and atmospheric touch of the new era, but underneath he remained a romantic and somewhat sentimental mind. Leibl (1844–1900) in Munich developed independently in the same direction as Courbet did in France. The massive warmth of his paint, the directness of his vision, and his unfortunate tendency toward creating studies rather than compositions, all remind one of the Burgundian artist. He was a craftsman in paint whose love of his medium grew upon him until he seems, in his later studies, to elaborate the textures of his brush strokes with the minute care of a jeweler (Fig. 105). His followers, Trübner and Schuch, expanded his manner into an elaborate display of brushwork. They are examples of a tendency which rapidly developed in objective realism, to make up for the loss of imposing subject matter by an exhibition of the artist's technical skill.

In Dresden was one of the best figure painters of the period, von Rayski (1806–1890), who gave a richness and amplitude to portraiture that make him seem, like Carolus-Duran in Paris, one of the last to uphold with dignity that declining branch of painting.

In America the same problems of light and of the esthetic value of objective facts were attacked by two great objective realists, Winslow Homer (1836–1910) and Thomas Eakins (1844–1916). Homer's work falls into two periods: an early manner before 1881, precise and rather detailed in style, extremely objective and direct in observation; and a later phase, in which he painted consciously heroic themes with rather liquid color and broadly atmospheric touch. He learned his art by doing illustrations for the pictorial weeklies which appeared on this

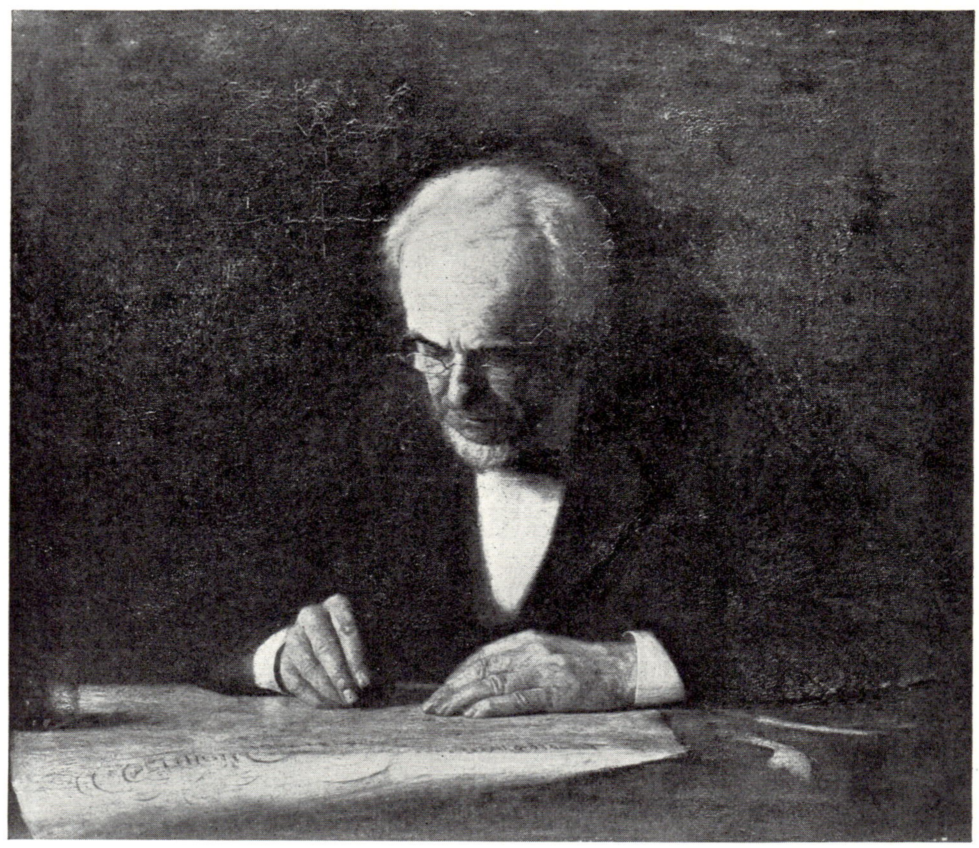

109. *Eakins: The Writing Master.* 1882

side of the Atlantic in the later fifties. Illustration was not at that time
tied to the printed matter. Homer was free to take for his subjects
whatever interested him in American life, and he ranged from a scene
at Newport to life on an Adirondack farm or in a New York opium den.
His instinct for the character of a scene developed into an ability to sum
up in one straightforward factual image all that there was to say about
a place, a phase of nature, an aspect of life. Like the other great realists
of his generation he enlarged the mind of his time, discovering esthetic
value in things which had never before been seen in such a way —
the southern negro, the sea, the intense sunlight of an American
summer day, the blazing light of the tropics, and, most important of
all, the frontier between man and nature. Homer is almost unique
in art in turning a pictorial intelligence of the first order to the mascu-

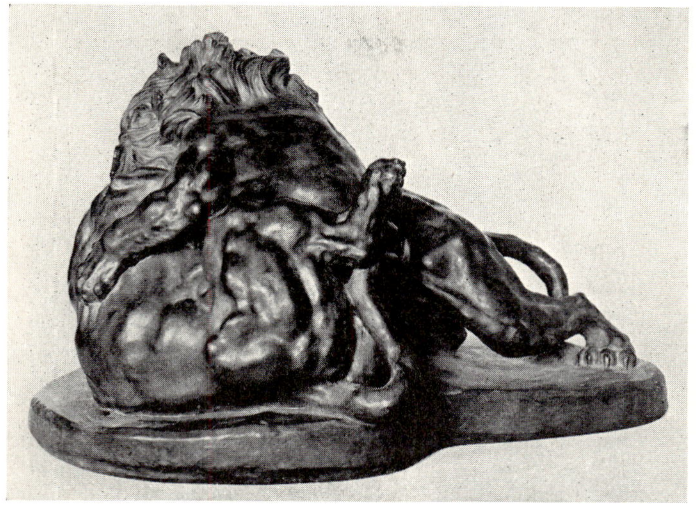

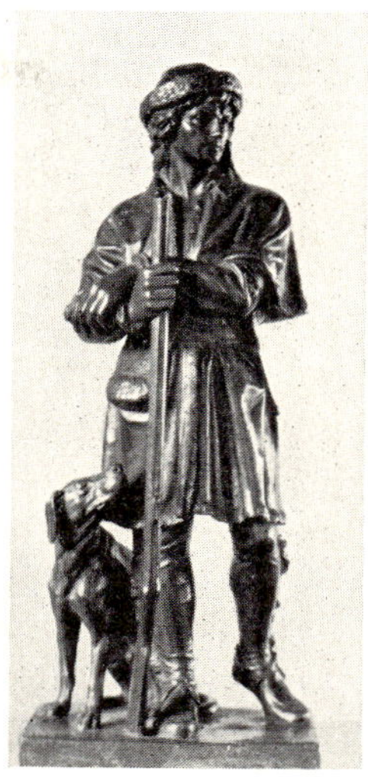

110. Rimmer: Fighting Lions. 1874

111. Ward: Simon Kenton. 1884

line life whose conquest of the continent from the wilderness was one of the great American achievements of the century. His "Huntsman and Dogs" (1891) in Philadelphia (Fig. 106), in which dogs and sullen, silent hunter are part of the vast solitude of mountain and forest, is the great painting of the American frontier. Like Mark Twain and Kipling, who dealt with the same objective and wholly masculine world, he is often looked down upon by introspective intellectuals because of his subject matter. In his early work he developed his own technical idiom for the brilliant sun of this continent, which is quite different from the soft, diffused light of the Seine valley where the French Impressionists worked out their idiom. In his later grandiose style he was closer to French Impressionism, using a broad, fluid touch and liquid color to achieve his atmosphere. His later style is seen at its best in his water colors, which, with the force and authority of oils, retain the freshness of eye that marked his early work (Fig. 107).

Thomas Eakins applied the same searching, objective study to the life of a city. He studied in Paris under Gérôme and absorbed from him the French plastic understanding of the human figure, as well as his teacher's factual technique. But instead of devoting his gifts, like his teacher, to the manufacture of dubious historical reconstructions, he

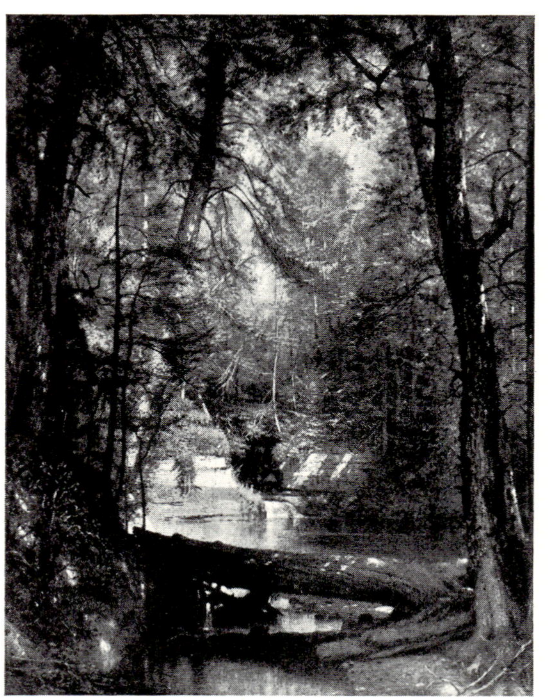

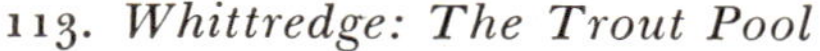

113. *Whittredge: The Trout Pool*

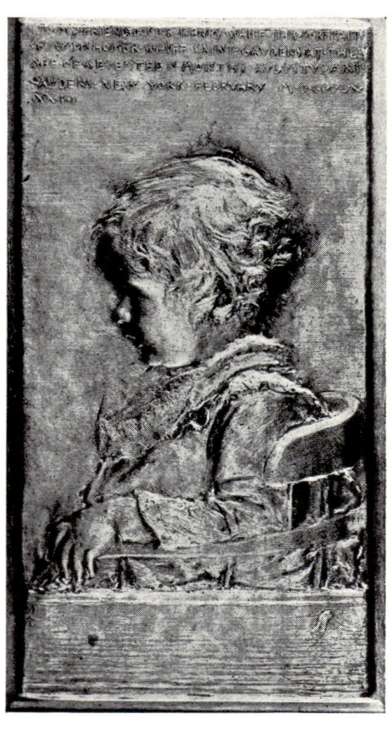

114. *Saint-Gaudens: Homer
Schiff Saint-Gaudens.* 1882

poems which were coming into music) unity of emotion took the place of a complex formal structure (Fig. 112). Inness explored every phase of sunlight from dawn to dusk. Wyant (1836–1892) was content to stay within a more limited range. The spacious solitudes of the early land-scape school are still found in his early work, as they are in the early period of Homer Martin, but both turned in the eighties to an exquisite exploration of light within a limited, and often slight, motive. In solemnity and spacious silence the early work of Whittredge (Fig. 113) creates a unique note in nineteenth-century landscape; but the power seems to evaporate from his later work, when he too gave up his distinctive golden atmosphere for the cool palette and divided tones of the French Impressionists.

Impressionism in the strict sense (that is to say, the broken-color technique which stemmed from Monet and Pissarro) began to win the allegiance of artists in the eighties and was presently carried all over the world. It was taken into Germany by Liebermann (1847–1935), whose forceful personality was of greater value to German art than his facile and often careless painting. The spontaneous and vivid art of Slevogt (1868–1932; Fig. 115) and the violent energy of Lovis Corinth (1858–1925; Fig. 116) form a strong German branch of the movement. The decorative turn given to French Impressionism in England by Whistler was not unlike the outcome of French influence in America. The first American to study under Monet was Theodore Robinson, who, with Hassam, Twachtman, and Dewing, developed the fastidious and muted decorative style that seems to represent the spirit of the nineties. The formation of the group of Ten American Painters in New York in 1895 created a kind of academy to perpetuate this style. It included Dewing, Tarbell, Benson, De Camp, Weir, Twachtman, Metcalf, Simmons, Hassam, and Reid; Twachtman, who died in 1902, was succeeded by Chase, whose early Munich palette had given way to Impressionist color (Fig. 117).

The magnificent brush stroke was another outcome of the growth of a painterlike freedom of touch. It found its masters at the end of the century in men like Sargent (Fig. 118), Zorn, and Boldini. Sargent's extraordinary sweeping brush and impassive mind, which seemed to consider the whole world merely as a series of objects reflecting light, were the culmination of one tendency in objective realism. There is no need to depreciate the superlative skill of such men as he, or Zorn, who have left us in their brilliant, secure, and confident portraits an admirable image of their generation.

As one looks at the work of the Impressionist period, its imagery of a world bathed in summer sunlight seems perhaps superficial, but very charming. It is an art that in most cases springs from no very profound emotional source. It floats on the surface of what seems today a halcyon age, reflecting the pleasure of life in images always fresh, always delightful and serene. There were other forces at work beneath the surface of its pleasant world, and a later generation of artists revolted from it as too easy and too shallow a reflection of life. But who can say whether the combination of sensitiveness and absence of great ideas that marked

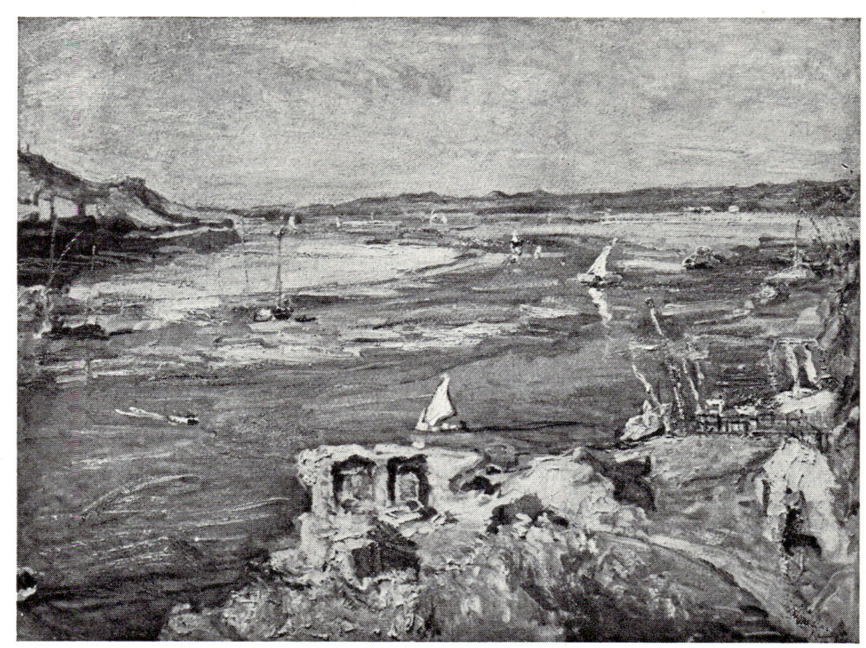

115. *Slevogt: The Nile at Assuan.* 1914

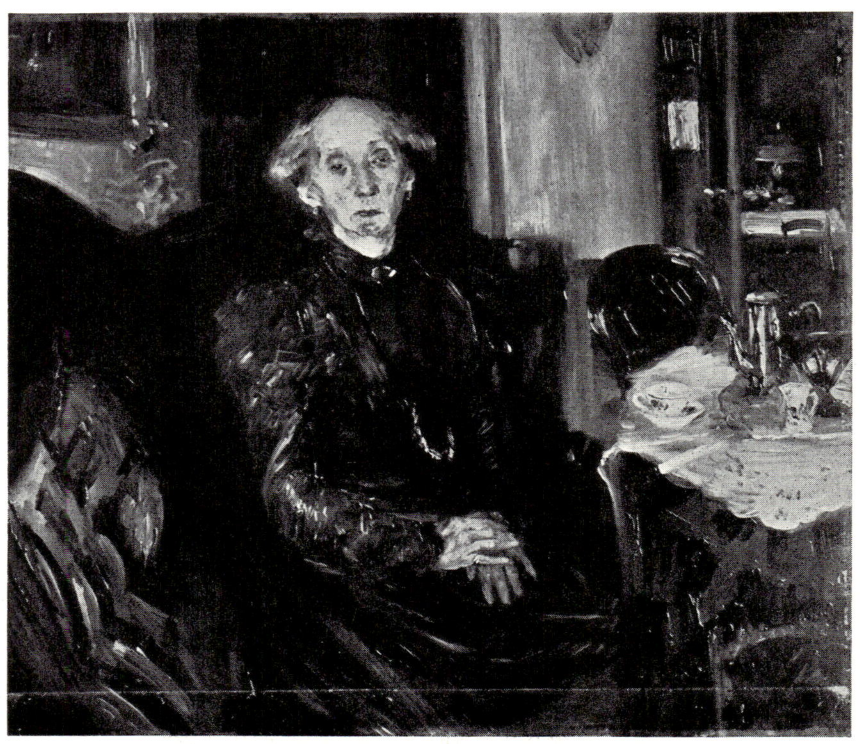

116. *Corinth: Frau Rosenhagen.* 1899

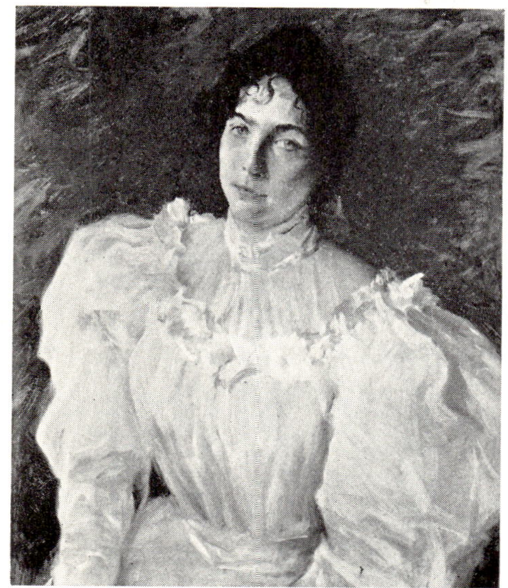

117. *Chase: Virginia Gerson*

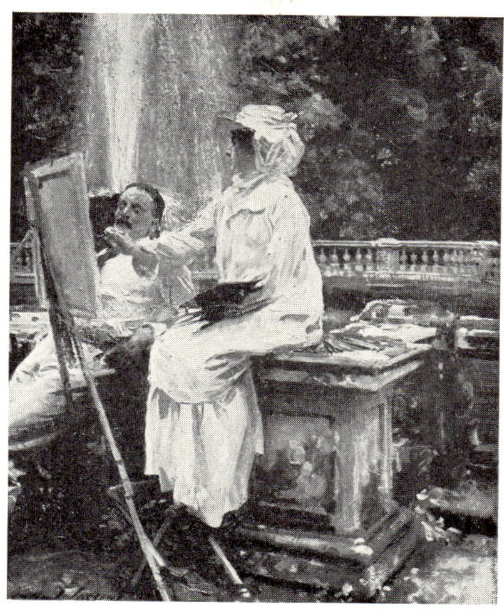

118. *Sargent: The Fountain,*
Villa Torlonia

this period was the cause or the result of the enormous change which it worked in the world's thought? For the nineteenth century was one of those centuries, like the twelfth and the fifteenth, during which the western world paused in its line of development to absorb from outside itself a vast mass of new knowledge. Although museums had appeared as great national storehouses at the beginning of the century, it was the Impressionist period which created the museum movement; and with the appearance of scholarly connoisseurship came an amazing widening of the mental horizon. Archaeology began to resurrect forgotten civilizations from the earth, like a magician lifting rabbits from a top hat — Egypt and Assyria, Babylon, Mycenae and Crete, the Stone Age, Celtic and Teutonic art, the Migration Period — until the length of recorded history had been doubled. At the same time there began a mental exploration of arts which had been before that time despised or but vaguely known. The Byzantine and Romanesque periods of Europe's own past, Japan, followed by China and India, then the primitive arts of America and Africa and the South Seas, were discovered as worthy of serious attention (Figs. 119 and 120). All these arts were collected in museums, were studied by artists and scholars, and worked their way gradually into the mind of the age. The change produced by this process was enormous. The age induced an eclectic internationalism which undoubtedly destroyed much that was of value and produced much that was superficial. Nonetheless, it changed the world.

119. *Whistler: The Ocean*

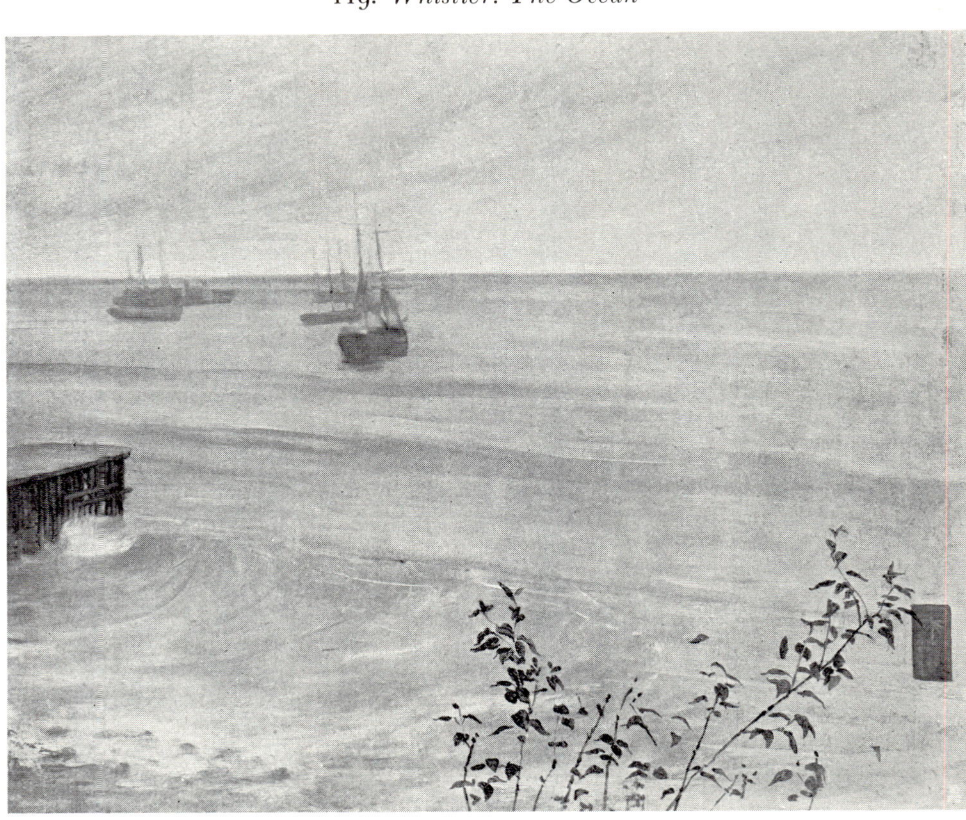

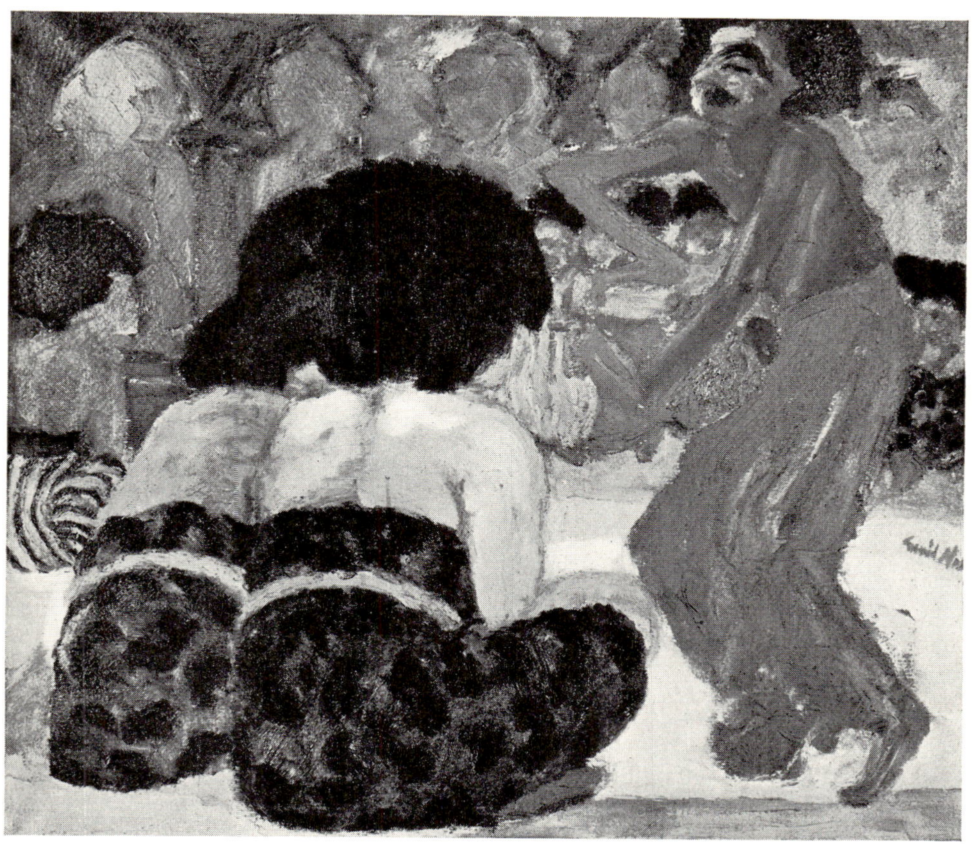

120. *Nolde: South Sea Dancers.* 1915

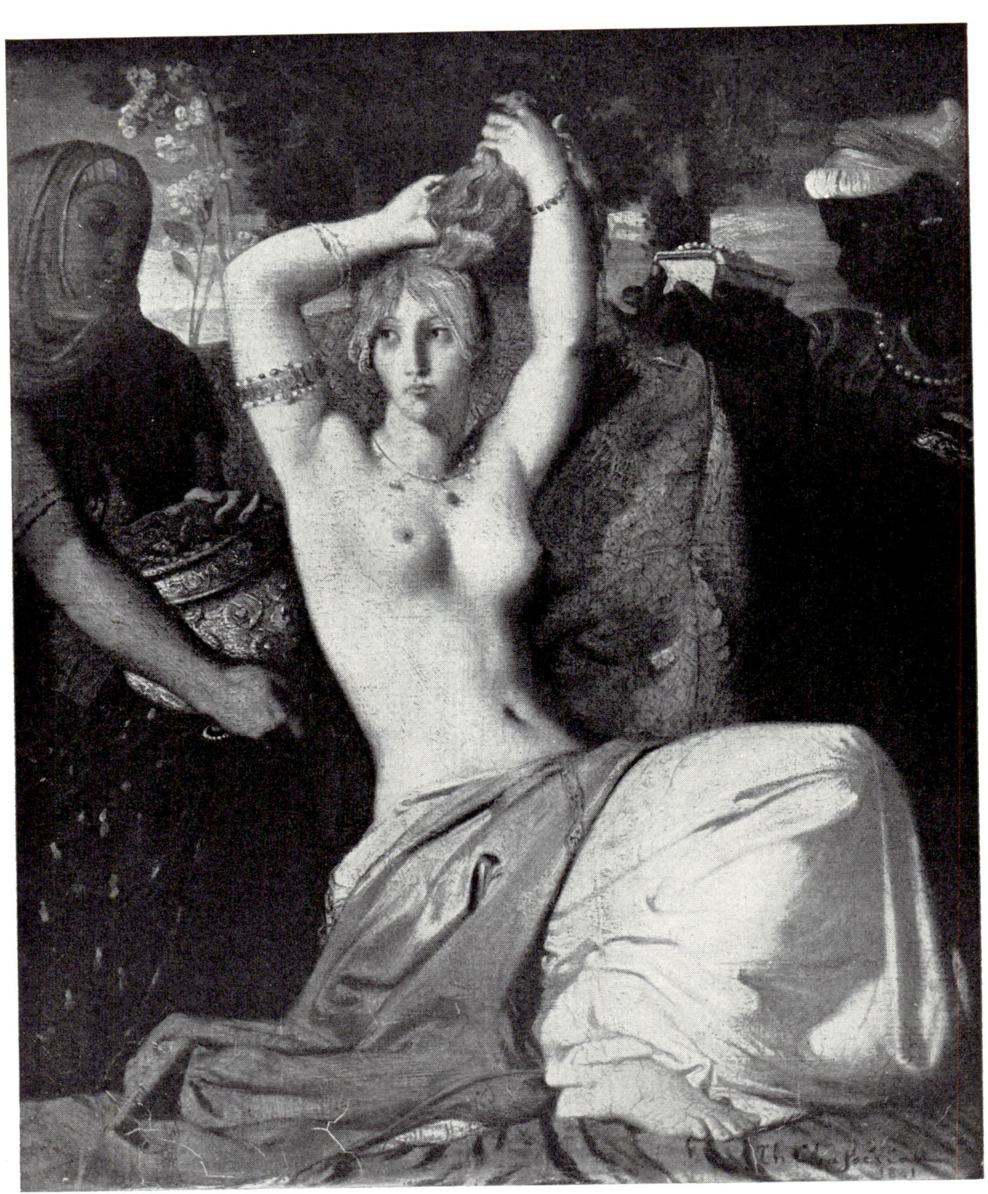

121. *Chassériau: Esther.* 1842

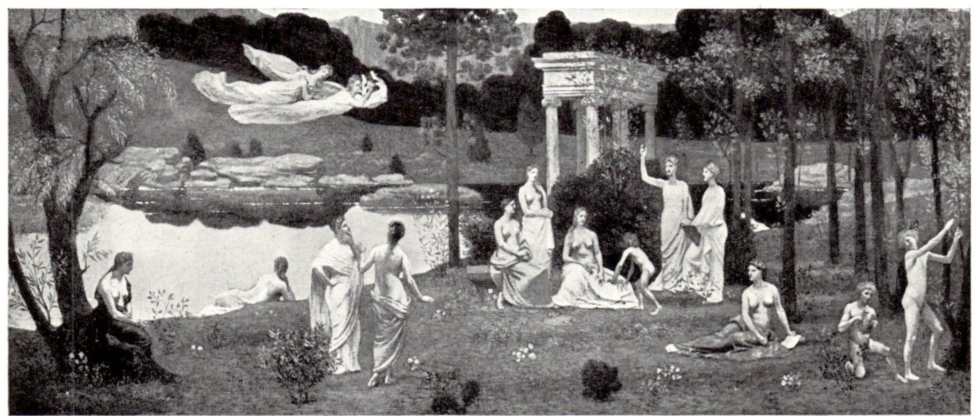

122. *Puvis de Chavannes: The Sacred Grove*

CHAPTER V

LATER IDEALISM AND THE RISE OF POST–IMPRESSIONISM

THERE WERE artists, however, who were made to deal with a more complex culture and a more spiritual subject matter than they found in the life of either the Second Empire or Bismarck's Germany, Prince Albert's England or the America of the Reconstruction Period. They were born too late to be either romantics or classicists, for they lived when the liberal dream was fading and the old ideals were dying, in an age of cynical empire-building and materialistic scientists. The men of this generation I have grouped under the rather makeshift title of the "later idealists." A characteristic of their work is that they gathered up what was left of both idealistic traditions and made a fusion, in form and content, of classicism and romanticism. It is also characteristic that, as idealists living in an age which gave neither outward nor inner occasion for their faith, they share a certain air of artificiality and frustration. Henry Adams in his *Education* gives one a realization of the dilemma in which a man trained to look on life as a matter of moral attitude found himself in an age that believed only in economics and machinery. The wave of factual thinking which was rising around led them also to approach their monumental and decorative problems with a naturalistic technique. The wonder is, perhaps, that they accomplished as much as they did.

In the 1840's a brilliant but short-lived pupil of Ingres, Théodore Chassériau (1819–1856), formed a mural style which was to distinguish the rest of the century (Fig. 121). Chassériau had Ingres's grace of line together with a remarkable ability to turn the beauty of a model into an ideal type without sacrificing the freshness of life. Ingres had been at his best in fairly small canvases; in big pictures he was never able to achieve more than the effect of a collection of separate figures. Chassériau learned from Delacroix to use color and atmosphere (as well as the charm of Oriental subjects) to achieve a unity which was entirely beyond Ingres. Unfortunately, he died young, and of the decorations in oil for the Palais de la Cour de Comptes in Paris, which he executed in 1844, only a few fragments survived the fire of 1871 to show the mingled elegance, languor, and passion of his art.

Puvis de Chavannes (1824–1898) became the great figure of the movement which Chassériau had begun (Fig. 122). Puvis gave up the attempt to paint directly upon the wall and returned to the Venetian method of painting in oil upon canvas, which was later to be applied to the wall; his method has been followed by most mural painters since. He gave great study, however, to Giotto's monumental style and returned to the emphasis upon the wall plane, which the baroque decorators had painted away into space. In an effort to achieve the flat transparent color of Giotto's fresco he toned down oil paint with white until its distinctive oily quality was gone; the pallor of his color is to his advantage, however, for it undoubtedly plays a part in creating the strangely moving silence and melancholy of his compositions.

It is one of the chief proofs of the strength of French culture at that time that Chassériau and Puvis de Chavannes had the power of style and distinction of mind to give life to their abstract compositions. For with a true instinct for monumental art they kept to monumental ideas: the Seasons, Peace, War, the Story of Christianity. They lived when the old conceptions of the world and the old humanistic imagery of thought were being dissolved by science, which substituted for it the confused mixture of minute natural detail and vast cosmic forces that has baffled modern efforts to generalize. And when neither the philosopher nor the scientist has been able to achieve a new synthesis of thought, it

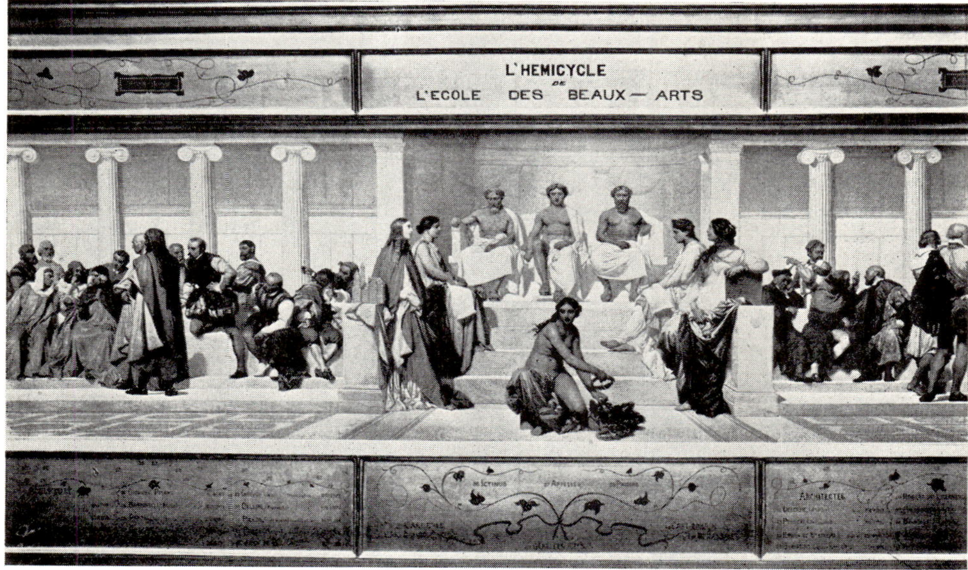

123. *Delaroche: Hemicycle of the Arts (detail).* 1853

is ungrateful to deny the achievement of artists able at least to make the old imagery of thought living and impressive.

A more superficial fusion of classic drawing and romantic subject matter was made by men like Paul Delaroche (1797–1856; Fig. 123) and Couture (1815–1879). The latter's theatrical "Romans of the Decadence" in the Salon of 1847 was an international sensation of its year. Anyone can remember a dozen other such brief reputations, in France and elsewhere, based upon vast canvases executed in this popular fusion of Ingres's drawing and the dubious theatrical grandeur of the romantic stage. It is not necessary to follow later idealism to its final decay in Gustave Moreau, but there is one more great French artist who must be mentioned here.

Corot's later landscapes and figures (after 1845) are as essentially ideal as those of Claude or Poussin. They are generalizations of nature, executed in formal harmonies of grey and green and quite as arbitrarily composed as a baroque landscape. But in place of Claude's grandiose quality Corot's landscapes have a dreamlike character which he himself indicated by calling them *rêveries*. Their deliberate evocation of emotion through formal harmonies, their appeal to tradition and to the

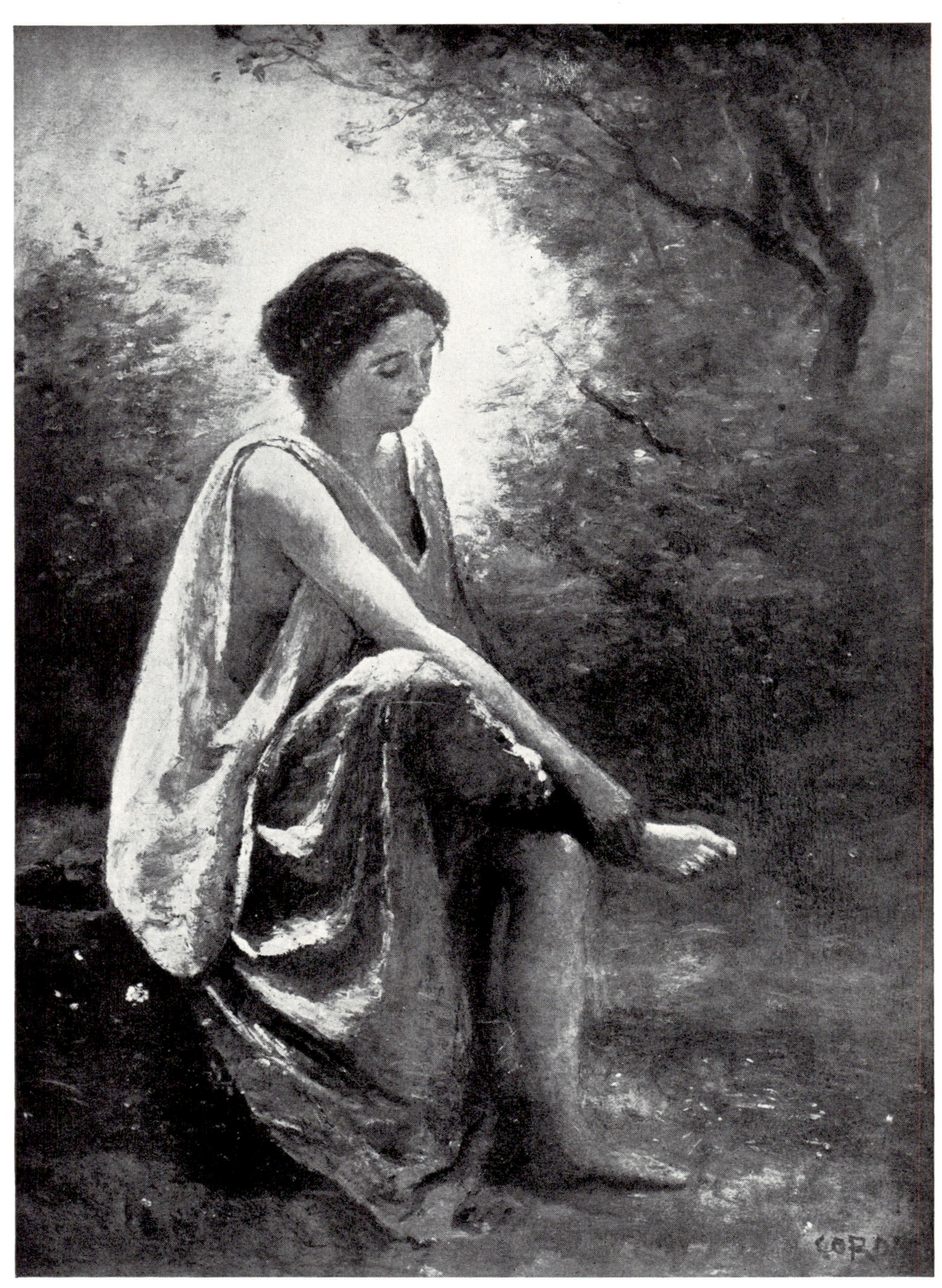

124. *Corot: Wounded Eurydice*

associations of Latin poetry, set Corot apart from the objective young minds rising around him in landscape painting. Yet without his cool and luminous palette, and his exploration of atmosphere, Impressionism would have lacked one of its chief sources (Fig. 124).

In English life the powerful ethical and religious forces of the Oxford revival, the great Victorian literary movement, and the influence of Ruskin created the foundation of an idealistic style. But the lack of form which had characterized the early ninteenth-century figure painters continued to prevent any strong growth. The Pre-Raphaelite Brotherhood, founded in 1849 by Rossetti, Millais, Holman Hunt, and others, was organized, as has been pointed out, by pupils of the naturalist, Ford Madox Brown (Fig. 100). They thus flung themselves headlong at the problem that plagued all the later idealists: how to create works of pure imagination by means of an exact naturalistic technique. It was impossible that they should not be affected by the realism around them; it was equally impossible that they could be content with naturalism; and, after an early phase of objective realism, they passed over into an idealistic style. Rossetti (1828–1882), the most influential of them, achieved something like a solution of the problem of combining naturalism and non-naturalistic subjects in his early work, like the "Annunciation" (Fig. 125) in the National Gallery; but later he lost himself in the murky, repetitious, sentimental style which one usually associates with him. It has been suggested that the maladjustment of an exile had something to do with the morbid sentimentalism of his later work, in which he repeated again and again the figure of the model whose peculiar beauty formed a kind of pseudo-Botticellian ideal for the whole group. Half a century later Aubrey Beardsley was still doing a neurotic parody of her heavy hair, long neck, and full lips.

Rossetti's sentimental types were passed on to Burne-Jones (1833–1898), who exerted a large influence through his decorative designs for stained glass and for William Morris' tapestries.

George Frederick Watts (1817–1904) and Alfred Stevens (1818–1875) came closest of all the Englishmen of the second half of the century to a generalized and monumental style. Watts, as his admirable

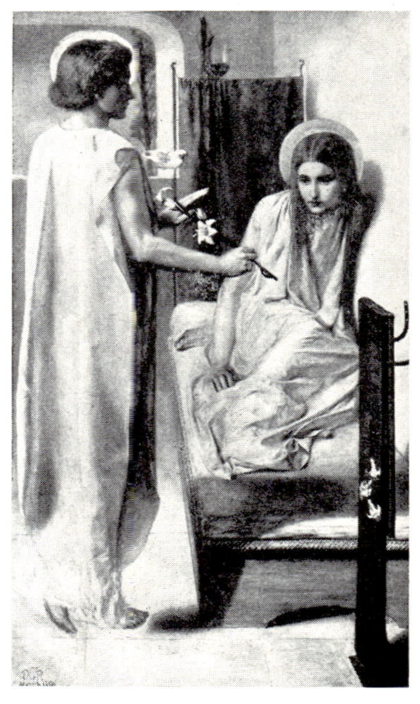

125. *Rossetti: Annunciation.*
1850

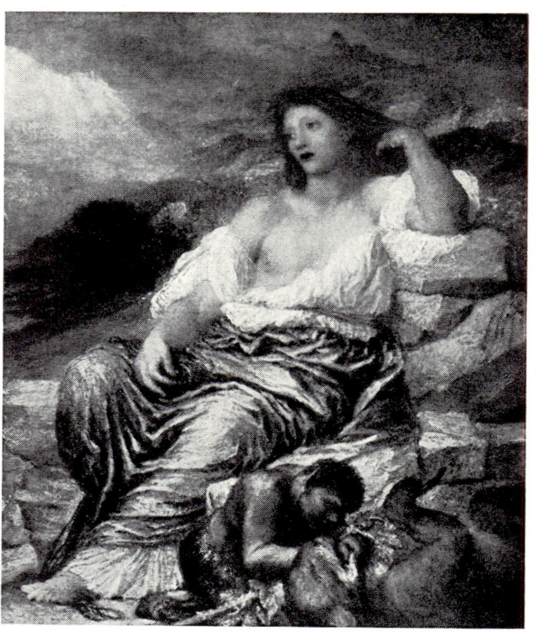

126. *Watts: Ariadne in Naxos.* 1894

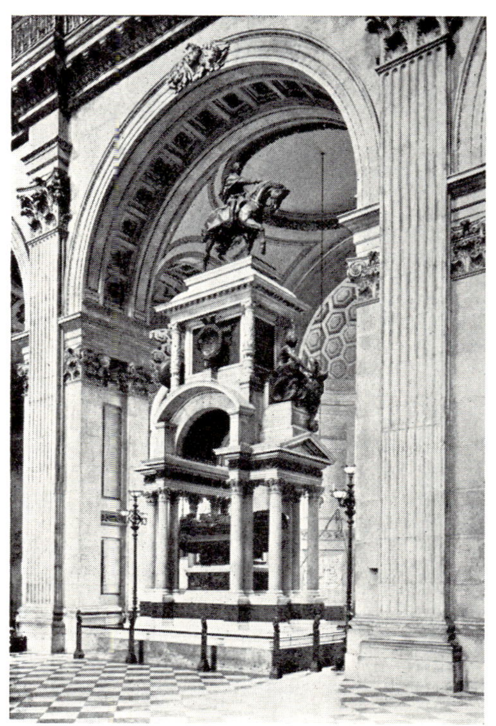

127. *Stevens: Tomb of Wellington,
St. Paul's, London*

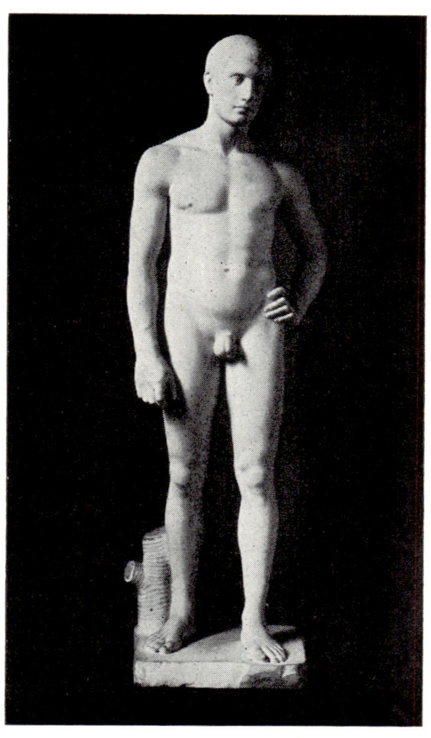

128. *Hildebrand: Young Man
Standing.* 1884

portraits show, really succeeded, like Manet, in creating form through color (Fig. 126). But, failing to find an opportunity to do monumental decorations, he turned after 1880 to allegorical painting, and in works such as "Hope" (1885) he exhibits, unfortunately, the worst rather than the best phase of English sentiment. Stevens was both painter and sculptor. His tomb of Wellington (Fig. 127) in St. Paul's Cathedral shows a plasticity and energy all too rare in nineteenth-century sculpture, but his career, like that of Watts, was frustrated by lack of opportunity and by the isolation of idealist thought in this age. A bloodless pallor of over-refinement and eclecticism seems to mar the most intelligent and cultured of English painters at this time.

The men who, in a naturalistic, factual-minded epoch, stood for the independent creative activity of the mind worked under tremendous difficulties. A greater or less degree of frustration also marks the later idealists in Germany, Feuerbach, Marées, and Böcklin.

The Swiss painter, Böcklin (1827–1901), showed in his early landscapes a great admiration for the formal, architectonic tradition of Poussin and Dughet, for he had in extreme form the yearning for the South that runs through German art. He not only loved the Italian landscape but saw the world through a mental lens of determined myth-making, peopling his canvases, like a baroque painter, with fauns and nymphs. When he carried out his baroque visions with an unmelodious brilliance of color and a coarse naturalism of detail, however, the result was a seriocomic and quite implausible mixture (Fig. 129).

Feuerbach (1829–1880) likewise spent as much of his life as possible in Italy, and tried to combine a richer color than that of the Nazarenes (in this case, the color of the Venetians) with the classic ideal of form. But like Couture, under whom he studied for a time, he chose to paint in a grandiose theatrical mood, with which the airless exactitude of his style clashes rather disagreeably (Fig. 130).

Hans von Marées (1837–1887), a far bigger personality, was a colorist who dreamed of covering great walls with frescoes and who left from a curiously fruitless life only one work that shows his true stature. This is his decoration of the library in the Aquarium at Naples (Fig. 131).

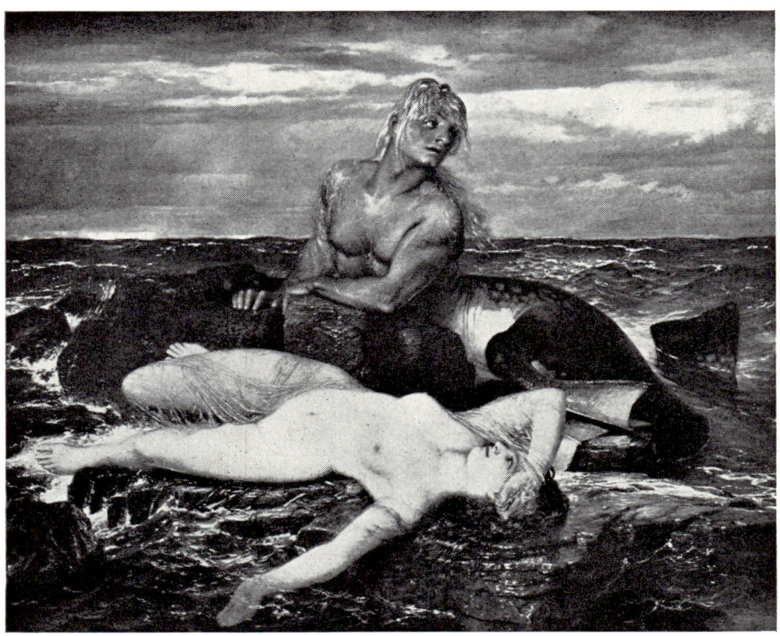

129. Böcklin: Triton and Nereid. 1875

The plan of these frescoes reveals the naturalism of the time. The themes are taken from the life of the Neapolitan fishermen. Each of the four walls is conceived as a huge window giving a view unconnected with the other walls; the pilasters which break up the two long walls into panels are treated as if they cut across the realistic view like the columns of a porch. Yet Marées showed that it was possible not only to create form (as Manet also did) by the strong, glowing, clear colors of the Impressionist period but even to give an epic treatment to simple, natural things without destroying their naturalness. Marées' solution of the problem of his generation, isolated in a little-seen library room in Naples, had nothing like the influence of Puvis de Chavannes's work in Paris, nor was he ever able again to achieve a similar success; but as an achievement of nineteenth-century mural painting these frescoes can be compared only to the work of Puvis.

The sculptor, Adolf von Hildebrand (1847–1921), was Marées chief successor. His "Young Man Standing" (Fig. 128), begun in 1884 (the year when Rodin began his great monument of dramatic Impressionism, the "Burghers of Calais"), marks a turning point in German art.

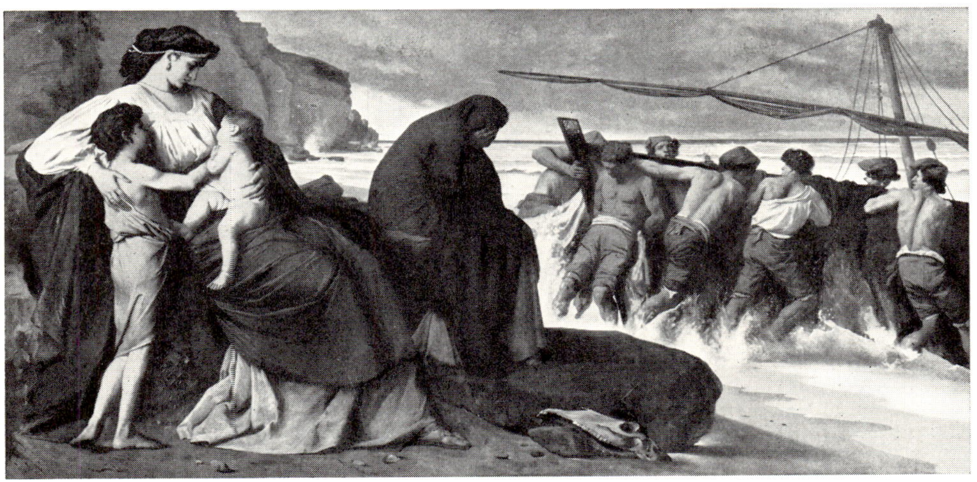

130. Feuerbach: Medea. 1870

Hildebrand cut through the crossed strands of naturalism and painter-like effects which confused the contemporary sculpture of Germany, and brought the art back to its own problem of plastic form. Sculpture was to him the human figure, seen as a three-dimensional harmony of shapes to be translated into the serene stillness of stone. External and cold as his work seems today, it put forward a living idea; from his purely plastic conception of his art rose the school of sculpture which is a leading achievement of twentieth-century Germany.

In the United States there were also artists of this temperament, who struggled to reconcile form with luminous color, imaginative subject matter with naturalistic detail. Through the influence of the great architect, H. H. Richardson, they also were led to the problem of monumental murals. Richardson had created a monumental style of architecture and for the first time in America had erected buildings of such emotional vitality that mural decoration was essential to give them completeness. He turned to John La Farge for the decoration of the interior of Trinity Church, Boston. January 31, 1876, the date of the completion of these decorations, marks the beginning of a second great attempt by American artists to create a monumental art.

The most important figures in this movement were John La Farge,

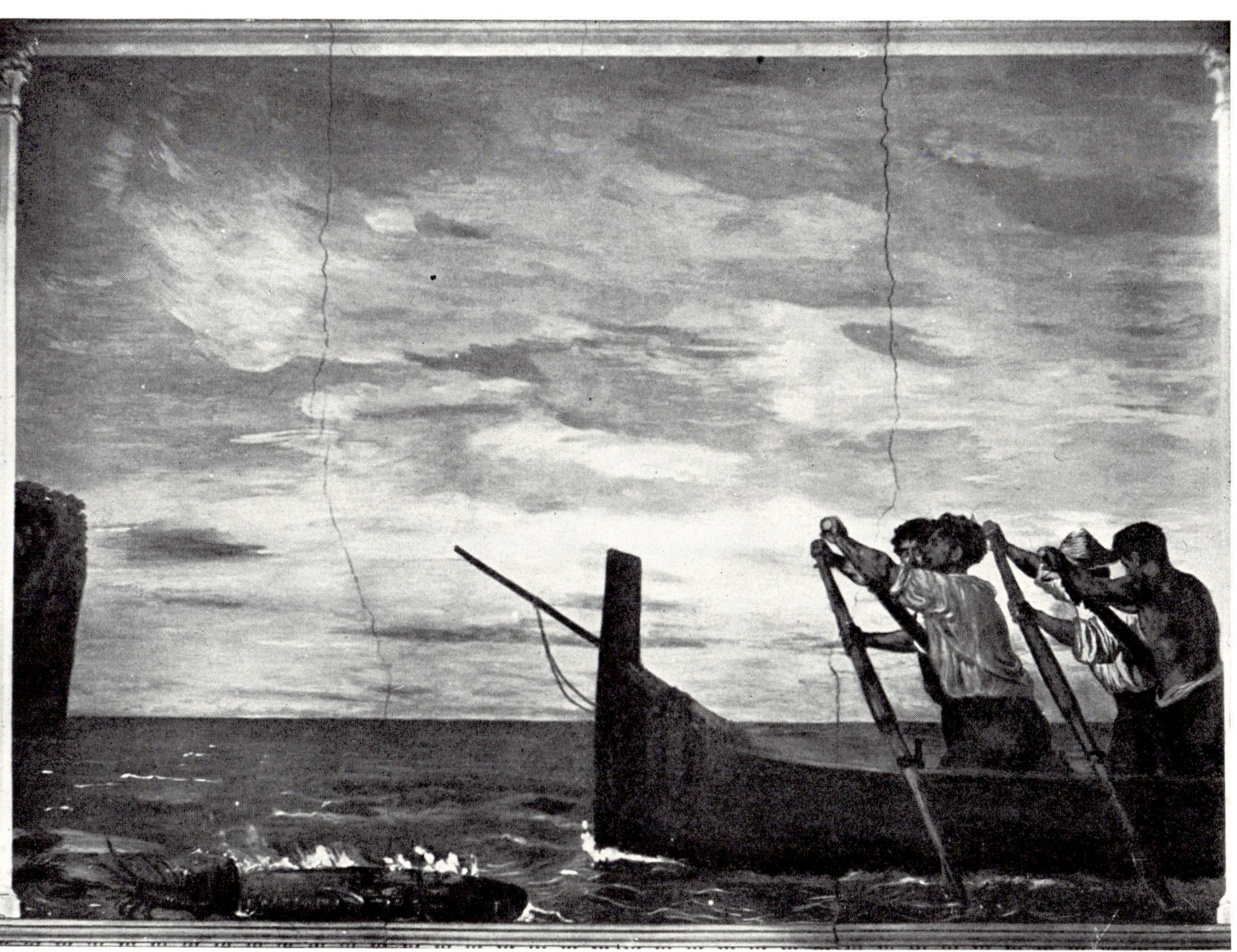

131. *Marées: The Rowers.* 1873

William Morris Hunt, and Elihu Vedder. Hunt's decorations for the New York State Capitol in Albany, which cost him his life, were ruined by the collapse of a ceiling (Fig. 134). Elihu Vedder spent most of his life in Rome, where he could nourish his dreams upon the rich air of an ancient culture. Vedder is an example of the heavy handicap which the later nineteenth century put upon the imaginative (as distinguished from the realistic) artist. Having no great public faiths or imaginative concepts to use as subject matter, he was forced to fall back upon illustrating poems such as the *Rubáiyát* or upon purely personal fantasies; his creations have a certain quality of mystery, but as ideas they were too personal to support a monumental style (Fig. 132).

The only great achievement was that of John La Farge (1835–1910), for he actually succeeded in creating a formal and imaginative art. One would suppose that he was of all painters the least likely to do so. He seems a man of fine taste rather than a creator; his frail health and his desultory training in art (which he studied for the sake of appreciation rather than with the aim of becoming a painter) seem the weakest kind of preparation for his difficult task.

When Richardson built Trinity Church, Boston, he wished to make the church an esthetic experience which should, by its solemn splendor, eliminate the everyday mood of one entering the building and prepare the mind for worship. La Farge's decoration of the interior with strong colors and solemn forms marked a new point in American culture, however much the walls may suffer by comparison with his later work. His two great works are the "Ascension" in the Church of the Ascension, New York, and the "Athens" in the Walker Art Gallery of Bowdoin College. In the figures of each one can see the naturalism of detail which is so striking in some of his smaller works, like the Samoan water colors; while the intricate modulation of every spot of surface, characteristic of the Impressionist period, gives a nervous quality to his draperies. Yet the vast space within which his figures stand removes the taint of fussiness. La Farge, like Marées, had learned to create form through luminous color. In the "Ascension" the figures rising into the cloudy, amethystine sky achieve a grave and noble solemnity. In his "Athens" (Fig. 136) the symbolical figures (which in the surrounding

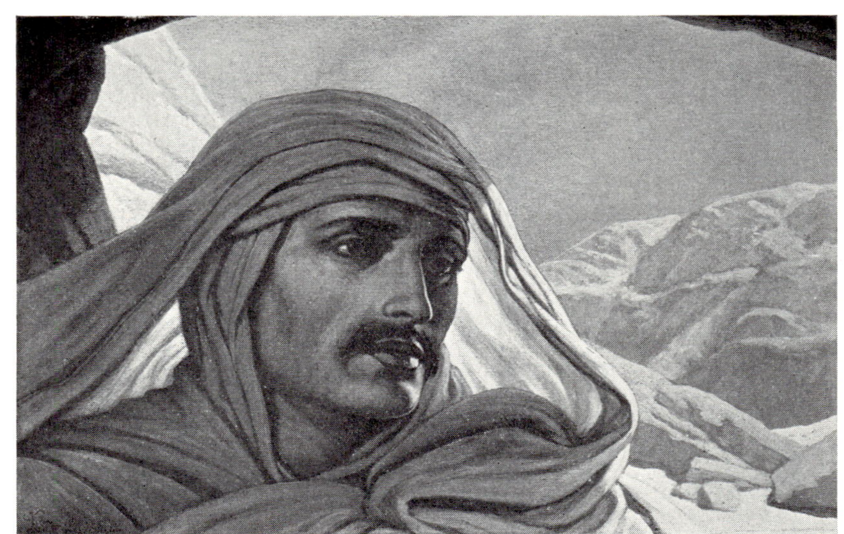

132. *Vedder: Lazarus*

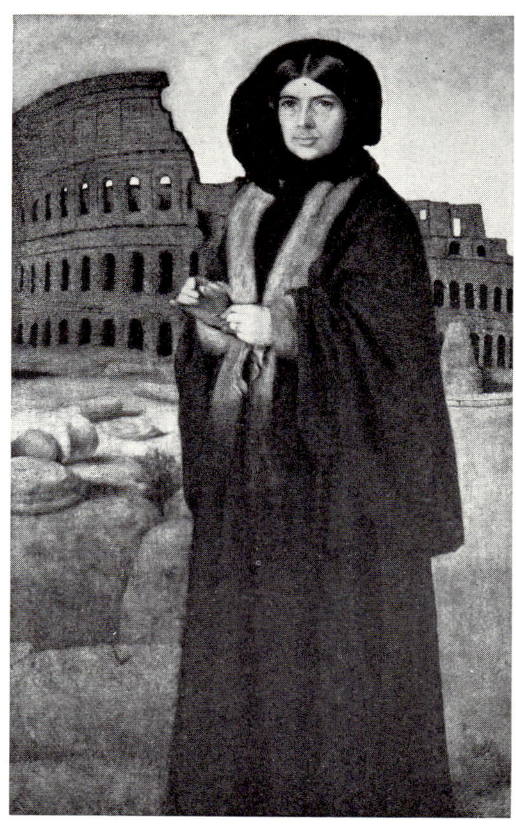

133. *Page: Portrait of the Artist's Wife.*
1861

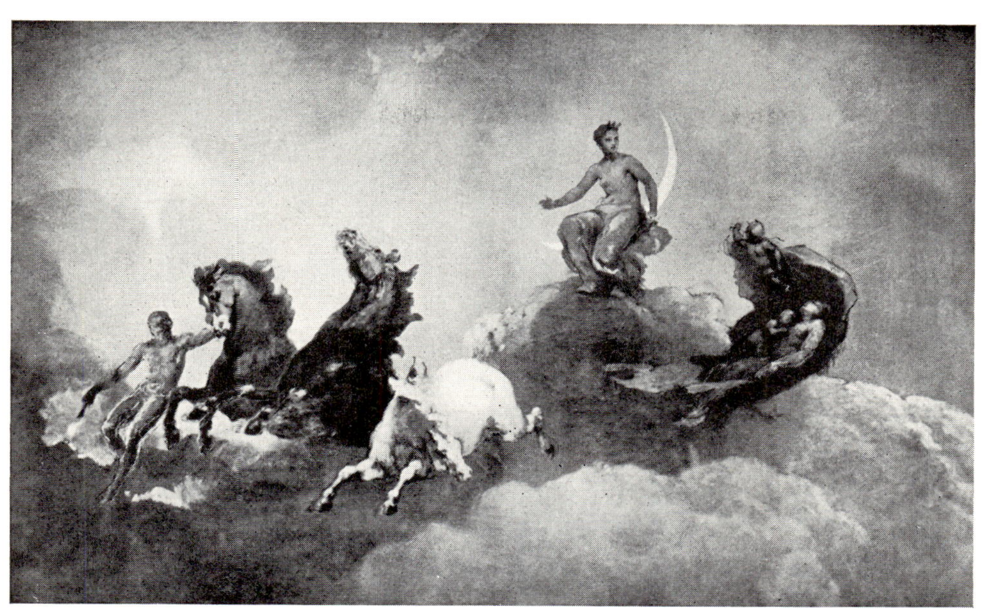

134. *Hunt: The Flight of Night (cartoon)*

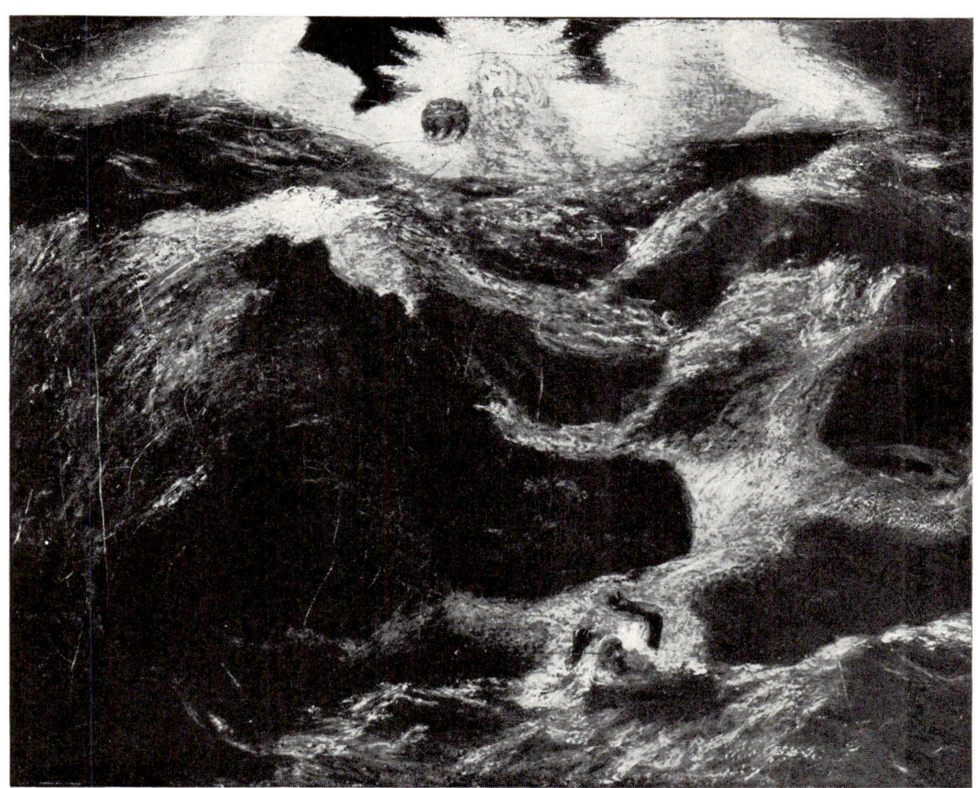

135. *Ryder: Jonah*

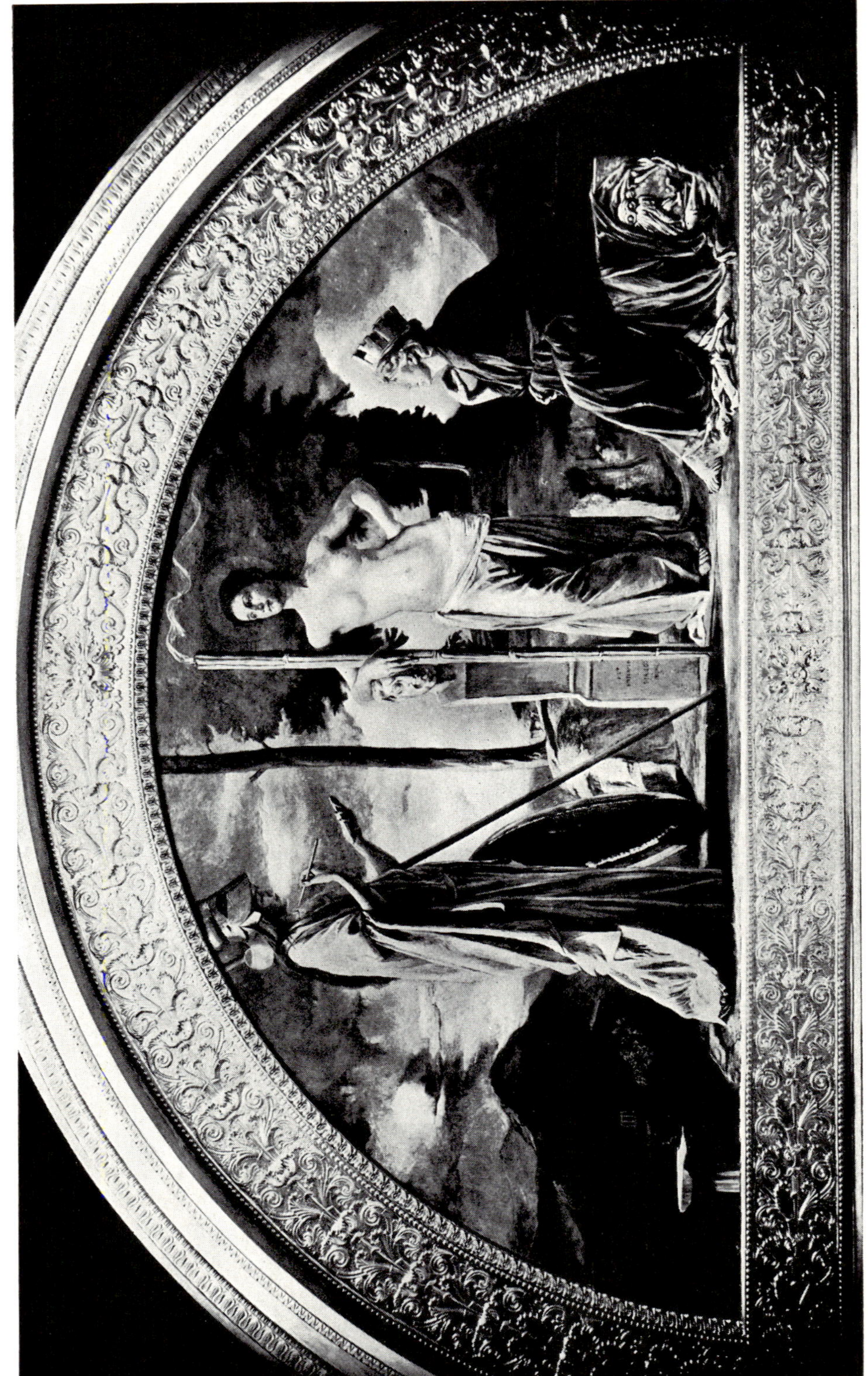

136. *La Farge: Athens.* 1898

lunettes by other artists are so much pasteboard) become embodiments in deep and splendid color of the august Virgilian calm: *vera incessu patuit dea.* La Farge's stained glass was also, in its own way, a major contribution to the nineteenth century's search to create monumental forms out of Impressionist color.

The mood of revery introduced into American art by Allston remained one of the source springs of the idealistic tradition. William Page (1811–1885), the pupil of one of Allston's pupils, was the first, perhaps, to develop independently in this country a new conception of monumentality and luminous color. His talent was unfortunately too uneven to achieve what these later men did, but his portrait of his wife (Fig. 133), painted in Rome against the background of the Colosseum, remains a living expression of his aim — for he, too, returned to original sources of inspiration for an art of monumental calm touched with the Virgilian note of revery.

The lyrical art of A. P. Ryder (1847–1917), although tiny in scale, is likewise important. Ryder was a born solitary, who lived in his room in New York City as isolated from the world as if he were in a hermit's cell. He created his own technique of thick, glowing paint, in whose deep impasto lurked the mystery of his imagination (Fig. 135). George Fuller, Blakelock, and Dewing, with varying degrees of success, also filled the need for an art of sentiment, of silence, and of meditation, qualities which the main stream of art in that day ignored.

The sculptor, Augustus Saint-Gaudens (1848–1907), by one work, at least, also achieved major stature in this movement. In most of his monuments one can see only the realism and the Impressionist technique of the time. But in his Adams Memorial in Washington he transcended objective realism in what seems one of the outstanding imaginative achievements of the century (Fig. 137).

Objective realism, dominating the close of the century in its later phase of Impressionism, thus provoked a long and dogged opposition. The men whom I have just mentioned have tended to fall into obscurity because they formed no school which lived and broadened into the great revolution of the twentieth century. Impressionism found its most

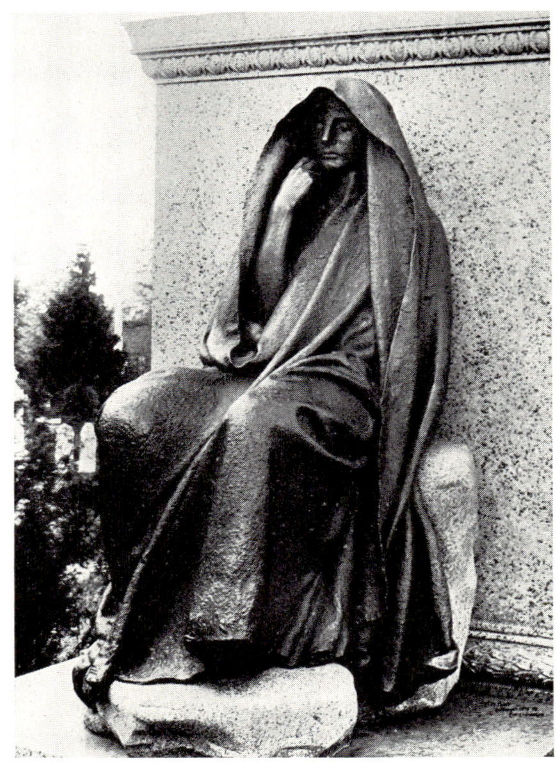

137. Saint-Gaudens: Adams Memorial

influential enemies in its own great recruits, who accepted its palette but rejected both the shallowness of its vision and the naturalism of its detail. In order of time, the first to break away was Cézanne; in point of influence, Van Gogh and Gauguin were felt by younger artists while Cézanne was still living forgotten in Aix.

The brief, intense activity of Vincent van Gogh (1853–1890) was crowded into the last years of the 1880's. It is an odd irony that his life should have coincided with the activity of Herbert Spencer. Beside Spencer's mechanical and complacent theory of the survival of the fittest and Nature's ruthless elimination of the unfit as the rule of progress in the universe, one has the spectacle of Van Gogh's little flame of spirit burning within the most helpless and unfit person that humanity could probably produce; yet we should not care to do without that tragic, helpless spirit. The passionate sensibility that drove him from one episode to another of his unhappy life unloosed a torrent of emotion into the calm pool of summer reflections that was the Impressionist view of life. No other painter is so perfect an example of the romantic dream of the artist as a being beyond control, who is seized by inspiration and pours it out in frenzied activity. The Impressionist technique was too calm and slow for Van Gogh. He fairly poured the paint on the canvas; in his hurry to set down his ideas he lengthened the tiny brush strokes of a Monet into long dashes of paint that often stand in great ridges upon his canvas, and fired the cool Impressionist color with incandescent flames of emotion. His work has all the virtues, and also the defects, of such spontaneity. In contrast to the calm, formal, and intellectual tradition of French painting, his canvases represent the response to life of a passionate, intuitive sensibility in the tradition of the Netherlands. He wrote of his famous "Café à Nuit" (Fig. 138), "I have tried to express the idea that the *café* is a place where one can ruin one's self, run mad, or commit a crime. So I have tried to express as it were the powers of darkness in a low drink shop, by soft Louis XV green and malachite, contrasting with yellow green and hard blue greens, and all this in an atmosphere like a devil's furnace of pale sulphur" (Letter 534). *To express the powers of darkness* — what a phrase to come from the decade of Herbert Spencer!

Van Gogh seems a Dutch rather than a French artist, in spite of the fact that he found himself only after he came into touch with the Impressionist technique of Paris. Paint was for him a means to express spiritual states of being: he was far more truly the descendant of Rembrandt than of Poussin. His chief companion among French artists was the violent, barbaric Gauguin, half Peruvian in blood, who also was striving toward an intuitive, emotional comprehension of the world.

Gauguin (1848–1903), however, gave the revolt against rationalism a different form. With his generation began the flight to the primitive, as an escape from the fastidious elegance of art for art's sake and the arid materialism of nineteenth-century thought. In the same decade with Gauguin's flight to Tahiti there began the Irish Renaissance of Yeats and Lady Gregory. It was a sign of the times that there arose a yearning for life close to earth and close to essential humanity, a

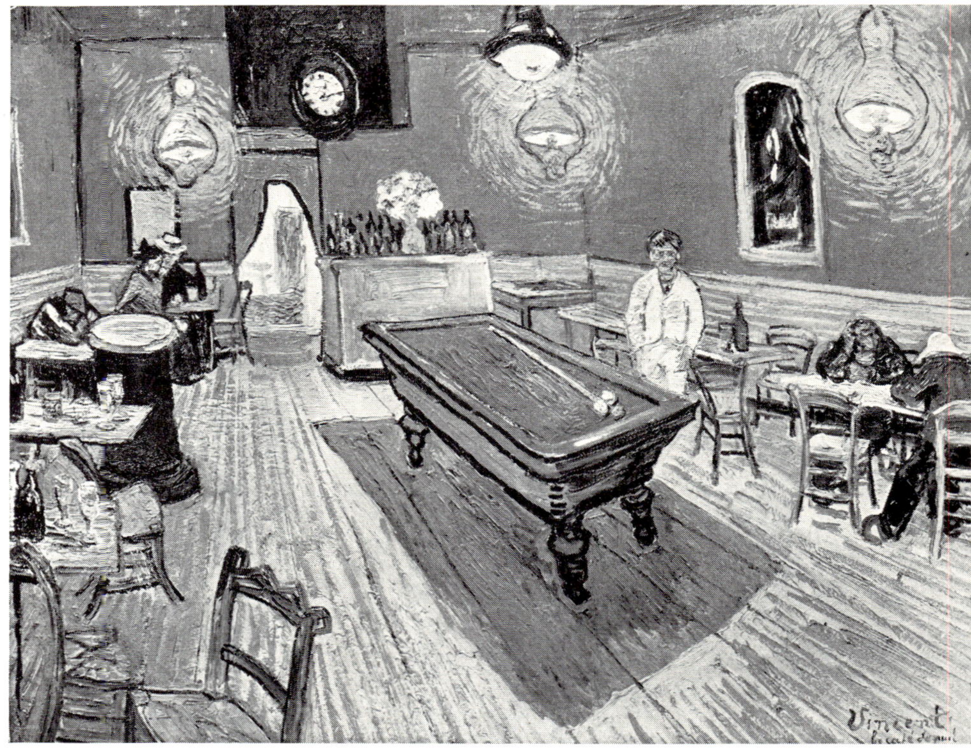

138. *Van Gogh: Café à Nuit.* 1888

wave of sympathy among men of the intellectual life for simple people
in whom the old emotions of wonder, terror, and faith still created the
ancient poetry of man's relation to nature. Gauguin learned the Impressionist technique from Pissarro, but he learned more from peasant
crafts, from medieval stained glass, from the primitive arts of the South
Seas. He broke away from realism to an archaic, two-dimensional style
using heavy outlines and broad areas of pure color. His attempt to
recapture the somber mystery and power which he felt at the heart of
primitive art was, however, of less weight among the younger French
painters than the sultry magnificence of his decorative effects: painting
moved under his influence closer to the abstract sense of style which
was to dominate the beginning of the new century (Fig. 139).

Cézanne (1839–1906) in his student days went through all the ideas
which were current in the sixties and seventies. He imitated Courbet's
directness of vision, Monticelli's massive pigment, the chiaroscuro and

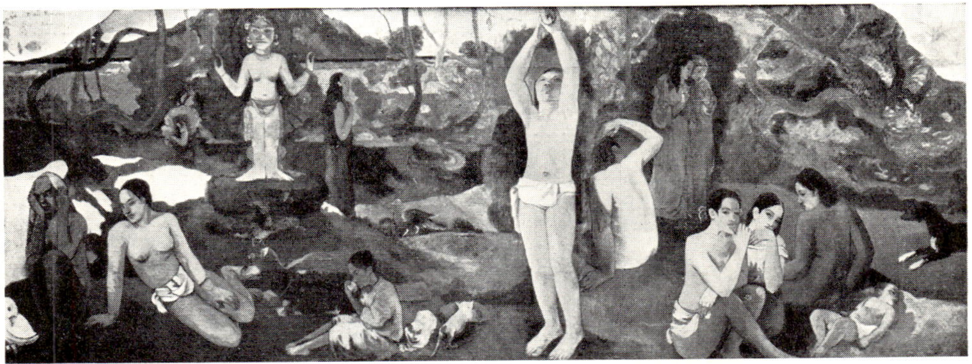

139. Gauguin· Whence Come We? What Are We? Where Are We Going?

romantic drama of Delacroix and Daumier. Then, in 1872, he came under the influence of Pissarro and abandoned his early dark palette for the division of tones and the atmospheric vibration of Impressionism. But although he accepted the Impressionist practice of painting out of doors in full sunlight and directly before the model, the dependence upon nature of a realist like Monet was deeply shocking to his instincts. He began the difficult work of reconciling realism and idealism. He did not go back to the subjects of Delacroix, or Poussin, or Signorelli, whom he admired. He retained the complete naturalness of eye and the absence of "idea" as well as the luminous color of the realists; but within these limits he reëstablished the conscious grandeur of the classic style.

First of all, he was a great colorist who added weight and chromatic richness to the Impressionist palette. The Impressionists were tending to sacrifice the form and solidity of painting to atmosphere and the vibration of color. It was Cézanne's double aim to combine the new transparent color of his age with the traditional solid, three-dimensional form of western art; and to combine the naturalness of vision, the close sympathy with nature, and the absence of anything but a visual idea, which were characteristic of nineteenth-century realism, with the grandeur of style of the old masters. Two famous utterances express this very clearly: "We must make of Impressionism something solid like the art of the museums." "What we must do is to paint Poussin over again from nature." (Fig. 140).

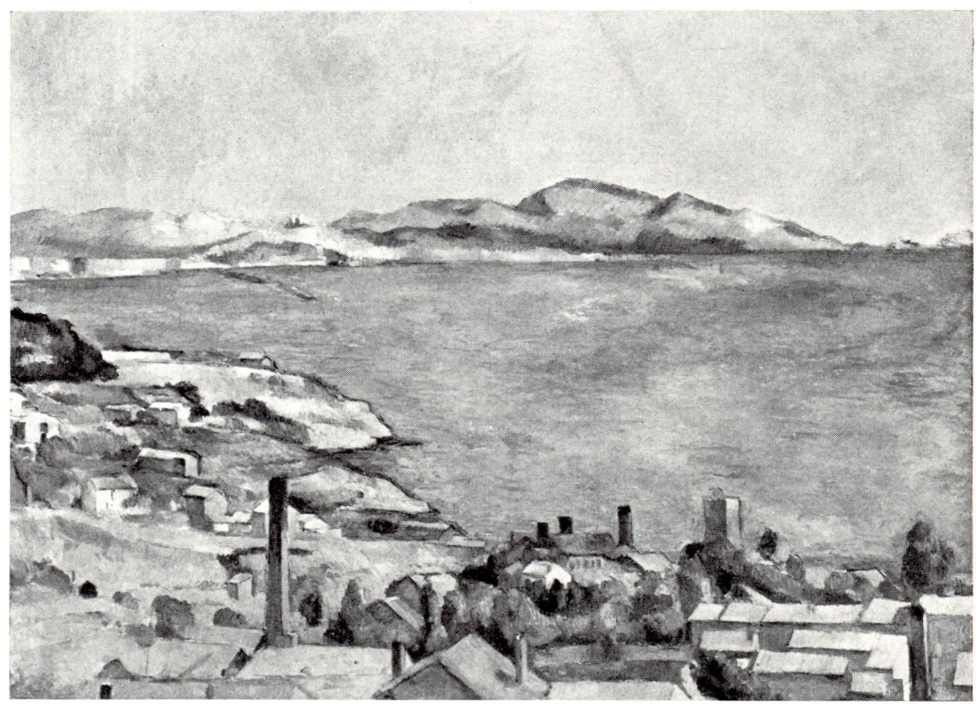

140. *Cézanne: L'Estaque, c. 1883–85*

The emergence of his style in the eighties and nineties was thus a restatement of the Latin instinct for order within the new vision of nature opened up by the achievements of nineteenth-century realism. "Art," said Cézanne in a remark already quoted, "is a harmony parallel to nature," repeating almost the very words uttered by Michelangelo three hundred years before. From Masaccio onward western artists had imposed their conscious harmonies upon nature without destroying the essential reality of their images. Why then, one must ask, did Cézanne go so far away from nature that in a later generation the Cubists could point to his example as justifying an attempt to eliminate all traces of nature and to make painting wholly an abstract order? It must be remembered that Poussin and Claude could create their noble and disciplined art in harmony with the taste of their time, for to their cultivated audience nature was something to be disciplined and controlled by the human mind. "It would be illiberal," wrote Sir Henry Wotton of the newly invented camera obscura, "to make landscapes

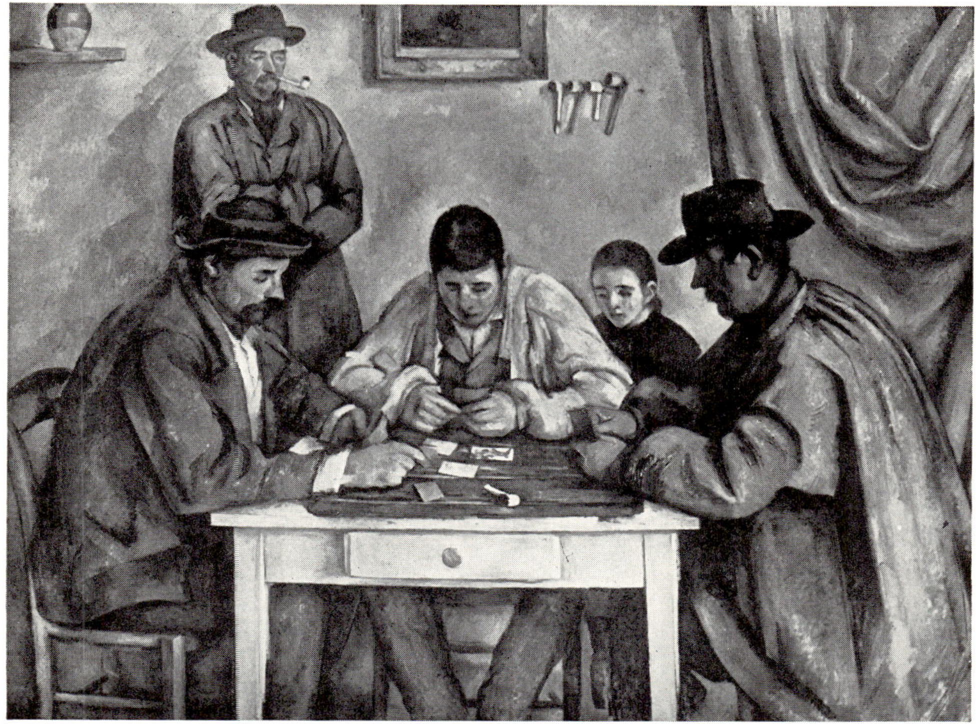

141. *Cézanne: The Card Players*

by it, though surely no painter can do them so precisely." Cézanne, however, had to maintain the liberality of the spirit against the fact-minded-
ness of his day, against the camera (which bore so heavily upon even
such a talent as Fantin-Latour's), and against the often fantastically bad
taste of an artistically illiterate population. It is no wonder, perhaps,
that a man who had to fight all the forces of the world about him should
show a somewhat grim and uncompromising face. But to treat Cézanne
as an abstract painter, as some twentieth-century critics have done, is
to ignore his repeated adherence to the humanistic tradition and, what
is worse, to ignore his pictures. He was an artist of deep sensibility,
through whose painting one comes to a knowledge of the soul of his
Provençal countryside, with its shrewd, dry peasants and its noble
poetry of sun and mountains and sea (Figs. 141, 142) as one comes
through Poussin and Dughet to understand the majesty of the Campagna and the Alban hills, or through Rembrandt to understand the
misty skies and the sturdy humanity of Holland.

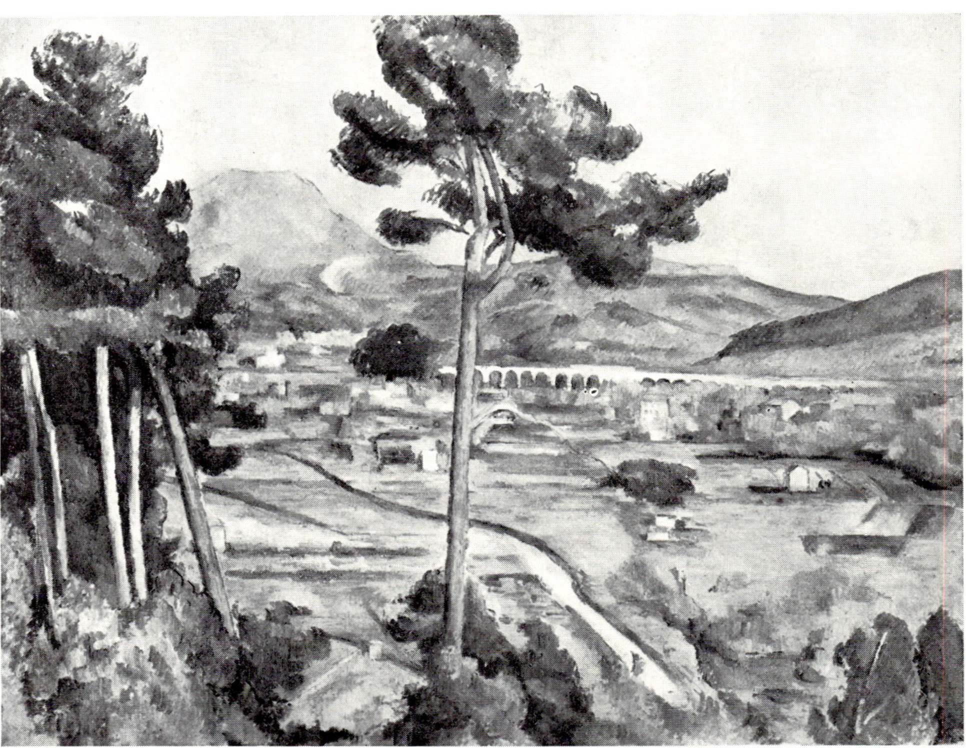

142. Cézanne: Landscape with Mont Sainte-Victoire, c. 1885–87

Seurat (1859–1891) also represents in a more theoretical form the reaction of the French intellect from Impressionism. His short life was devoted to the creation of a system of painting, called *pointillisme*, which he believed capable of reducing lines, colors, and tones to fixed values, like those of a chemical formula. To eliminate the transitory and personal quality of art he reduced the broken color of Impressionism to an exact system, stylized his brush strokes into a mosaic of minute round dots, simplified figures into geometric shapes. His schematic and almost mechanical method was the antithesis of naturalism; but he had time in his short life for only seven large and a score of small canvases, and one wonders if in a more fortunate time he would have been forced to erect such a laborious method in order to achieve style. His small landscapes and drawings are filled with an exquisite sensibility, which pleases our taste today better than the abstract monumentality of his large compositions (Fig. 143). It was the formal geometry of his

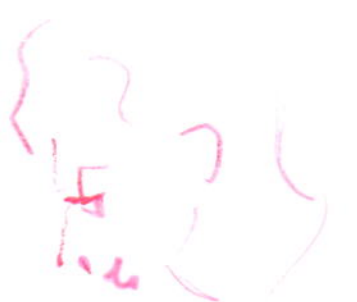

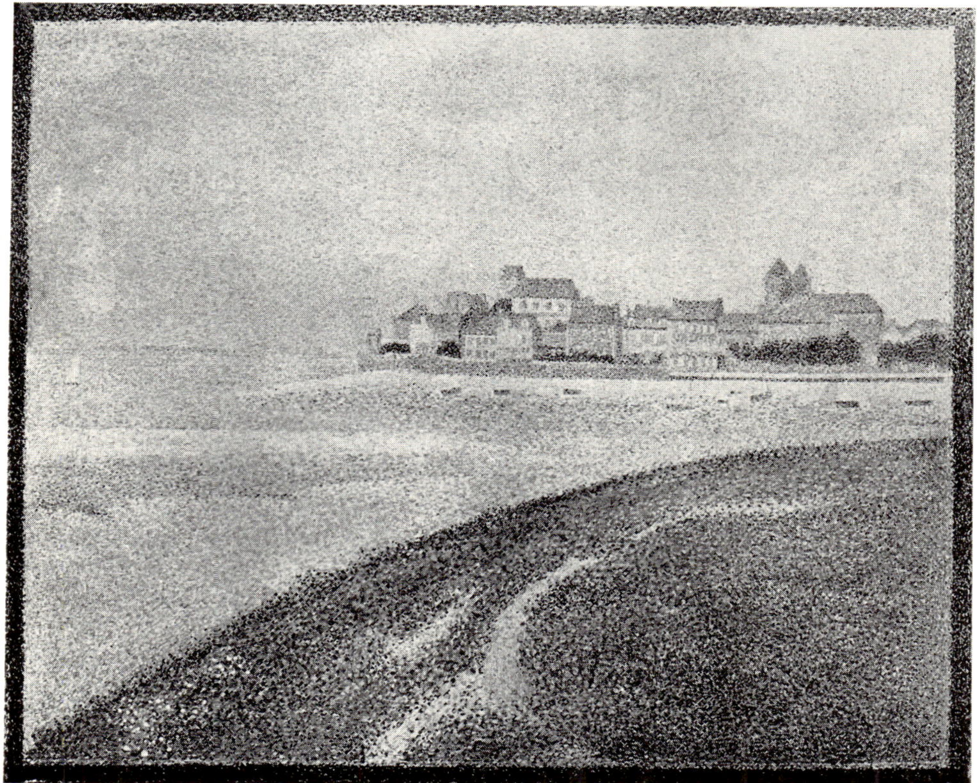

143. *Seurat: La Crotoy.* 1890

style, however, which made him admired by the generation of abstract painters that came after. One can almost hear, as one looks at these big creations of the later eighties, the twentieth-century war cry of "painting as architecture."

The elaborate study of the structure of painting which constitutes Post-Impressionism, the tendency toward geometric forms, the emphasis upon weight, mass, and space which one finds in Cézanne and Seurat especially, is truly a revival of the inner architecture of painting as it had been understood in the seventeenth century. It had its parallels in the art of building. It is true that, as one looks at the eclectic architecture of the later nineteenth century, one sees predominantly the reign of an Impressionist style that fills every part of a design with the flicker of light and shadow — wall faces broken into innumerable pro-

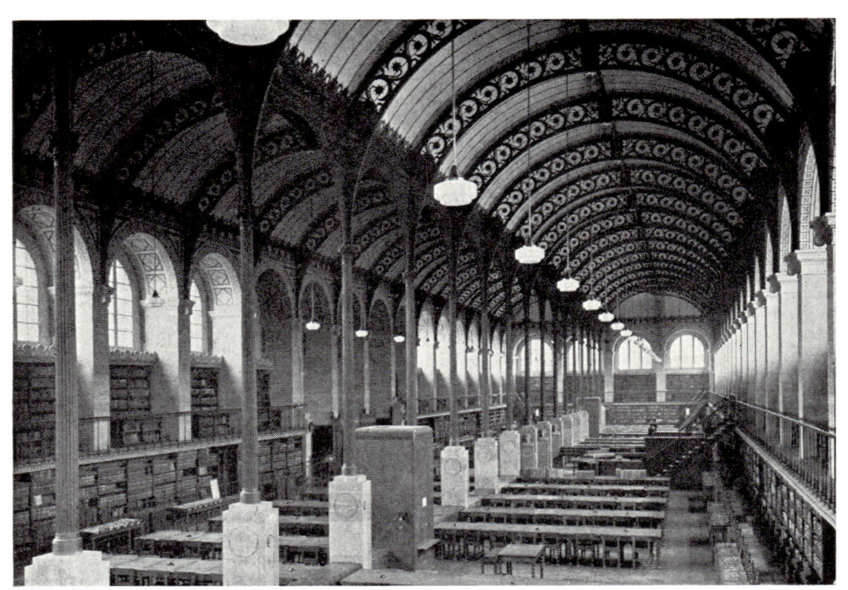

144. Labrouste: Bibliothèque Sainte-Geneviève, Paris

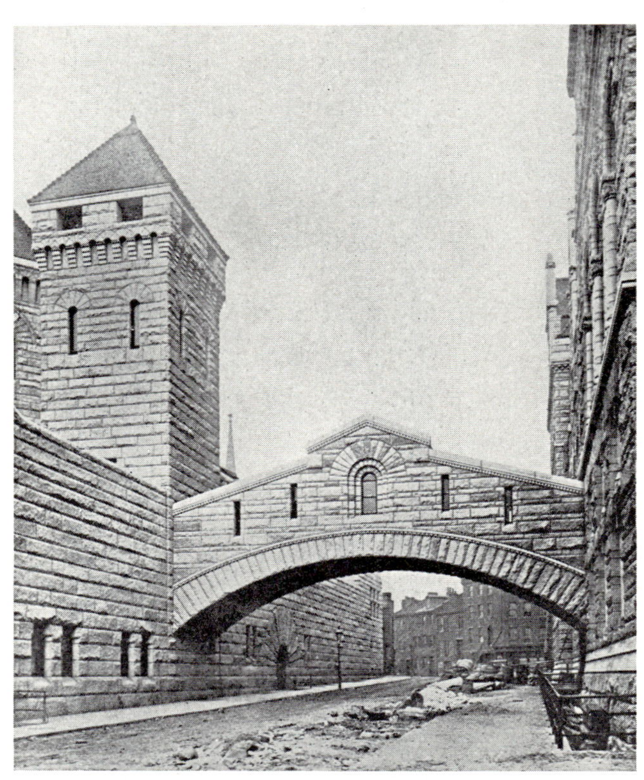

*145. Richardson: Alleghany County Buildings,
Pittsburgh, Pennsylvania. 1884–86*

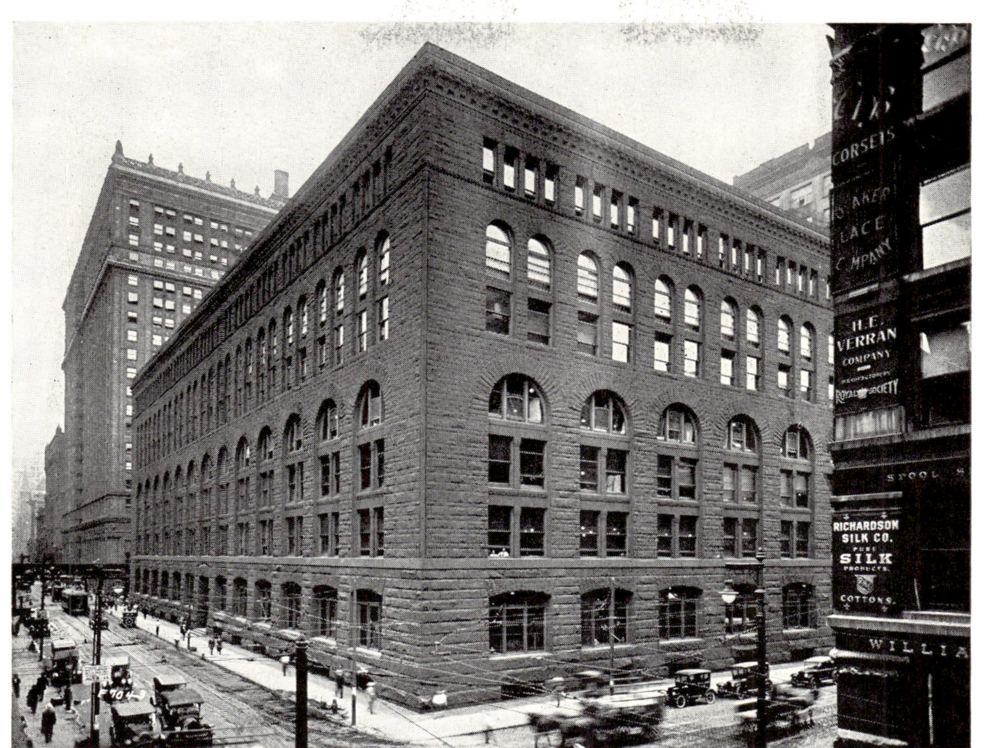

146. *Richardson: Marshall Field Wholesale Store, Chicago. 1885–87*

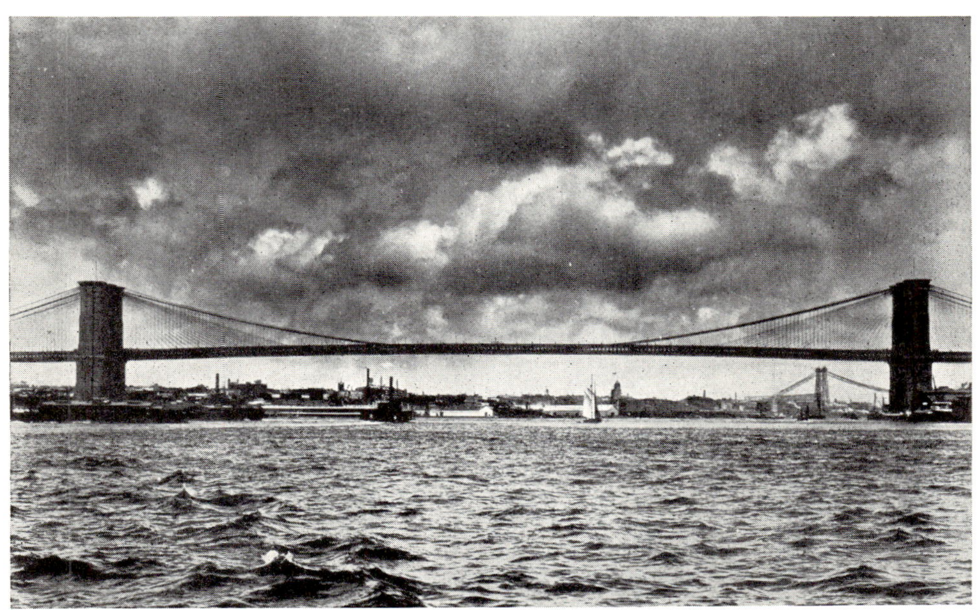

147. *John A. and Washington A. Roebling: Brooklyn Bridge. 1870–83*

jections, crowned with towers and pinnacles, irregular roof lines, and frequently a filigree of iron work against the sky — while every possible spot of the interior and furniture was correspondingly covered with ornament. Impressionism in architecture achieved some of its most fantastic and entertaining expressions in American wooden buildings, but it dominated the whole eclectic period (Fig. 148).

Nevertheless, the pioneers of a new sense of structure were at work. This was the period of Labrouste (1801–1875) whose reading-room of the Bibliothèque Sainte-Geneviève is a masterpiece of austere form and frank structural expression (Fig. 144). A sense of formal structure was the outstanding characteristic of his pupil, H. H. Richardson (1838–1886), who outgrew his Trinity Church, Boston, to achieve the magnificent, solemn geometric order of the Alleghany County Court House (Fig. 145) buildings in Pittsburgh (1884) and the Marshall Field building (Fig. 146) in Chicago (1885). Richardson made his architecture as rich in color and texture as any of the period, but the coloristic richness is the skin of a great structural architecture.

The Brooklyn Bridge (1870–1883; Fig. 147) built by the Roeblings, the Monadnock Building in Chicago designed by John Wellborn Root, the development of the steel-frame skyscraper in Chicago, and the early

148. *Villa of Charlotte Cushman, Newport*

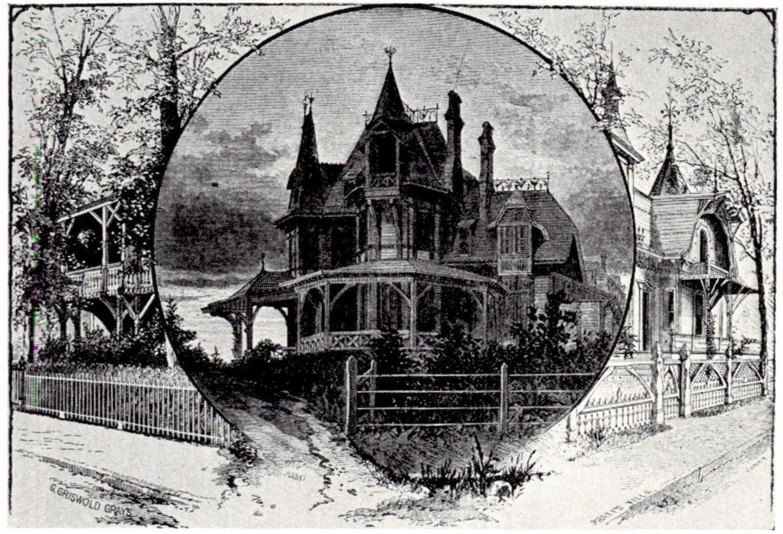

functionalism of Sullivan united to form a tradition of structure and of purely formal design which Frank Lloyd Wright passed on to the twentieth century. It was in no sense, however, a doctrinaire or mechanical functionalism, for from Richardson onward American architects have all worked with a consciousness of the romantic splendor of their art; it was a true revival of the formal, constructive spirit.

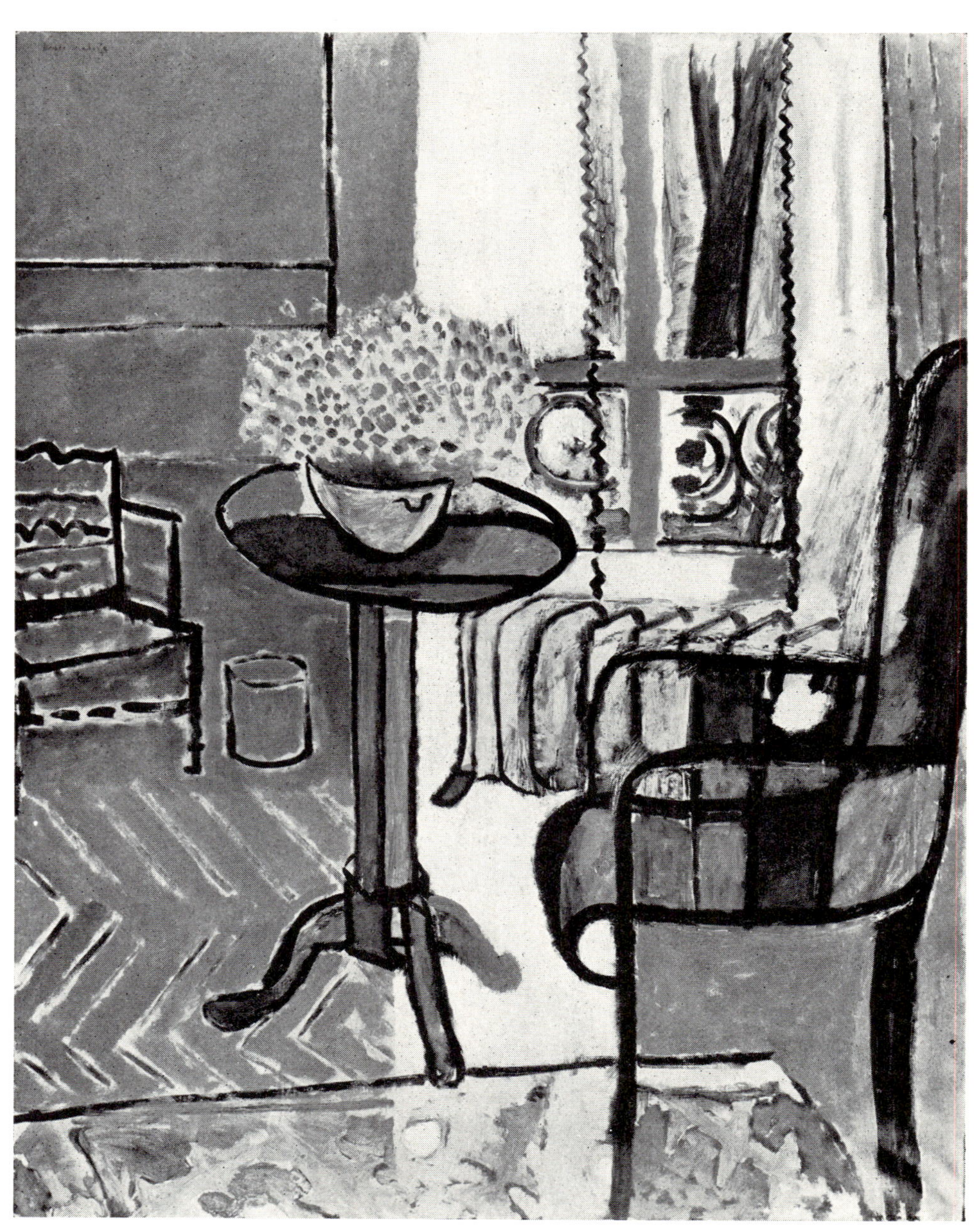

149. *Matisse: The Window.* 1907

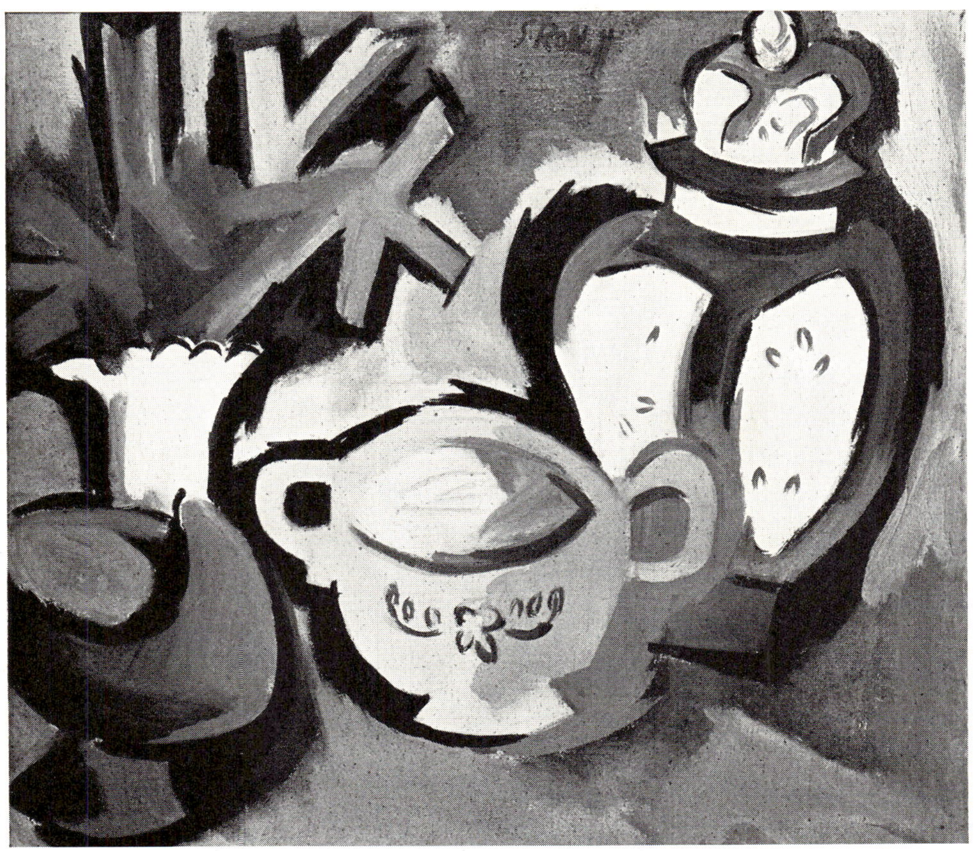

150. Schmidt-Rottluff: Still Life with Crockery

CHAPTER VI

THE TWENTIETH CENTURY

THE MEN who led the realistic movement which was the "modern art" of the fifties and sixties were of a vigorously national mind. Manet and Courbet, Homer and Eakins, Menzel and Ford Madox Brown, represent a simple, rather narrow, but highly developed national life. The men who led the new movements of the twentieth century had their mental roots in the world-consciousness created by the end of the nineteenth century. This is the greatest difference between the preceding revolts and the one that boiled and fermented in the early years of the twentieth century.

The great Post-Impressionists had bequeathed to the twentieth century two problems. Cézanne, Seurat, and Gauguin had raised the question of style as a projection of the artist's mind upon the raw material of nature. Gauguin had the strongest immediate influence in France. His mysticism interested the French much less than his new manner of painting. His canvases composed in bold, two-dimensional color areas revealed possibilities of greater brilliance of color than even the Impressionists had reached. He had freed drawing from the task of naturalistic representation and given it a decorative value, assigning it the same part that the lead plays in early medieval stained glass. Cézanne's influence was not felt until after the retrospective exhibition of his work at Paris in 1904. Seurat was first discovered by the Cubists. The second problem was an escape from objective realism. Van Gogh had discarded realism to make painting the expression of one's subjective response to nature. Child of the age of science, he had no tradition or philosophy to arrange or control his expressions, and fell back upon a naked sensibility.

The more intellectual and stylistic examples of Gauguin, Seurat, and Cézanne were preferred by the French. Van Gogh's subjectivity was of special influence in Germany, where it was reinforced by the brooding art of the Norwegian painter, Edward Munch, and by the dramatic, forceful expressionism of the Swiss, Hodler.

Nevertheless, a greater gap separates the young rebels of the twentieth century from their predecessors than exists between any of the nineteenth-century movements, because the leaders of the twentieth-century revolt were intoxicated by a flood of new influences. The fruit of a hundred years of western empire-building was being gathered in an enthusiasm for all the non-European arts which had been discovered during that expansion — Japanese prints, Chinese scrolls, Coptic textiles and Near Eastern pottery, Egyptian and Negro and Oceanic sculpture, as well as the arts of the Romanesque and Byzantine Europe in which our barbaric and Oriental inheritance is strongest. The Renaissance, the classical Mediterranean world, faded before the glittering host of a thousand new inspirations. Practically all these arts are stylistic in drawing, two-dimensional in color, intuitive rather than rationalistic in character. Since the beginning of the fifteenth century western painting had maintained steadily two characteristics: it had created an effect of deep space and of solid, three-dimensional objects within that space; and it had drawn the human figure more or less according to the humanistic conventions inspired by Greek and Roman realism. The greatest of the rebels of the nineteenth century — whether Manet or Cézanne, Homer or Marées — had devoted themselves to trying to realize these ancient ideals with the new luminous palette of the seventies. But in the twentieth century these conventions were discarded in favor of new non-western models. Deep space was set aside for two-dimensional modes of painting, and a half-century's search for the most intense color possible with the new palette came to a climax shortly after 1900 under the influence of Islamic pottery and twelfth-century stained glass. Homely realism found itself challenged by exotic style; objective observation by the mysterious, dark fire of primitive mysticism. It is hardly to be wondered at that the new manner of painting achieved by the twentieth century should be radically different from anything put forward in a narrower and simpler world.

151. *Prendergast: Landscape with Figures*

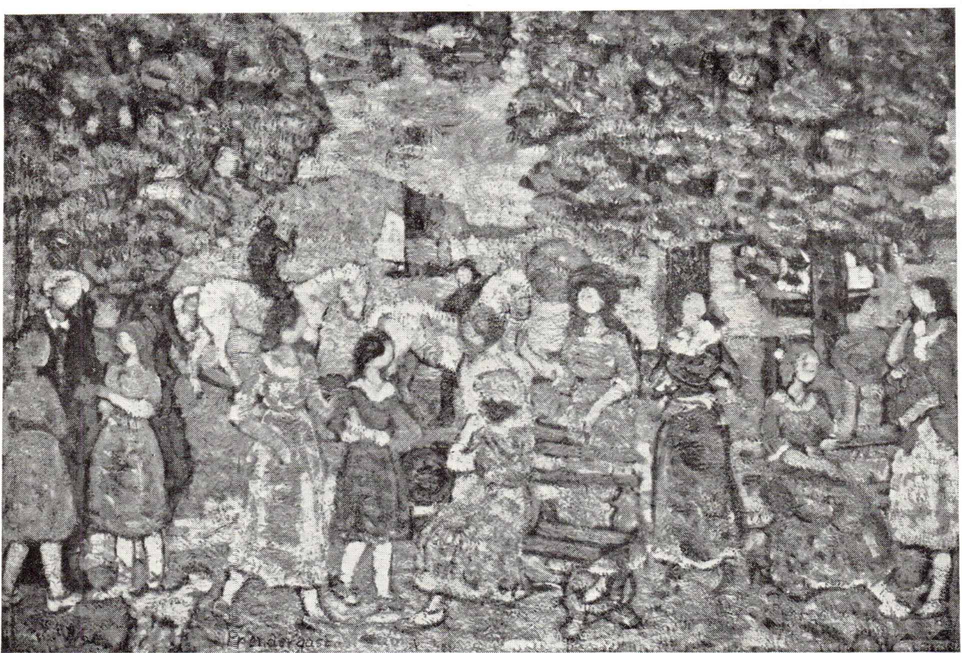

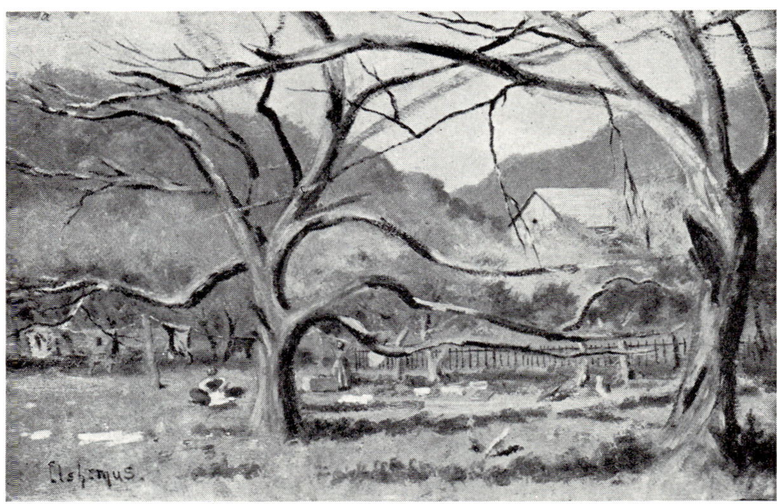

152. *Eilshemius: Landscape*

To a large extent one can describe the initial movement of the twentieth century as the revolt of the colorists. But there was a deeper and more universal strain in it. It was a revolt from the preciousness of *l'art pour l'art* and the pessimism of nineteenth-century materialistic thought toward an emotional, intuitive, and, above all, positive attitude toward life.

The turn of the century really came in 1905 and 1906 with the almost simultaneous appearance of three militant groups of young artists — the Fauves in Paris, the Brücke in Dresden, the Eight in New York.[1] They were alike in their essential aim, to break away from second-generation Impressionism and to make art an expression of energy, of daring, and of masculine strength. Beyond that the divergences begin. The Fauves, who received this insulting nickname at the Salon d'Automne in 1905, included the colorists Matisse, Braque, Derain, Dufy, Vlaminck, Friesz, and Rouault. The Brücke was formed about the same time as an artistic brotherhood, whose members shared in common both living and working quarters and enthusiasms for Van Gogh and primitive art. Schmidt-Rottluff, Heckel, and Kirchner were the original members; Pechstein, Nolde, and Otto Müller were later added. The

---

[1] Augustus John and his followers, who represent the same tendency in England, were at work then also but were not really felt as a force until their exhibitions of 1910 and 1911.

Eight, who exhibited together at the Macbeth Galleries in 1906, were Henri, Glackens, Sloan, Luks, Shinn, Davies, Prendergast, and Lawson; Bellows was shortly added to the group. In addition to these groups there were many other figures who formed their art during that decade and contributed as individuals to the movement of the times. The great Viennese painters, Klimt and Kokoschka, and Christian Rohlfs on the Lower Rhine, helped notably to create what the German critics called Expressionism. Rousseau le Douanier, Segonzac, and Utrillo were at work in Paris. Augustus John introduced a salutary vigor into English painting. In America artists like Eilshemius (whose best work was done in this period) and Prendergast were part of the colorists' movement, translating realism into a style of pure color. Prendergast had, in fact, achieved a two-dimensional mosaic-like style before 1900.

Both Matisse and Schmidt-Rottluff are typical of their respective groups. The aim of Matisse, as he expressed it at this period, was almost pure decoration. An exhibition of Near Eastern ceramics and miniatures held in Paris in 1903 seems to have opened the road to him for his escape from naturalism. To achieve a similar brilliance of decorative pattern he eliminated the traditional three-dimensional modeling and drew with heavy outlines, filling the areas between outlines with clear, pure color in map-like areas. His subjects were the familiar nudes and still lifes of French studio tradition, but his ideas were those of a Persian potter (Fig. 149). Most of the Fauves followed him in simplification of nature into gorgeous color patterns.

Schmidt-Rottluff (Fig. 150) had perhaps the most inventive color sense among the members of the Brücke. He, too, abandoned a mild Impressionism for a flat style with slashing outlines and powerful hues. He, too, used color with an understanding of its resonance and power to create a mood by direct appeal to the senses. Matisse wished his hues to be "an appeasing influence . . . like a good armchair" for the tired brain. Schmidt-Rottluff's raw, strong colors were, on the other hand, violent and exhilarating. He was important also in the development of a new two-dimensional graphic style in Germany.

At the same time certain painters in America, notably Prendergast (Fig. 151) and Eilshemius (Fig. 152) were moving toward two-dimen-

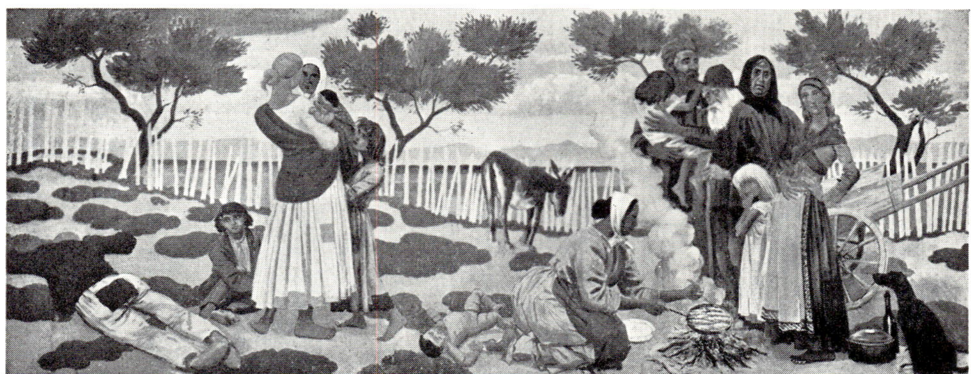

153. *John: The Mumpers*

sional patterns of very clear, transparent colors, in harmonies of a lyrical quality that was characteristic of the American school.

The colorists depended upon an instinctive sense of style in simplifying nature into their novel color patterns (Fig. 153). They had no European tradition nearer than Gothic painting to show the way to such bold simplifications. They developed no clear-cut formulas of style, such as the Cubists developed. Their art was intuitive rather than programmatic, and it resulted in a complete exploration of the

154. *Klimt: The Kiss.* 1911

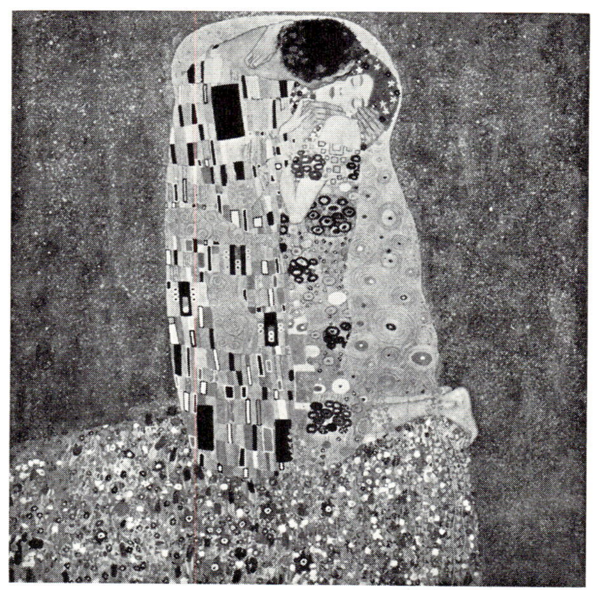

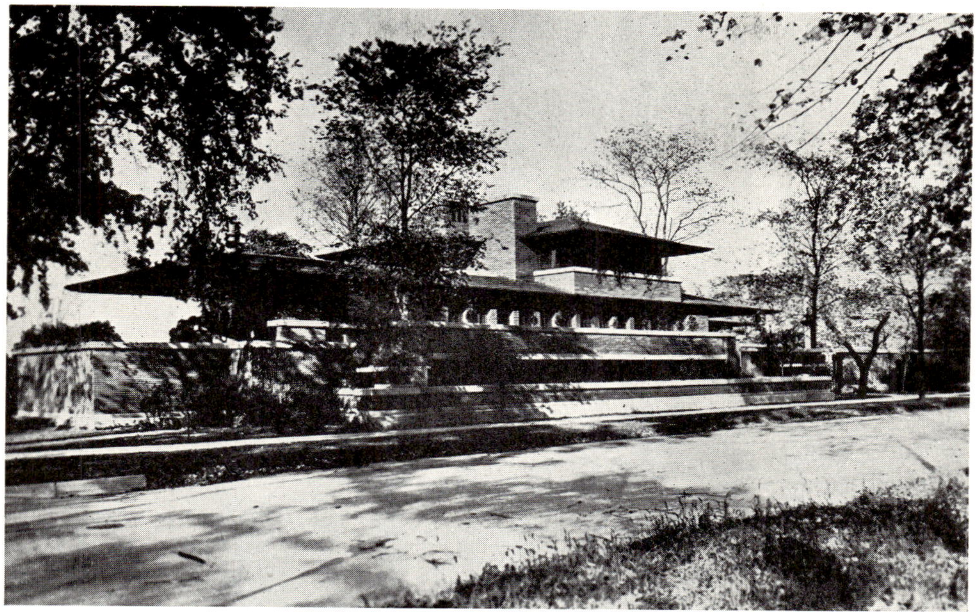

155. *Wright: Robie House, Woodlawn Avenue, Chicago.* 1908–09

sensuous values of color. It was in this respect analogous to the Imagist movement that took place at the same time in poetry. It was also allied through Klimt (Fig. 154) with the Secession movement in Austria, which carried the process of simplification and stylization into architecture and the decorative arts. The Secession movement spread rapidly through Germany in the first decade of the century. The new movement in architecture is too complicated to introduce here: I can only mention that in America the prairie style of Frank Lloyd Wright (Fig. 155) introduced in the decade 1900–1910 new ideas of space and simplified geometric form, which were not fully explored until after the war.

The principle for which all the artists of the twentieth century fought was the concept of art as a formal order, derived from the mind rather than from nature. It had been inevitable that a generation should come which would strive to recapture the values of style after the naturalism of the later nineteenth century. It was the influence of non-European models which drove this movement (which we can recognize as another form of idealism) so far out of the normal line of western development,

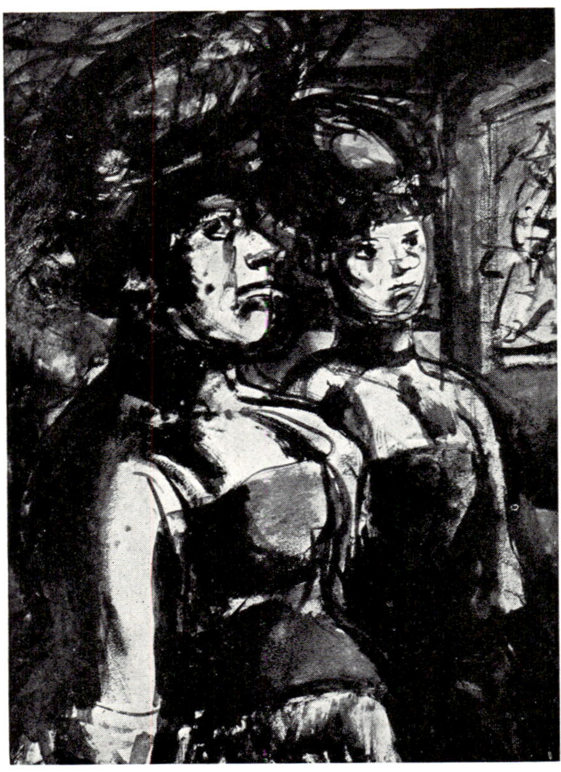

156. *Rouault: Au Theatre.* 1906

toward flat "unnatural" colors and "distorted" drawing. The camera undoubtedly also played a part in discrediting the mechanical excellences of academic drawing and fostering a return to a primitive manner. Derain, one of the most thoughtful of the Fauves, said, "Fauvism was our proof by fire. I never lost touch with the masters and, at eighteen, I knew all the reproductions of masterpieces possible. What does one gain by lack of culture? There were certainly obscure causes for our restlessness at that time, for our need to do something other than what every one saw. It was the epoch of the camera. That may be a source of influence, which counted in our reaction against everything that resembled clichés borrowed from life." [2]

Much of the neo-primitive work of that movement now seems thin and dated, possessing neither the disciplined craftsmanship nor the inner conviction that gives validity to the genuine primitive. These

[2] Georges Duthuit, *Le Fauvisme*, Cahiers d'Art, IV (1929), 268.

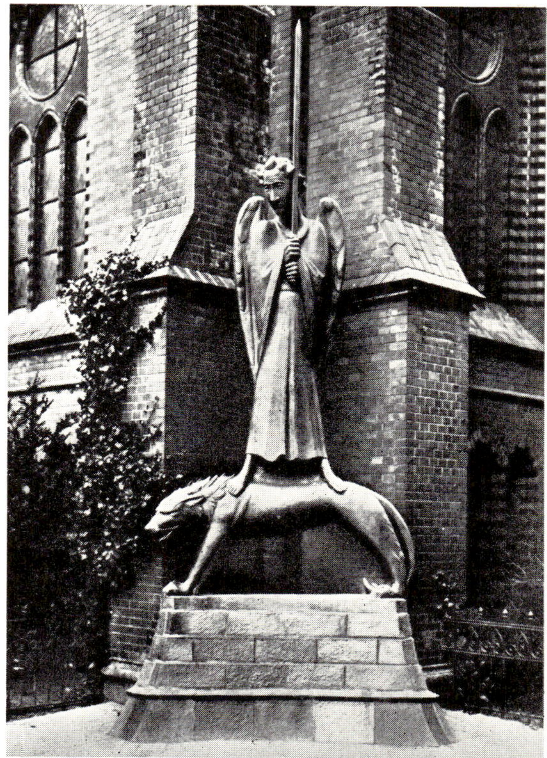

157. Barlach: Memorial in Kiel

artists were not primitives but highly cultured representatives of the
most civilized nations of the world. Once their principle was established
— that art is a language of pure imaginative creation, springing from
within the mind and not from objective reporting — it is not surprising
that many of them, like Kokoschka or Derain, should return later to the
western three-dimensional style. Yet the splendor of color, and the
results of their study of materials and textures, remained to enrich
twentieth-century style, as in literature the poetic vocabulary was re-
freshed and renewed by the Imagists.

Moreover, the study of the deeply religious arts of the Middle Ages
and of the Orient and the passionate imitation of primitive work represent a profound psychic need. It broke through the hard shell of
materialism and pessimism which had overlain western thought in the
late nineteenth century, and there welled up again to the surface of
modern society ancient springs of emotion and imagination that had

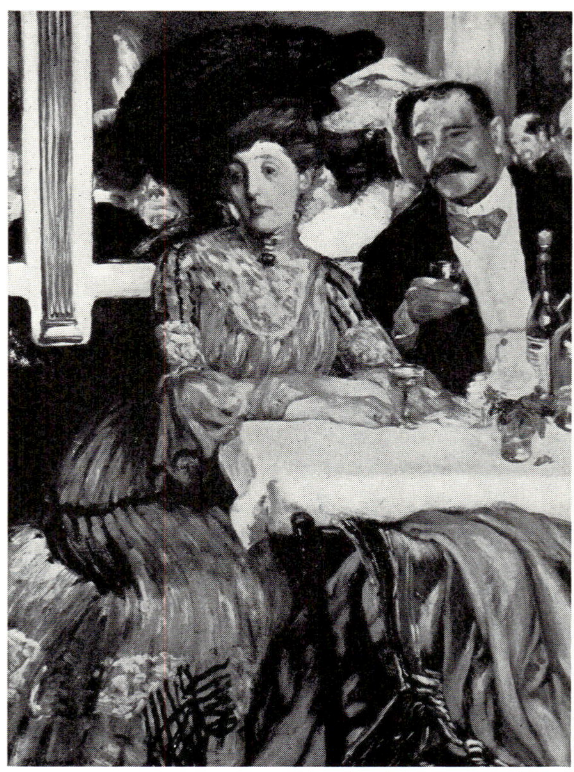

158. *Glackens: Chez Mouquin.* 1905

been dry for centuries. Not all the artists of the colorists' revolt were neo-primitive. Some began naturally at a point which others only tried self-consciously to reach. In France Rousseau le Douanier was a genuine primitive, by a sport of nature born to set an example of pure and naïve sentiment among the intellectuals of the Paris studios. But there are more important examples than he of men who belong completely and naturally to their own generation, yet are nourished by ancient racial sources of poetic intuition. One cannot, for instance, call Rouault (Fig. 156) a neo-primitive. In his murky, violent images the shadowy and melancholy imagination of his Celtic ancestors reappears once more. So, too, in the case of the north-German painter, Nolde (Fig. 120), born of old seafaring and peasant stock on a farm in Schleswig, or with the sculptor Barlach (Fig. 157), also from the North Sea rim, one feels oneself in the presence of the ancient beserk imagination of Teutonic folk poetry. Their imaginations are those which conjured up

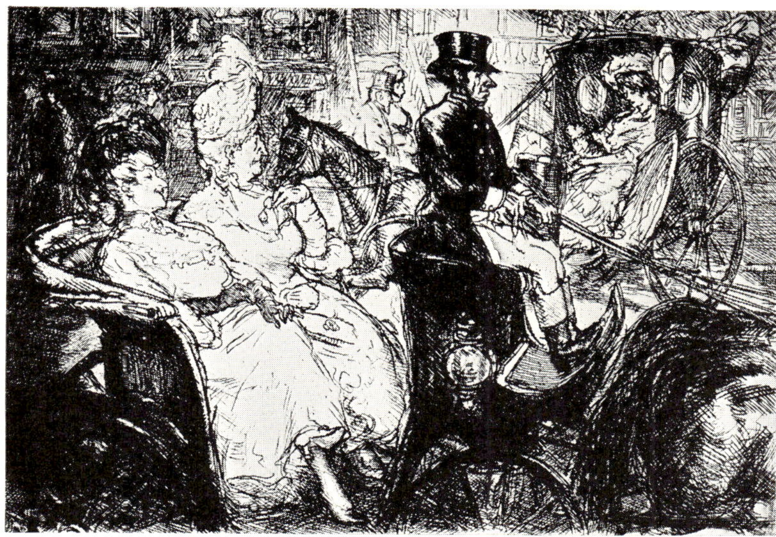

159. Sloan: Fifth Avenue Critics (etching)

the heroes and the monsters that stalk the moors or haunt the sea depths
in *Beowulf.* I will return to this point in speaking of the development
of sculpture.

The emotional comprehension of the world took also another form.
In Vienna (which was to give the world its post-war obsession or religion
of abnormal psychology) a neurotic introspection appeared in Klimt,
whose sumptuous, arbitrary style was one of the strongest forces in the
Viennese Secession. Under Klimt's influence Kokoschka, in the years
before the war, developed a portraiture of extraordinary subjectivity.
Nolde and Rouault were wholly subjective, Expressionist painters. In
America the development of the introspective mood (the eighteenth
century would have called it sensibility) had its representatives in the
delicate evocation of sentiment by Davies or Eilshemius.

But in the United States the revolt against the nineteenth century
took a special form, first of all through the influence of Eakins' teaching
and secondly from the expatriate temper of the preceding generation.
The temper of American painting in the nineties, as represented by the
Ten American Painters was one of fragile preciousness. The most
famous leaders of that generation — Whistler, Sargent, Henry James —
preferred to live abroad and looked upon America as a spiritual desert.

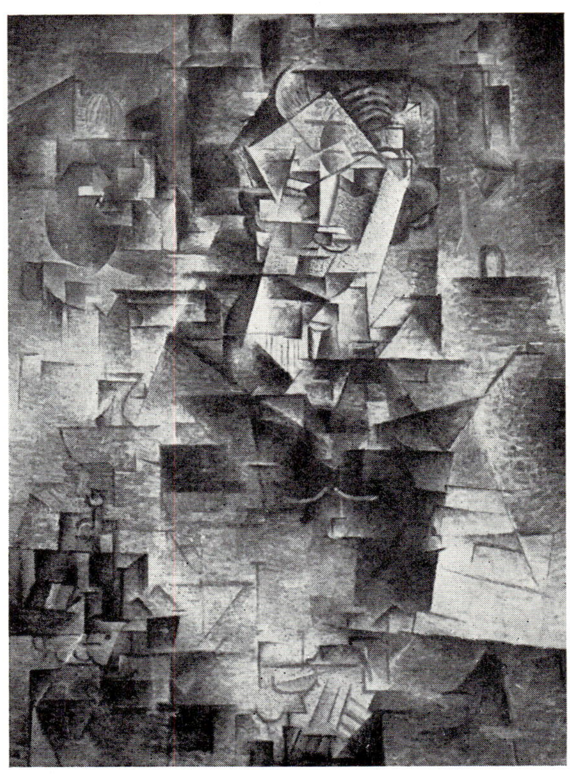

160. *Picasso: Man with Pipe*

Among the young artists who expressed the reaction of the twentieth century against this generation there were colorists like Prendergast and Lawson and Expressionists like Davies. The most conspicuous group, however, led by Robert Henri, were largely Philadelphia-trained men, who had come to New York to work as illustrators of magazines and newspapers. They were realists by temperament, who took as their credo the esthetic richness of everyday American life: "The esthetic significance of the elevated and the skyscraper, city crowds and rows of flat houses" was how one of them phrased their ideal. Time has made certain weaknesses of their work only too evident. They were betrayed by the same zest for life which was their strength into caring too little for style, as perhaps the Fauves cared too much. Henri's personality was of more importance than his hasty, slashing painting. The swift, sure observation of Glackens (Fig. 158) and the gaiety of his color were a distinguished contribution, but his later work seldom equaled his

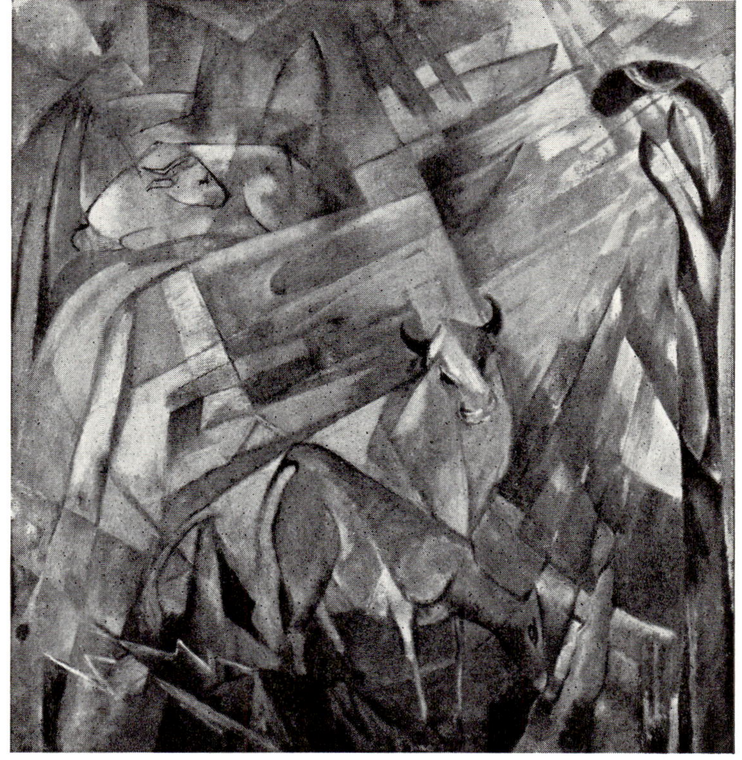

161. *Marc: Cattle in the Jungle*

early, pre-war painting. George Luks's Gargantuan enjoyment of life
never found an adequate expression in paint. Sloan (Fig. 159), Bellows, Kent, Hopper, shrewd observers and able men, produced brilliant graphic art, but their oils are marred by carelessness of handling.
Their rich and energetic humanity burst out, nonetheless, in a great
chorus in praise of life which was of the greatest importance for the
spiritual development of American art.

The abstract movement replaced an interest in color by an interest
in form. The exhibition of Cézanne's work in Paris in 1904, just before
his death, helped to turn attention away from the two-dimensional
Fauve style. At that time Braque was a Fauve and Picasso a romantic
colorist of peculiar psychological power in a macabre Spanish fashion.
Shortly after the Cézanne exhibition the discovery of Negro sculpture
offered examples of an absolutely objective and emotionless art, created

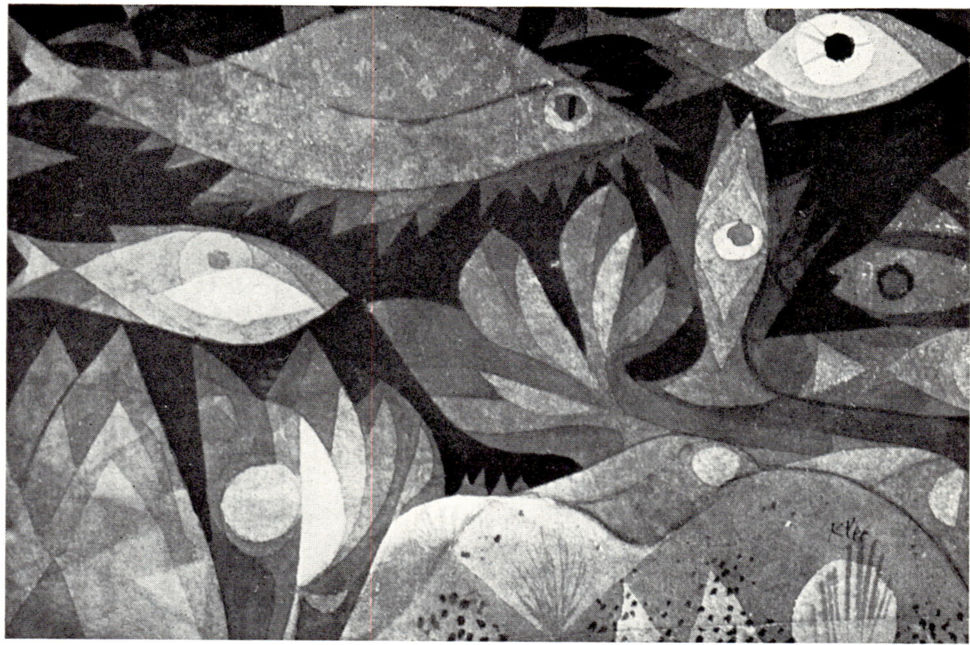

162. *Klee: Fish in the Sea.* 1921

by the exercise of an extraordinary freedom in transforming the human form into abstract geometric designs. About 1908 Picasso and Braque began the process of breaking whatever they painted into geometric forms, which was to lead to Cubism.

Cubism brought to a climax, about 1912–1913, the reaction against nineteenth-century naturalism (Fig. 160). Instead of the intuitive freedom of the Fauves, it offered an intellectual formula developed with all the clarity of Latin logic. Its program was to eliminate all elements of interest which a picture borrowed from outside itself through memory or association with nature. A picture was to be a "lyric fact," that is, an organization of shapes and colors which had no meaning except its own inner harmony. This theory was put forward by the apologists for Cubism, accompanied by an appeal to various authorities in the past. Plato's famous passage about the beauty of pure geometric forms; a chance remark of Cézanne that all the forms in nature could be resolved into the cone, the cylinder, and the cube; the examples of music and architecture — these were offered as justifications for making painting the music of the eye and treating painting as architecture. The relation of Cubism to the sense of form which we have traced throughout French painting is sufficiently obvious. The best justification for it, however, is that Picasso, Braque, Juan Gris really produced pictures without subject which are interesting; and its influence upon modern taste was enormous.

The years from 1911 to 1914 were filled with abstract movements which supplemented the stark intellectualism of Cubism. The organization of the Blue Rider group in Munich in 1911, by Marc (Fig. 161), Kandinsky, Klee, Campendonck, and Macke, brought the resources of German sentiment and Russian mysticism into the movement. The Russian, Kandinsky, was a colorist who tried to build a nonrepresentative art out of color, giving spatial, decorative, and emotional values to his different hues. Marc stylized animal subjects into geometric color shapes, but filled his kaleidoscopic designs with an excitement and enthusiasm that was far removed from abstraction. Klee (Fig. 162) in Switzerland and Feininger (Fig. 163) in northern Germany achieved unique decorative effects with color and textures, and Klee, especially,

163. *Feininger: The Side-Wheeler.* 1913

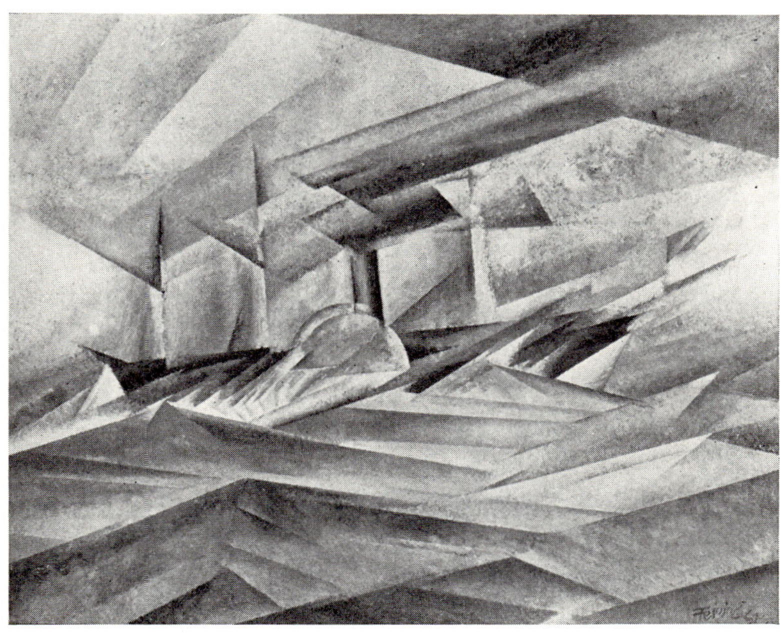

filled his abstract designs with overtones of fantasy, humor, and natural beauty.

The Italian abstract movement called itself Futurism. It made its public debut in 1910 before three thousand people in a theater in Turin, announced by a manifesto of the poet Marinetti. The Futurists' method was also one of geometric simplification of nature, but for them the geometric manner was a means to the dynamic representation of the stream of life, which they believed a static, realistic image could not represent. They introduced the principle of simultaneity, which was to be of great importance in the twentieth century's development of an intuitive rather than a naturalistic method of representing the world. A subject suddenly remembered, they said, presents itself in the mind as a medley of impressions, all true and necessary to a complete understanding, yet not all formed at one time nor from a single point of observation. The Futurists began boldly to paint this composite image that the mind forms rather than the realistic view, taken at a single moment from a single spot. In order to do so, they introduced the important device of the simultaneous representation of all significant aspects of a subject, which carried into painting something comparable to the stream of consciousness technique of literature. The painter

164. Bourdelle: Herakles   *165. Haller: Park Figure*

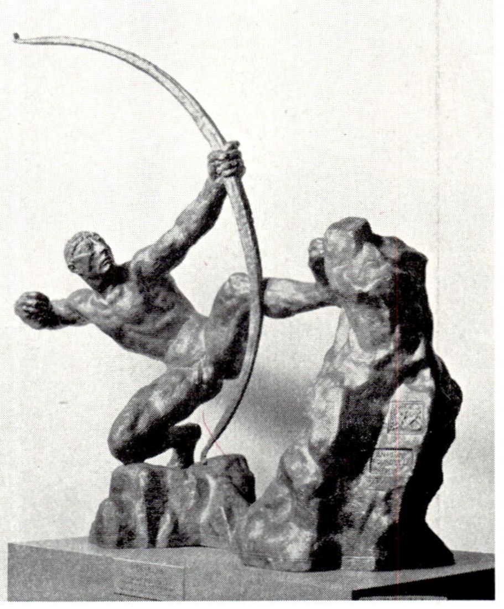

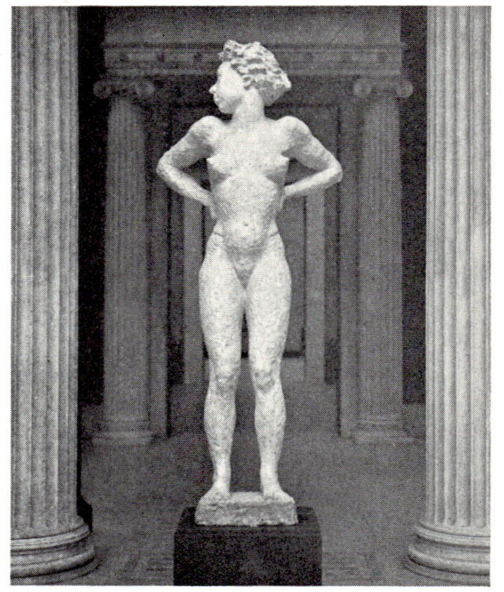

Severini was more successful in carrying out this program on canvas than was Boccioni in sculpture. But at least, like Cubism and German abstraction, Futurism offered a way out of naturalism to a conception of art as an expression of the creative faculty of the mind.

The English version of the abstract movement was Vorticism, which had no single definite principle except a revolt against the tyranny of factual thinking. Ezra Pound, Wyndham Lewis, and Gaudier-Brzeska, the sculptor, who was killed on the western front, were the most prominent Vorticists. Meanwhile in Paris two Americans, Morgan Russell and Macdonald-Wright, had formed a style of color abstraction called Synchromism.

On this side of the Atlantic the whole century of the Parisian formal tradition, from Delacroix and Ingres to Picasso, was shown for the first time in the famous Armory Show of 1913, arranged by the Independent Artists under the presidency of Arthur B. Davies. This panorama of revolt, which was unfolded before an astonished public, provoked furious discussion. Some American painters, notably Davies,

166. *Despiau: Mlle Bianchini*   167. *Lipchitz: Pegasus.* 1929

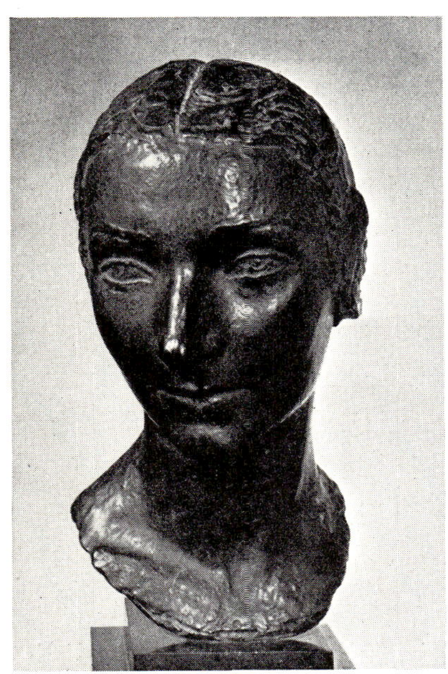

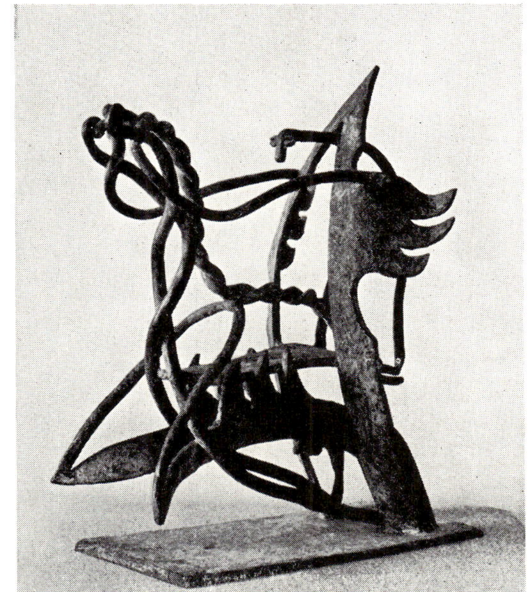

experimented with an abstract style, but Arthur Dove is the only man who can be said to have developed an independent abstract style in this country.

The significance of abstraction varied in each country. It reached its extreme form of objectivity in Paris; its widest influence was from 1919 to 1925 or 1926, coinciding with the brilliant international culture that followed the war. Paris, home of a long intellectual tradition from Poussin to Seurat, was its center and focus. Elsewhere it overflowed its rigid boundaries and mingled with the subjective movement of the colorists. Its influence upon taste was tremendous, for as subject disappeared the attention was transferred to the painted surface itself, and the eye developed a razor-sharp sensitiveness to color nuance, to quality of line, and to texture of surface.

The sculpture of the generation which formed its style before the war felt the same driving forces as painting — the search for a way out of naturalism, the study of qualities of the medium as the basis of expression, the rebirth of ancient racial feeling, the intuitive approach to life. But while there was some neo-primitive sculpture and some abstract, most sculptors applied themselves to the oldest and most familiar theme — the human figure — treated in quite a real manner. That is not to say that one finds realism in the nineteenth-century sense, but one does not find the extremes of revolt against realism that occur in painting. The detached, single human figure is the chief subject of the twentieth century, as it had been of the Renaissance and of Greece.

Among Rodin's successors in France, only Bourdelle wished to continue his dramatic quality, and even Bourdelle made his drama more athletic and formal than psychological (Fig. 164). The others, Maillol, Bernard, Despiau, created a calm, plastic style, devoid of introspection, that forms an oasis of peace in the modern world. Maillol reacted from Rodin's passion to a conception of sculpture as something primarily solid, weighty, and timeless. His figures became harmonies of full volumes, whose smooth surfaces are bathed in full light. After Rodin's Impressionism his grave and heavy compositions seem to breathe per-

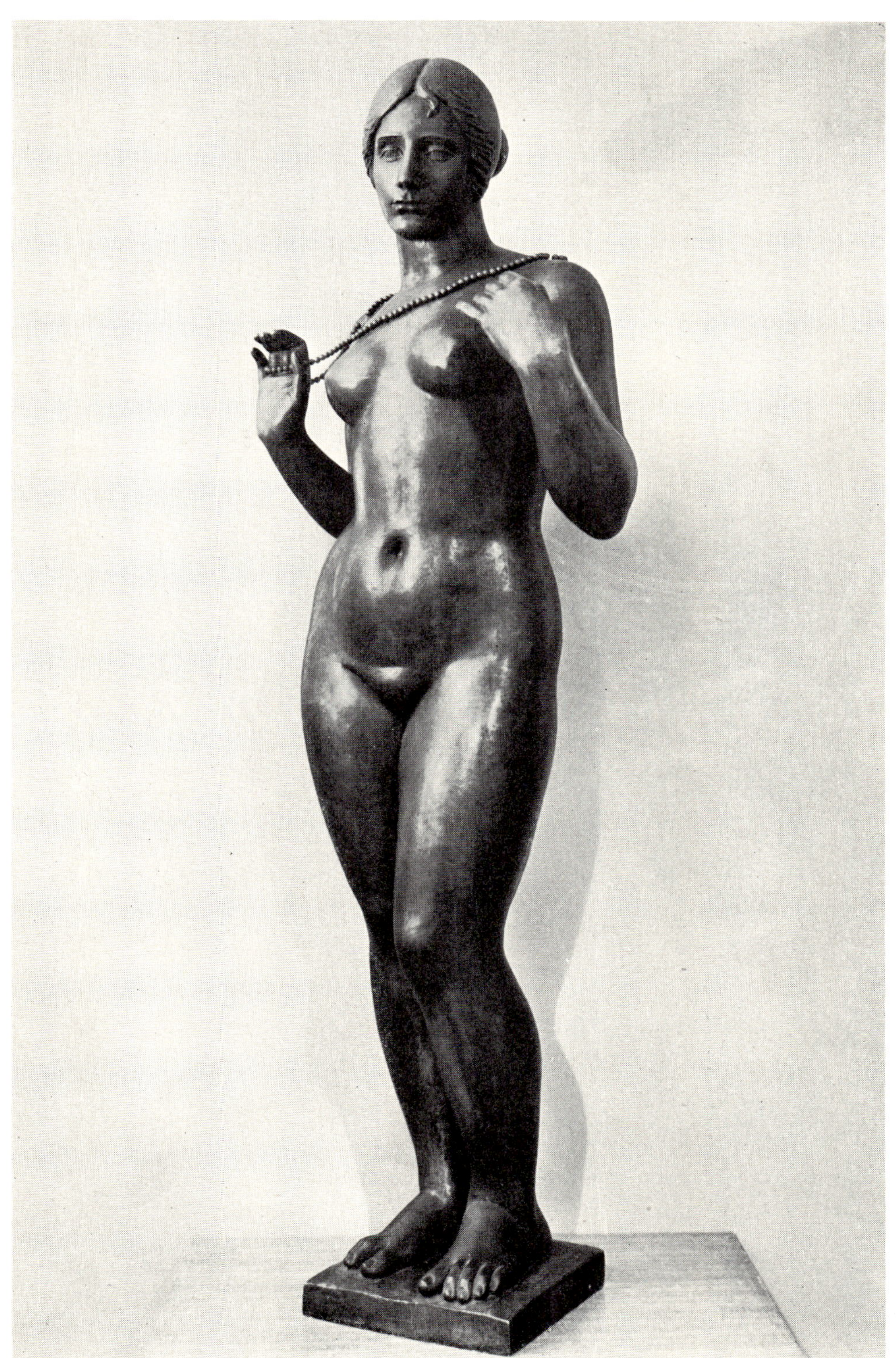

168. Maillol: Woman with a Necklace

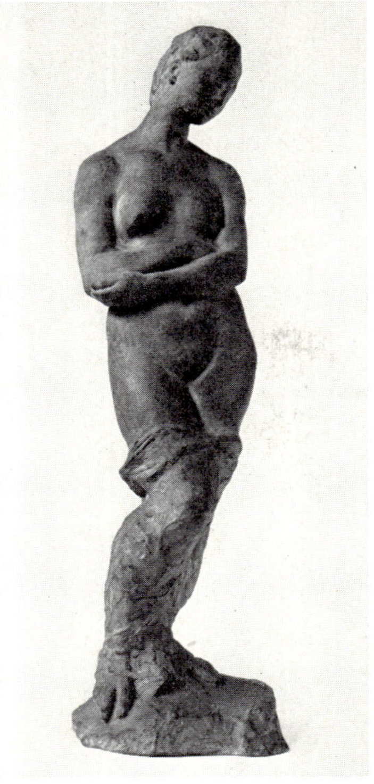

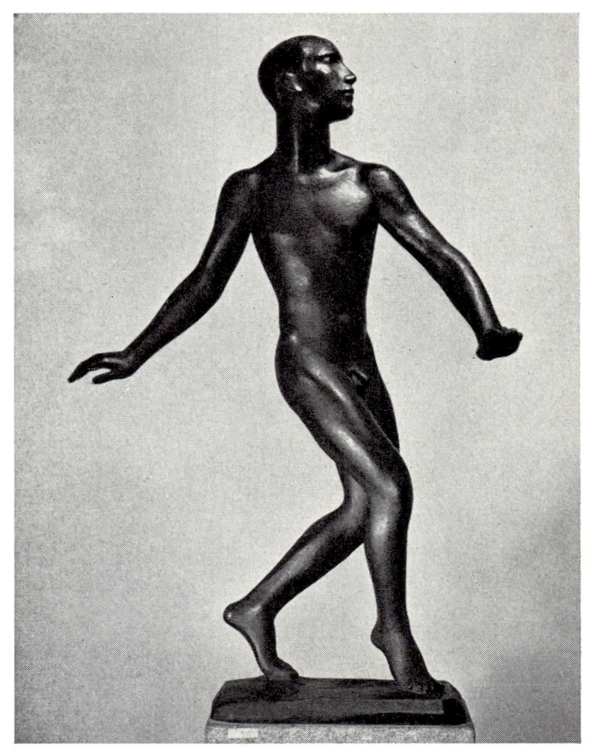

169. *Lehmbruck: Draped Figure*

170. *Kolbe: Nijinsky.* 1912

manence and calm. His art is not antique, for it shares the simplifications and plastic emphasis of the twentieth century; but in the air of well-being and repose that emanates from his figures it seems to achieve an antique serenity. Maillol was, curiously enough, the son of a peasant of the Mediterranean littoral and thus sprang from the ancient pastoral and vine-raising life which has remained unchanged since the days of Theocritus. One feels, looking at his figures, as if an ancient root had quietly put forth a new shoot (Fig. 168).

Despiau worked for a time as a stonecutter for Rodin. In his independent work he retained his master's subtle surfaces and his study of the inner life of his subject. But Despiau's sculpture also shows the emphasis upon volume and plastic solidity that marks his generation. He is the most acute and sensitive of modern French portraitists, having rescued the portrait bust from the depths of banality and restored it to

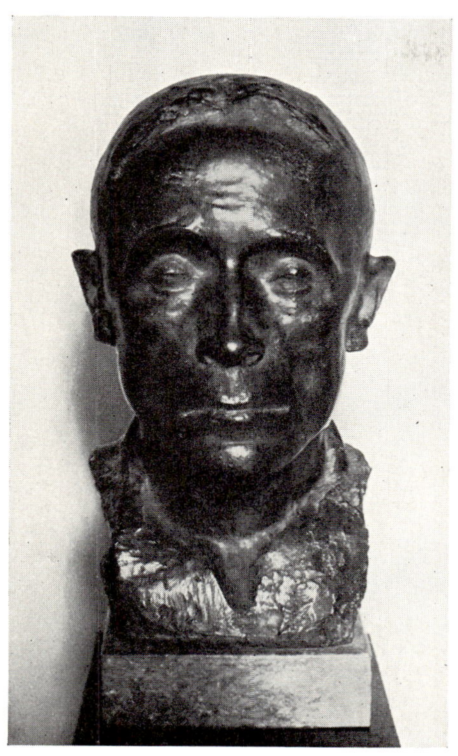

171. *Scheibe: Self-Portrait*

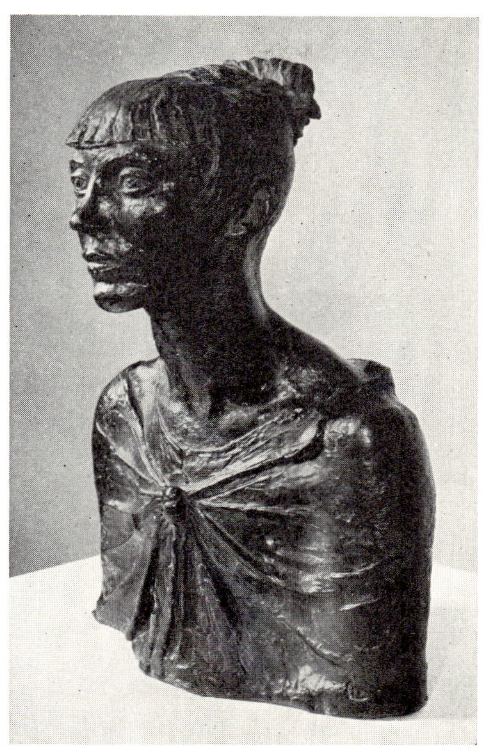

172. *Epstein: Bust of Mlle Gabrielle Soene.* 1921

the front rank of creative effort. Nowhere does one find the modern study of personality more happily expressed than in his heads (Fig. 166). When he turns from the head to the complete figure, one finds oneself thinking (in spite of differences of style) of the harmony and grace of a Tanagra figurine. Bernard also expressed, with great charm, the profound classic instinct of France.

In contrast to these men, the sculptors of abstraction were recruits to the school of Paris from outside of France. Manolo, the Spaniard, made the human figure a completely impassive subject for composition of plastic volumes and weights. Brancusi, born in Rumania, found the audience for his study of pure form in Paris. Lipchitz, the most interesting sculptor of the Cubist movement, is a Pole (Fig. 167).

In Germany Hildebrand had already restated the problem of sculpture as a formal problem. The twentieth-century generation empha-

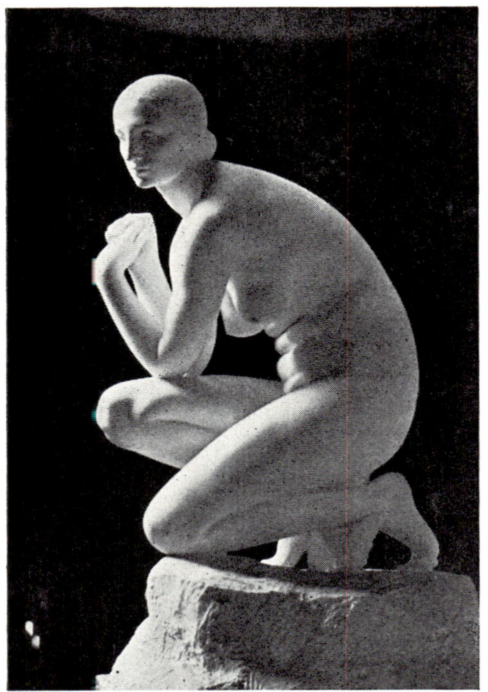

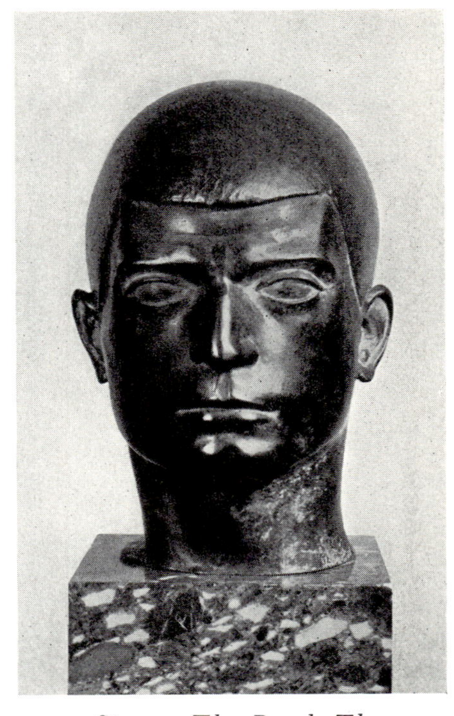

173. Barnard: Rising Woman   *174. Sterne: The Bomb Thrower.*
1909

sized clear, definite form, but it used also the delicate, subtle surfaces which Impressionism had introduced. The distinguishing characteristic of central European sculpture, however, is its lyric quality. In the Gothic period German work had been distinguished from the more architectonic French style by its psychological life. The same contrast returns in the twentieth century to separate Maillol, Bernard, and Bourdelle from the German school. It would seem as if the need that is so deep-rooted in the history of Germany, to assimilate the plastic form of the South to its own brooding introspection, had achieved a successful synthesis in this remarkable generation of sculptors. Lehmbruck's melancholy, pensive art (Fig. 169), the poetry of movement in Kolbe's work (Fig. 170), Haller's acute animation (Fig. 165), the gentle sadness of Scheibe (Fig. 171), the Gothic visions of Barlach are all given purely plastic expression, but their unique qualities are psychic. A small number of sculptors, among whom Mataré is notable, devoted themselves to more purely formal aims.

In England the Expressionist Epstein (Fig. 172) and the Vorticist, Gaudier-Brzeska, whether or not they are authentic geniuses, served to break the hold of naturalism upon English thought and prepare for the strong development of English post-war sculpture. The same part was played in American development by Manship's study of decorative surfaces and Hunt Diedrich's silhouettes. George Grey Barnard, in his early work (Fig. 173), and Maurice Sterne (Fig. 174) likewise clarified the medium by their emphasis upon volume and mass.

The year 1914 is an arbitrary close for this essay, for the main currents of art continued through and beyond the war period with less change than we commonly suppose. As the reader will have noticed, it has been necessary to choose more than one illustration from among the work done later in order to show the fulfillment of what was before only a promise. But there must be an end, and the twenties are still too close for a historical perspective.

The early years of the twentieth century present an extraordinary spectacle of experiment and change. The epoch was a riot of profuse and fertile energies in which little groups of artists formed, split up, absorbed one another or disintegrated, and credos were shouted one day, to disappear the next. The single constant characteristic was that eye, ear, and mind were subject to constant surprise. The *vie de Bohème* manner in which these movements were conducted seems curiously young and naïve as one looks back. They moved in an atmosphere of manifestoes and shocked outcries, of noise and good humor and alcohol; they were buoyed up by a sublime, ridiculous, and touching self-confidence. There was much confusion of aim and much promise that went unfulfilled. But if the eager innovators of the early twentieth century showed sometimes a tendency to announce when it might have been better to reason, and to reason when it would have been better to do, and if the pleasures of shocking and of change for its own sake were also to some extent present, it is still too easy, now that the effervescence has settled down, to pass severe judgments upon them. It is not only too easy, but superficial. Such happenings do not occur without a reason, and the impulse behind them was important. The excitement and restlessness of the time correspond to some inner need.

Let one ask one's self what was happening during this period in other fields of life. Was it not the era during which greater and more profound changes in the organization of life took place, outside the sphere of politics, than in any other? What a prodigality of invention and discovery carried men along on its onrushing torrent. Life in many of its essential elements passed through greater changes than have occurred during the whole preceding course of western civilization. All means of communication, of work, of movement, man's relations with space and time itself were altered. By new devices men worked miracles: they flew through the sky and sailed beneath the sea, they sent instantaneous messages crackling through the air and caused the living voices of the absent, even of the dead, to speak from within a little machine. In all this era of change should art alone remain placid, unruffled, unaltered? It is no wonder, I think, artists shared a desire for change, felt that in order to create they must first invent new means of expression and a new style of utterance, to transform language itself into a new thing. But if, afterwards, all has not turned out as these artists expected, one may still admire in them their idealism, their faith in art and humanity, their ardor, and their confidence that they were building a brave new world.

Postscript

It is no part of my purpose to attempt the ungrateful task of describing the post-war world in which we live. But there are certain observations which may be made at the close of such a survey as this. The sense of style developed by the first twenty years of the century continued to grow and expand its influence, as the men old enough to be interrupted rather than formed by the war continued their work. Wars seem to quicken the interest of peoples in the world outside themselves and to be followed by a period of international culture. The first ten years (1919–1929) after the World War were a brilliant example. The sharp, strong color and hard, clean forms, the new understanding of materials and of space produced by the early ferment spread throughout the world, shaping the development of American skyscrapers and German housing developments, Viennese decorative arts and French furniture. The western tradition may be said to have achieved a *style*, in the meaning of a world spirit evident in a unified aspect of all the arts, during these years.

But the important thing, to my mind, is not that. Nor is it the world-wide reaction from the freedom of Fauve and Expressionist painting to a firm, precise, controlled manner, which may be found in all countries beginning in the twenties. It is rather the turning inward upon itself of the western mind. In the 1920's Viennese psychologists were the prophets to whom all men listened. The confident idealism of the young century gave way to the introspective, troubled, and uncertain attitude which we know so well. The new mood is well represented and most familiar in literature. The sadness and divided mind of the post-war world are recorded with extraordinary sensitiveness in the later books of *The Forsyte Saga*, for example. The confidence of Shaw and Wells in man as a rational being who is in control of himself and is capable of securing his own future by the exercise of his reason in the form of applied science began to seem a little naïve to men who had known the World War. Nor did one need to go to primitive art to find mystery: there was plenty of it in the riddle of things as they are. In the theater the delicate fantasy of Barrie and Dunsany was replaced by Eugene O'Neill's harsh sense of the blind tragedy of man. One may say that in America we were carried onward in the boom years by a complete confidence in material things: need one add that American artists were united in a bitter crusade against this confidence, which made the whole literature of the twenties one of protest?

The striking post-war phenomenon in Paris is the conquest of objective art — Cubism — by abnormal psychology, which produced Surrealism and the late, macabre work of Picasso.

One of the marked characteristics of post-war painting in all countries is its sadness. The melancholy of the younger Parisian painters finds its counterpart in the bitter satirists of post-war Germany and in many Americans.

The movement has been away from the attempt to make a work of art complete in itself, a "lyric fact" (which is, after all, the twentieth-century version of "art for art's sake"), back to a contemplation of the human mind and human life. But as a result of the modern intense study of the psychological, we have what may be called a subjective realism, which reflects the world through the lens of imagination and attains at its best a haunting penetration into personality.

I made the point, in speaking of objective realism, that it was a break with the great tradition of art as an expression of the mind. Whether formal or emotional, French or not French, art was before the age of science a record of the mind, a language, a creation of imagination, not a transcript of what one sees. Since that time art has made a great effort to assimilate its new discoveries: first (by the Post-Impressionists) to assimilate color and the new meaning of nature, then to absorb the influence of the non-European world and the appearance of the camera. Western art has zigzagged wildly in its time of development since Winckelmann persuaded us that art should represent only an ideal beauty that is not to be found in nature. Art has gone through great revolutions and survived devastating changes. It is not becoming for anyone to try to sum up in neat generalizations the mystery of this present world, but if we can discern, here and there, an art which with acute sensibility deals with our own inward feelings, an art whose instruments of expression have through recent experiments in style become highly supple and enriched, we may feel that the art of our day has reached a by no means negligible point.

INDEX

INDEX